Democracy in Africa

This book provides the first comprehensive overview of the history of democracy in Africa and explains why the continent's democratic experiments have so often failed, as well as how they could succeed. Nic Cheeseman grapples with some of the most important questions facing Africa and democracy today, including whether international actors should try to promote democracy abroad, how to design political systems that manage ethnic diversity, and why democratic governments often make bad policy decisions. Beginning in the colonial period with the introduction of multiparty elections and ending in 2013 with the collapse of democracy in Mali and South Sudan, the book describes the rise of authoritarian states in the 1970s; the attempts of trade unions and some religious groups to check the abuse of power in the 1980s; the remarkable return of multiparty politics in the 1990s; and, finally, the tragic tendency for elections to exacerbate corruption and violence.

Nic Cheeseman is the Associate Professor of African Politics at Oxford University. He is the co-editor of the collections *Our Turn to Eat* (2010) and *The Handbook of African Politics* (2013). He is also the editor of the journal *African Affairs*, a member of the advisory board of the UNICEF Chair on Communication Research (Africa), and an advisor to, and writer for, Kofi Annan's African Progress Panel.

New Approaches to African History

Series Editor
Martin Klein, *University of Toronto*

Editorial Advisors
William Beinart, *University of Oxford*
Mamadou Diouf, *Columbia University*
William Freund, *University of KwaZulu-Natal*
Sandra E. Greene, *Cornell University*
Ray Kea, *University of California, Riverside*
David Newbury, *Smith College*

New Approaches to African History is designed to introduce students to current findings and new ideas in African history. Although each book treats a particular case and is able to stand alone, the format allows the studies to be used as modules in general courses on African history and world history. The cases represent a wide range of topics. Each volume summarizes the state of knowledge on a particular subject for a student who is new to the field. However, the aim is not simply to present views of the literature; it is also to introduce debates on historiographical or substantive issues and may argue for a particular point of view. The aim of the series is to stimulate debate and to challenge students and general readers. The series is not committed to any particular school of thought.

Other Books in the Series:

1. *Africa since 1940* by Frederick Cooper
2. *Muslim Societies in African History* by David Robinson
3. *Reversing Sail: A History of the African Diaspora* by Michael Gomez
4. *The African City: A History* by William Freund
5. *Warfare in Independent Africa* by William Reno
6. *Warfare in African History* by Richard J. Reid
7. *Foreign Intervention in Africa* by Elizabeth Schmidt
8. *Slaving and Slavery in African History* by Sean Stilwell

Democracy in Africa

Successes, Failures, and the Struggle for Political Reform

Nic Cheeseman
University of Oxford

CAMBRIDGE
UNIVERSITY PRESS

CAMBRIDGE
UNIVERSITY PRESS

32 Avenue of the Americas, New York, NY 10013-2473, USA

Cambridge University Press is part of the University of Cambridge.

It furthers the University's mission by disseminating knowledge in the pursuit of education, learning, and research at the highest international levels of excellence.

www.cambridge.org
Information on this title: www.cambridge.org/9780521138420

First published 2015

Printed in the United States of America

A catalog record for this publication is available from the British Library.

Library of Congress Cataloging in Publication Data
Cheeseman, Nicholas, 1979– author.
Democracy in Africa / Nic Cheeseman.
   pages   cm. – (New approaches to African history; 9)
Includes bibliographical references and index.
ISBN 978-0-521-19112-8 (hb) – ISBN 978-0-521-13842-0 (pb)
1. Democracy – Africa – History.   2. Democratization – Africa – History.
3. Africa – Politics and government – 1960–   4. Africa – Politics and government – 1945–1960.   5. Political parties – Africa – History.
6. Elections – Africa – History.   7. Political participation – Africa.
I. Title.   II. Series: New approaches to African history; 9.
JQ1879.A15C536   2015
321.8096–dc23   2014044909

ISBN 978-0-521-19112-8 Hardback
ISBN 978-0-521-13842-0 Paperback

For my parents

If a [democratic] society displays less brilliance than an aristocracy, there will also be less wretchedness; pleasures will be less outrageous and well-being will be shared by all.

"If a democratic republic similar to that of the United States were ever founded in a country where the power of a single individual had previously subsisted, and the effects of a centralized administration had sunk deep into the habits and the laws of the people, I do not hesitate to assert, that in that country a more insufferable despotism would prevail than any which now exists in the monarchical States of Europe, or indeed than any which could be found on this side of the confines of Asia."

Alexis de Tocqueville, Democracy in America, 1835

Contents

Figures

Tables

Acronyms

ABAKO	Alliance of Bakongo
ACFODE	Action for Development
AMISOM	African Union Mission in Somalia
ANC	African National Congress
APRM	African Peer Review Mechanism
ASP	Afro-Shirazi Party
AU	African Union
BDP	Botswana Democratic Party
CAR	Central African Republic
CCM	Chama cha Mapinduzi
CDR	Coalition for the Defence of the Republic
CDRs	Committee for the Defence of the Revolution
CIA	Central Intelligence Agency
CIAT	International Committee in Support of the Transition
CNDD-FDD	National Council for the Defense of Democracy–Forces for the Defense of Democracy
CNPC	Chinese National Petroleum Corporation
CODESA	Convention for a Democratic South Africa
CONAKAT	Confederation of Tribal Associations of Katanga
COSATU	Congress of South African Trade Unions
CPDM	Cameroon People's Democratic Movement
CPI	Corruption Perception Index
CPP	Convention People's Party
DfID	Department for International Development
DRC	Democratic Republic of Congo

DTA	Democratic Turnhalle Alliance
EC	European Commission
ECK	Electoral Commission of Kenya
ECOMOG	Economic Community of West African States Monitoring Group
ECOWAS	Economic Community of West African States
EIDHR	European Initiative for Democracy and Human Rights
EU	European Union
FEC	Federal Executive Council
FH	Freedom House
FNL	Palipehutu National Liberation Forces
FOCAC	Forum of China-Africa Cooperation
FORD	Forum for the Restoration of Democracy
FPI	Front Populaire Ivoirien
FPTP	First Past the Post
FRELIMO	Liberation Front of Mozambique
FRODEBU	Hutu Front for Democracy in Burundi
GDP	Gross Domestic Product
GSU	General Service Unit
HDI	Human Development Index
HSRC	Human Sciences Research Council
ICC	International Criminal Court
ICG	International Crisis Group
IMF	International Monetary Fund
KADU	Kenya African Democratic Union
KANU	Kenya African National Union
LDP	Liberal Democratic Party
MDC	Movement for Democratic Change
MMD	Movement for Multi-Party Democracy
MMM	Mauritian Militant Movement
MNC	Congolese National Movement
MNC – K	Congolese National Movement – Kalonji
MNC – L	Congolese National Movement – Lumumba
MONESTO	Togolese National Movement of Students and Trainees
MONUC	United Nations Organization in the Democratic Republic of Congo
MOSOP	Movement for the Survival of the Ogoni People
MOU	Memorandum of Understanding
MP	Member of Parliament

MPCI	Mouvement Patriotique pour la Côte d'Ivoire
MPLA	Popular Movement for the Liberation of Angola
MPR	Popular Movement of the Revolution
MRND	National Revolutionary Movement for Development
MUZ	Mineworker's Union of Zambia
NaRC	National Rainbow Coalition
NCA	National Constitutional Assembly
NCNC	National Council of Nigerian Citizens
NCP	National Congress Party
NDC	National Democratic Congress
NEC	National Electoral Commission
NEPAD	New Partnership for Africa's Development
NGO	Non-Governmental Organization
NP	National Party
NPC	Northern People's Congress
NPFL	National Patriotic Front of Liberia
NPP	New Patriotic Party
NRA	National Resistance Army
NRM	National Revolutionary Movement
NURTW	National Union of Road Transport Workers
OAU	Organisation for African Unity
ODM	Orange Democratic Movement
OECD	Organisation for Economic Co-Operation and Development
ONEL	Observatoire National des Elections
ONUC	United Nations Operation in the Congo
PAC	Pan-African Congress
PAI	African Independence Party
PAIGC	African Party for the Independence of Guinea and Cape Verde
PCD	Communist Party of Dahomey
PDCI	Democratic Party of Côte d'Ivoire
PDP	People's Democratic Party
PDS	Senegalese Democratic Party
PF	Patriotic Front
PNU	Party of National Unity
PRC	People's Republic of China
PRPB	People's Revolutionary Party of Benin
PRSP	Poverty Reduction Strategy Paper
PS	Parti Socialiste du Sénégal

RDR	Rassemblement des Républicains
RENAMO	Mozambican National Resistance
RND	National Democratic Rally
RPF	Rwandan Patriotic Front
RTP	Rally of the Togolese People
SACP	South African Communist Party
SADC	Southern African Development Community
SAP	Structural Adjustment Programme
SLPP	Sierra Leone People's Party
SMC	Supreme Military Council
SNC	Sovereign National Conference
SNM	Somali National Movement
SPLA	Sudan People's Liberation Army
SPLM	Sudan People's Liberation Movement
SWAPO	South West Africa People's Organisation
TAA	Tanganyika African Association
TAC	Treatment Action Campaign
TANU	Tanganyika African National Union
UDF	United Democratic Front
UGCC	United Gold Coast Convention
UIC	Union of Islamic Courts
UNAMSIL	United Nations Mission in Sierra Leone
UNAVEM	United Nations Angola Verification Mission
UNDP	United Nations Development Programme
UNIP	United National Independence Party
UNITA	National Union for the Total Independence of Angola
UNMIL	United Nations Mission in Liberia
UNOB	United Nations Office in Burundi
UPC	Uganda People's Congress
UPRONA	Tutsi Union for National Progress
UPS	Senegalese Progressive Union
USAID	United States Agency for International Development
USSR	Union of Soviet Socialist Republics
UWONET	Uganda Women's Network
ZANLA	Zimbabwe African Liberation Army
ZANU	Zimbabwe African National Union
ZANU-PF	Zimbabwe African National Union – Patriotic Front
ZCTU	Zambia Congress of Trade Unions
ZIPRA	Zimbabwe People's Revolutionary Army
ZNA	Zimbabwe National Army

Acknowledgements

It is difficult, if not impossible, to write a book about the history of a continent on your own. Even the most avid traveller would struggle to amass the knowledge and experience required to tell the many stories that can be found across Africa without a little help from their friends. This is particularly true if you are at the start of your career, when you have no option but to draw on the books and articles you have read, the talks and lectures you have attended, and the arguments and ideas of those around you. In this way, academic work is a form of collective endeavour.

This book is no different, and I am grateful to all of the colleagues who have helped me along the way. The idea for this manuscript was first suggested by William Beinart, one of my most valued colleagues at Oxford, who, along with Bill Freund, made helpful suggestions on the structure and content of the text. It was subsequently nurtured by Martin Klein, the editor of the *New Approaches to African History* series, who has shown quasi-parental levels of patience in the years that it has taken to bring this project to fruition. It gives me great pleasure to be able to repay at least some of their faith and kindness with the completion of this manuscript.

The task of summarizing 80 years of history in just 80,000 words is not an easy one, and it forced me to look for concise ways of characterizing complex periods and peoples without doing too much violence to life's rich tapestry. I did so by trying out ideas in seminars, lectures, and discussions whenever the opportunity arose. In this regard, I am particularly grateful to the participants of the African Studies

Association conferences in the United Kingdom and United States, and the students that have taken my Democratization and Multiparty Politics in Africa option paper at Oxford over the years.

The study of African politics has thrived over the last decade, and I have benefitted greatly from being able to discuss my work with a remarkable set of colleagues that includes Leo Ariola, Joel Barkan, Matthijs Bogaards, Catherine Boone, Jennifer Brass, Michael Bratton, Petet VonDoepp, Elliott Greene, Karuti Kanyinga, Nelson Kasfir, Adrienne LeBas, Andreas Mehler, Anne Pitcher, Rachel Beatty Riedl, Philip Roessler, Nicolas van de Walle, and Tom Young. I owe an even greater debt of gratitude to my mentors, Nigel Bowles, Gavin Williams, and David Anderson. Without the support of Nigel and David I would never have become an academic, and I continue to benefit from their guidance today. Gavin Williams casts a particularly long shadow where this project is concerned: by setting me on the path of African studies while simultaneously encouraging me to read Alexis de Tocqueville's *Democracy in America*, he was the intellectual godfather of this book. Thanks also go to the people that I have been fortunate enough to collaborate with since completing my doctorate; working with the likes of Rita Abrahamsen, Daniel Branch, Paul Chaisty, Svitlana Chernykh, Sarah Jane Cooper-Knock, Mark Eddo, Staffan I. Lindberg, Gabrielle Lynch, Joanne McNally, Tim Power, Nicole Stremlau, Miles Tendi, Job Wandalia, Peter Wanyama, Lindsay Whitfield, and Justin Willis is so interesting, and so much fun, that it rarely feels like work.

My friends at Oxford University have also played a major role in my work over the last few years. Completing research and book projects is much easier if you have supportive colleagues. Over the last few years, I have been lucky to teach alongside Christopher Adam, Jocelyn Alexander, Julie Archambault, William Beinart, Neil Carrier, Paul Collier, Patricia Daley, Stefan Dercon, Jan-Georg Deutsch, Miles Larmer, Tony Lemon, Raufu Mustapha, Helene Nevou-Kritcheback, David Pratten, Andrea Purdekova, Ricardo Soares de Oliveira, Jonny Steinberg, and Miles Tendi. Having spent my entire career at Oxford, I am often asked why I never left to see if the grass really is greener on the other side. The answer is that I cannot imagine a more stimulating and enjoyable set of colleagues with which to work.

As any academic knows, sometimes the most effective critics are your own students. At Oxford, I have also been blessed with brilliant undergraduate, masters, and doctoral students whose work has taught me a tremendous amount, and whose conversation and comments have helped to improve drafts of this book. Among them are Nana Antwi, Sarah Brierley, Dominic Burbidge, Michaela Collord, Ian Cooper, Diane de Gramont, Wambui Kamiru, Brian Klaas, Zoe Marks, Gillian McFarland, Halfdan Ottosen, Daniel Paget, Moizza Sawar, Michelle Sikes, Patrycja Stys, and Hannah Waddilove. Three students were so helpful that they became research assistants, and in different ways were critical to the completion of this manuscript. I am deeply grateful to Andrea Scheilber for her copyediting, Dan Paget for his work on the appendix, and Alisha Patel for her assistance in putting together the figures and tables and, most importantly, for her help with the index. As ever, any mistakes or errors of judgement are mine.

Although most academic work is a form of collective endeavour, writing a book can be a lonely time. To all the friends who have been forced to listen to me waxing lyrical about the joys of fieldwork/complaining bitterly about writer's block, I am forever grateful. In particular, Bieber, Dave, Hana, Jo, Julia, Juliet, Kristin, Lucie, Mat, Mo, Pete, and Thea have enjoyed/endured more than most. Thanks for reminding me that there is a world outside of work. Of course, no one has contributed more to making this all possible than my parents. I am not sure why I ended up being fascinated by Africa and democracy, but it does not seem too much of a stretch to think that having parents who travelled to West Africa and Papua New Guinea, and spent their lives working for charities, had something to do with it. Their advice, love, and support have been critical at every stage of my career, and I will be forever grateful to them for encouraging me to follow my dreams.

Finally, I would like to thank Santu Mofokeng for agreeing to let me use his wonderful photograph, 'Democracy is Forever', on the cover of this book. To my mind, he is one of the most challenging and powerful artists working today. In one striking image he is able to highlight both the wonderful promise of democracy and its sobering reality. It was exactly these contrasting emotions that inspired me when I started writing this book, and that I hope the reader feels upon ending it. They say that a picture is worth a thousand words – in this case, you can multiply that by eighty.

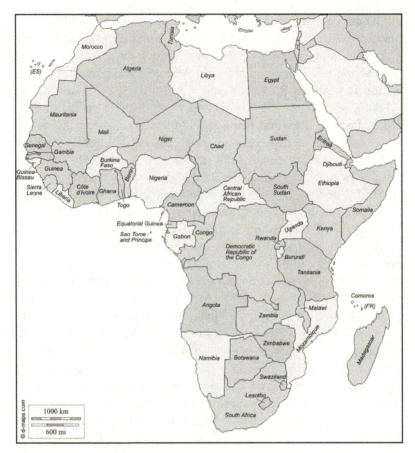

Map of Africa

Source: http://d-maps.com/carte.php?num_car=25459&lang=en

INTRODUCTION

Democratization Against the Odds

When I told people that I was writing a book on democracy in sub-Saharan Africa they often joked that it would surely be a very short volume, up there with the history of Swiss military victories and the compendium of great English cooking. Such a response is understandable. Since the reintroduction of multiparty elections in the early 1990s, the cause of African democracy has suffered a major setback in almost every round of elections. In the early-1990s, the return of party politics was closely associated with the resumption of the Angolan civil war in 1993 and the Rwandan genocide of 1994. In 1996, the reputation of Zambia's Movement for Multi-Party Democracy (MMD) – initially celebrated as one of the first opposition parties in Africa to defeat an authoritarian government at the polls – was undermined by a flawed election and evidence of widespread corruption. Four years later, Côte d'Ivoire, thought to be among Africa's most stable political systems during the single-party era, descended into civil war following a disputed election.

Sadly, these democratic breakdowns were not just the result of "teething problems": they continue to be a prominent feature of multiparty politics up to the present day. In 2007, election observers described the polls in Nigeria – the third to be held since 1999 – as some of the worst they had ever had the misfortune to witness. Just months later, accusations of electoral manipulation in Kenya – which by then was on its fourth competitive contest – led to a month of civil conflict in which more than 1,000 people lost their lives. The same year, President Robert Mugabe refused to accept defeat at the hands

1

of the Movement for Democratic Change (MDC) in Zimbabwe amidst the mass repression of opposition supporters. More recently, democratic experiments in Mali and South Sudan have been undone by violent conflict. It is therefore easy to see why so many commentators are skeptical as to the prospects for multiparty politics on the continent. Endemic poverty, weak infrastructure, and pronounced inter-communal tensions are unpromising foundations upon which to build successful democracies.

Yet in a number of countries democratization has resulted in a far more positive outcome. Those who depict sub-Saharan Africa as "A Hopeless Continent"[1] tend to ignore the fact that the region contains two states that have enjoyed uninterrupted multiparty politics since independence: Botswana and Mauritius. Indeed, cases in which elections have not led to civil conflict or political disorder are typically overlooked in favour of examples in which the body count makes for more eye-catching headlines. Yet Africa's success stories are every bit as important as those of Côte d'Ivoire and Rwanda. Despite a history of violent divide-and-rule politics, South Africa has managed a stable and relatively peaceful transition from apartheid to majority rule. Ghana's transformation from a political system marked by coups, military rule, and mismanagement to one of Africa's leading democratic lights is equally striking. The recent histories of Benin and Cape Verde are no less impressive, and these are not isolated examples: all told, around a quarter of sub-Saharan African countries can now be considered "free". Moreover, although African elections have typically been won by those already in power, limiting the extent of political change, many leaders have been forced to step down as a result of constitutional restrictions on their time in office. In the 2000s, elections and term limits replaced death and coup d'état as the most common ways in which African presidents and prime ministers left office.[2]

These more open polities did not emerge out of a vacuum; rather, reformers in countries such as Ghana and Senegal drew on previous elements of democratic practice and experience. Although authoritarian rule was the norm on the continent for much of the last century, few, if any, African societies have recognized the right of a government to exercise absolute power. As a result, building a regime that is

---

[1] This was the banner headline that famously ran above a picture of the continent on the front cover of *The Economist*, 13–19 May 2000.

[2] Posner, Daniel N., and Daniel J. Young. "The Institutionalization of Political Power in Africa". *Journal of Democracy* 18, 3 (2007), pp. 126–140.

both legitimate and popular – and hence can be maintained without the use of widespread repression – has required leaders to fulfil local expectations and to rule within limits. Thus, while the continent has endured more than its fair share of brutal dictators, Africa's history is also dotted with fragments of democracy. In the pre-colonial period, centralized states with hierarchical authority structures were rare; in most cases the power of leaders was constrained both by their limited territorial control and by local custom. Moreover, many communities, such as the Kikuyu in Kenya, developed a shared understanding of the appropriate relationship between leaders and their communities that gave rise to complex moral economies in which rulers were expected to provide for their followers in return for their support. These sorts of patron-client agreements served to legitimate highly unequal political and social arrangements, but nonetheless located norms of reciprocity at the heart of the social contract between the government and the governed. In doing so, they placed important, if limited, constraints on the abuse of power.

In some of the continent's more repressive political systems, these kinds of norms and expectations were frequently violated by unscrupulous leaders prepared to use violence to compensate for a lack of popular support, but this was not always the case. While the one-party states that mushroomed in the 1960s both centralized power and denied citizens a choice of ruling party, many continued to hold elections for constituency MPs, reflecting the desire of ordinary Africans to select their representatives. These regimes were far from being competitive democracies, but single-party systems in countries such as Kenya, Senegal, and Zambia were nevertheless significantly more open, tolerant, and responsive than was typically the case in their Latin American and Eastern European counterparts. As a result, African political systems were sometimes more democratic than they seemed. Although they are typically overlooked, these histories of more open politics are important, because they established norms regarding the appropriate – and inappropriate – actions of governments. In turn, these norms constrained authoritarian leaders and were later harnessed by pro-democracy campaigners, facilitating the process of political change.

But even when we factor in these prior experiences of electoral politics, the existence of democratic states in Africa is still remarkable. Political scientists have identified a long wish list of factors that make it easier to establish and consolidate a democracy. Towards the top of the list are a coherent national identity, strong and autonomous

TABLE I.1 *GDP per capita of selected African countries (1965 and 1995), current US$*

	1965	1995
Botswana	77	2,988
Burkina Faso	82	236
Chad	126	207
Congo, Dem. Rep. of	233	134
Côte d'Ivoire	206	774
Kenya	105	270
Liberia	183	65
Malawi	58	140
Nigeria	176	205
Niger	117	263
Rwanda	46	228
South Africa	555	3,863
Sudan	121	462
Zambia	297	393
Zimbabwe	297	611
Latin America	452	3,778
OECD	1,806	22,292
South Asia	118	385
sub-Saharan Africa	162	564

Source: World Bank.

political institutions, a developed and vibrant civil society, the effective rule of law, and a strong and well-performing economy. For example, Adam Przeworski has famously shown that countries that enjoyed a GDP per capita of more than $6,000 when they introduced democracy almost always succeed, while those with a GDP per capita of less than $1,000 almost always fail.[3] Both in the 1960s and in the 1990s, few African countries fulfilled this – or any other – wish list criteria (see Table I.1). Yet a quarter of them have nonetheless made significant progress towards establishing stable and accountable multiparty systems. In other words, a significant proportion of the continent is democratizing against the odds. Given this, Africa should not be thought of solely as an interesting context in which to analyse the fragility of democracy. Rather, it is a continent that has much to teach us about the different pathways through which even the poorest

[3] Przeworski, Adam et al. "What Makes Democracies Endure?" *Journal of Democracy* 7, 1 (1996), pp. 39–55.

and most unstable countries can break free from authoritarian rule. It turns out that a book about democracy in Africa needs to be longer than most people would think.

Democratization and Autocratization

Explaining the success and failure of democracy in Africa requires us to think about what facilitates political liberalization. Given the great power wielded by African political elites it is tempting to conclude that political reform occurs when leaders allow it to. In Ghana, Flight Lieutenant J.J. Rawlings responded to pressure to democratize by constructing an increasingly rule-bound political system that was responsive to people's needs. Faced with the similar pressures, President Daniel arap Moi of Kenya adopted a radically different strategy, manipulating state resources to fund his party's campaign of thuggery and intimidation. It is tempting to conclude that Rawlings was simply a better man than Moi; that Ghana was just luckier than Kenya. It is certainly true that African leaders demonstrated very different capacities to put the national interest first when faced with pressure to reform in the 1990s. In Côte d'Ivoire, Rwanda, Togo, and Zimbabwe, incumbents held onto power at all costs, even when doing so spawned widespread civil conflict. By contrast, Presidents Kerekou in Benin and Kaunda in Zambia gracefully accepted defeat following their "founding" elections.

Yet while Kaunda and Kerekou may have been made of stronger moral fibre than their counterparts, this was not the only reason for their willingness to cede power. Both presidents lacked the resources and international support required to overcome the sizeable opposition to their rule, and understood that repression was not a viable long-term strategy. At the same time, Kaunda and Kerekou found it relatively easy to walk away from power because they had not committed crimes that were likely to make them targets for domestic and international prosecution and because they trusted future governments not to persecute them. By contrast, leaders who were blessed with greater resources and who feared that losing power would lead to prosecution for corruption or crimes against humanity, such as Moi, naturally found it far harder to relinquish control. In other words, incumbent leaders did not decide how to act on the basis of moral backbone (or lack of it) alone, and it is possible to identify the main factors that encouraged them to accept, or reject, democratization.

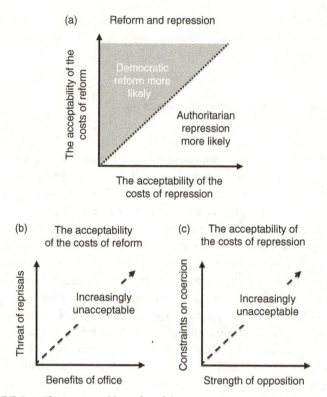

FIGURE I.1 The costs and benefits of democratization to incumbent leaders.

In building such a framework it is helpful to start with Robert Dahl's intuitive but important point that leaders are more likely to pursue political liberalization when they find the costs of reform to be more acceptable than the costs of repression. For example, if the danger of electoral defeat is more acceptable than the cost of repressing the opposition (which might include, for example, the loss of legitimacy that would ensue) incumbents are more likely to allow for free and fair elections.[4] This is illustrated in Figure I.1a, where the shaded area represents the conditions under which incumbents are most likely to choose democratization over autocratization. Although a given leader will evaluate the acceptability of a particular cost depending upon their own beliefs and values, I suggest that it is possible to

---

[4] Dahl, Robert. *Polyarchy: Participation and Opposition.* New Haven: Yale University Press, 1972, p. 15. Staffan Lindberg has also used Dahl's framework to look at the process of democratization in Africa.

distill some generalizations about the factors that render the costs of political liberalization more or less easy to bear.

The Costs of Repression

From the point of view of a sitting president the costs of repression are shaped by a broad range of factors, but the most important are the strength of the opposition and whether leaders have the funds and authority to be able to sustain their regimes through the use of coercion (Figure I.1c). In cases where pro-democracy forces are united, better funded, and supported by a vibrant civil society, an incumbent must expend far greater resources in order to contain the opposition (see Chapter 2). When the pro-reform movement is so strong that it can only be defeated through force, leaders must also factor in the likely loss of domestic and international support that will result. This was clearly the case in both Egypt and Tunisia in 2011, and similar processes have previously played out in a number of sub-Saharan countries. Moreover, in cases where the military refuses to participate in attacks on protestors, as was the case in Egypt during the protests against the regime of Hosni Mubarak, it may not even be viable for the president to suppress pro-democracy activists.

The unity of the opposition is also critical. In many countries, leaders were able to retain power by playing different factions of the opposition off against each other. Consider Kenya, where the regime of Daniel arap Moi actively encouraged different factions of the opposition Forum for the Restoration of Democracy (FORD) to register as separate parties (FORD-A and FORD-K) for the 1992 founding elections. Subsequently, a heavily divided opposition, in addition to the use of electoral violence and vote rigging, enabled Moi to win the election with just 38 per cent of the vote. One of the reasons that the Kenyan opposition became so fragmented was the refusal of different ethnic leaders to compromise on their personal ambitions – and the expectations of their communities – in order to build a united party (see Chapter 5). In this way, pronounced ethnic and religious identities can make it harder for a united opposition to emerge, and so reduce the cost of maintaining the status quo.

The cost of repressing the opposition also depends on whether a leader enjoys the machinery and resources necessary to rule through force. Where incumbents lack an effective police force and security service, and struggle to raise the finance required to meet the costs of repression, they are more likely to find reform acceptable. The strength of key political and judicial institutions is also important. In cases where institutions are particularly weak and undermined by informal patronage networks, the barriers to corruption and the use of violence are particularly low. However, where strong checks and balances exist on the executive, employing extralegal strategies and purchasing the support of key institutions such as the electoral commission is likely to cost the incumbent far more economic and political capital. Thus, the institutionalization of the rule of law places constraints on the use of coercion and hence improves the prospects for democratization.

The economic position of a government is equally significant. Even when the costs of containing the opposition are very high, incumbents may be willing to bear them if they can afford to sustain a high level of coercion indefinitely. This is one of the reasons that periods of economic decline are so significant to processes of political change. Recessions highlight the poor performance of the government and have a direct impact on jobs and wages, making citizens increasingly sympathetic to the opposition. At the same time, falling revenues forces leaders to make tough choices: they can reduce the pay of the security forces, dip into their personal reserves, or cut government spending elsewhere. Each strategy creates as many problems as it solves. The first increases the prospect of a coup or mutiny. The second eats into the retirement fund of the incumbent, and so undermines one of the main reasons for retaining power. The third requires the regime to cut back on the services it provides and/or the funds being channelled through its patronage networks. In turn, this reduces the number of people dependent on the government, and so makes it more difficult to stem the flow of defectors to the opposition. Consequently, as the resources available to the incumbent dwindle, the costs of repression become increasingly unacceptable (see Chapter 3). It is therefore unsurprising that incumbents blessed with vast oil wealth, as in Saudi Arabia or Sudan, have been far less responsive to demands for change than their counterparts in poorer states.

Well-targeted government spending can help to persuade voters, officials, and bureaucrats to stay loyal to a regime, even after it has begun to use repressive strategies. However, the extent to which this strategy is necessary and feasible depends on the socio-economic context. For example, in countries where democratic rules and values are ingrained, incumbents may find that money is a poor tool with which to influence political behaviour. The level of poverty and inequality is also important because, other things being equal, ruling parties in poorer countries are likely to find it less costly to buy votes and hence electoral victories. Similarly, the more unequal a society is, the cheaper it will be for those at the top of the ladder to buy the support of those at the bottom. Of course, poor communities regularly reject financial inducements to vote for a certain candidate, and support opposition leaders even when faced with the most brutal repression – as in Zimbabwe. But where politics is dominated by patron-client relationships, poverty and inequality make it less costly for leaders to provide the goods necessary to fulfil their side of the bargain. In turn, this makes it that much easier for leaders to maintain the status quo. If the strength of communal identities means that incumbents can rely on ethnic ties to mobilize supporters without financial inducements, the costs are further reduced.

The level of control that incumbents enjoy over their revenue streams is just as important as the amount of revenue available. In resource-rich economies, such as the Democratic Republic of Congo, Gabon, and Nigeria, incumbents typically enjoy a monopoly over trade taxes and so face few barriers to the exploitation of their nation's natural wealth. By contrast, where leaders are unable to rely on oil and gas deposits, collecting revenue may involve complex bargains that limit the incumbents' range of options. In countries where the government is dependent on tax revenue raised on the population through income tax or a form of sales tax, it may be forced to bargain with workers in order to secure a continual flow of revenue. For example, citizens who are highly taxed are more likely to demand a greater say in how their money is spent and so may be less willing to accept poorly performing regimes. Moreover, in countries with strong trade union movements or producers groups like South Africa and Zambia, workers were able to use their key position within the national economy to strike for higher wages and other concessions. In such cases, trade unions emerged as key players in the struggle for democracy, and by lending their economic leverage and organizational might to the opposition significantly increased the costs of repression.

Of course, the economic independence of a regime has an international component as well as a domestic one. When government revenues decline, incumbents become more economically dependent upon foreign lenders such as the International Monetary Fund and the World Bank, and on foreign donors, such as the United States, Canada, France, and the United Kingdom, and more recently Brazil, China, India, and Japan. In turn, the dependence of governments on financial assistance can confer great political influence on the international community, as Greece, Ireland, and Portugal have recently discovered. When the coffers of an authoritarian regime run dry, donors have the option of making access to their funds conditional on political reform. Many foreign governments were willing to prop up vicious regimes such as Mobutu Sese Seko's regime in Zaire during the Cold War, when security concerns won out over human rights. But following the collapse of the Berlin Wall in 1989 Western donors became more willing to use the economic weakness of African states to push for political liberalization, dramatically increasing the costs of repression (see Chapters 3 and 4).

The Costs of Reform

Even when the costs of repression rise, leaders are only likely to democratize when they find them less acceptable than the costs of reform. Quite how much a leader stands to lose by implementing reforms depends on what benefits they accrue from holding office and the likelihood that they will suffer reprisals from those who follow in their footsteps (Figure I.1b). The rampant corruption in many African states has naturally focused attention on the financial benefits that presidents can derive from holding office. In Nigeria, successive presidents are thought to have stolen more than $6 billion from state coffers; the benefits of retaining office could hardly have been greater. But control over jobs and business opportunities are important too. Where the government enjoys a monopoly over resources and jobs (such that opportunities for those outside of the regime are few and far between), as in many African countries, political control means economic control. Under these circumstances, loss of office implies a loss of financial opportunities not just for the leader, but also for their allies, family, and supporters. As a result, when leaders perceive that reforms could open the way for an opposition victory, they often conclude that the cost is unacceptable.

While financial rewards are important, they represent only a small part of the potential gains from office. Incumbency typically carries with it immunity from prosecution and the ability to protect allies. The more an incumbent fears that they and their friends and family will be prosecuted for past corrupt activities and human rights violations, the more valuable retaining office will appear and the less willing they will be to give up power. This is why declarations that leaders will be investigated for past actions, such as the attempted prosecution of President Bashir of Sudan by the International Criminal Court for crimes against humanity, may delay processes of reform. It is also why genuine democratization often comes only after incumbents and their closest advisors have been granted amnesty – as in South Africa. Significantly, the fear of prosecution may extend far beyond a sitting president. Where human rights have been systematically violated, the military and the police are likely to be vulnerable to retrospective prosecution. Under these conditions, leaders from the security sector may seek to veto reform in order to protect their own positions. Consider Zimbabwe, where some commentators believe that President Mugabe was willing to concede defeat to Movement for Democratic Change (MDC) leader Morgan Tsvangirai, but was prevented from doing so by hardliners within his party and the security forces on whom his regime had become dependent. The balance between hardliners and reformers within the ruling party can thus shape the decision facing the incumbent.

Of course, how incumbents perceive reform is also shaped by whether they believe that they will be able to control the consequences of opening up the political system. This is most obviously the case when the ruling party stands to gain by introducing small reforms without any threat to their hold on power. For example, in 1992 the Chama cha Mapinduzi (CCM) in Tanzania decided to return the country to multiparty politics because it wanted to boost the country's domestic and international legitimacy and was confident that it could dominate competitive elections. Even leaders facing electoral defeat may attempt to introduce reforms if they are confident that they can broker reliable deals that will protect their own interests in the future. However, such a strategy is only viable in a context where new legislation and agreements are likely to be honoured, such as when a leader receives a credible promise of amnesty guaranteed by a number of international actors as a reward for leaving office.

Incumbents may also pursue this kind of "defensive democratization" in order to constrain the ability of future leaders to exclude or persecute them. For example, leaders who fear defeat may deliberately create stronger democratic institutions because while these structures constrain their own actions in the short-term, they offer protection in the long-term. The willingness of the National Party government of F.W. de Klerk in South Africa to negotiate with the ANC over a return to majority rule is a classic case of defensive democratization in which an incumbent embarked on a process of reform having recognized that it was in their own best interests to do so (see Chapter 3). This is an important point, because it demonstrates that it is possible to build democracy without democrats. Leaders may begrudgingly implement far-reaching political reforms when faced with overwhelming pressure to do so, or seek to create stronger and more autonomous institutions as a strategy of self-defence, whether or not they value plural politics themselves.

However, sitting presidents are unlikely to take this course of action if they believe that institutions are too weak to protect them, and hence find the potential of reprisals to be unacceptably high. In countries where leaders have historically been able to use personal networks to undermine constitutional provisions, as in Gnassingbé Eyadema's Togo, incumbents have little reason to believe that any reforms they introduce will withstand manipulation by future regimes. From the point of view of an authoritarian incumbent, introducing democratic reform in such a context represents the worst of all possible worlds because it is likely to hasten the defeat of the ruling party (by creating a more open political system) without actually offering any significant long-term protection. This helps to explain why incumbents are so reluctant to engage in reform in the wake of civil wars or prolonged liberation struggles, where the combination of weak institutions, a history of violence, and the military capacity of different factions renders the political landscape particularly unstable and unpredictable and hence inflates the potential costs of reform. Given this, the high number of African leaders that came to power through the barrel of a gun reduces the prospects for government-led democratization (see Chapter 1).

The Barriers to Democratization in Africa

Drawing these points together, we can start to build a picture of the sorts of countries in which leaders are most likely to pursue political liberalization. Some factors are particularly significant to the process of democratization because they influence both the costs of repression and the costs of reform, and so have the capacity to radically change the incentives facing incumbents. Unrestricted access to vast natural resources makes it considerably easier for incumbents to meet the costs of repression, and, by increasing the benefits of office, raises the potential costs of reform. It is this "double whammy" that explains why such a high proportion of the world's oil economies are also authoritarian regimes. Compromised political institutions are just as significant. By reducing the constraints on authoritarian leaders, weak and pliant institutions render the costs of repression more acceptable. At the same time, poorly institutionalized political structures enable incumbents to misappropriate state resources and offer little protection from future reprisals, making it less likely that leaders will pursue defensive democratization. Only incumbents with a strong democratic impulse will consider the costs of reform to be more acceptable than the costs of repression under these circumstances. Finally, pronounced communal or ethnic identities render it less likely that reform movements will remain united, and less likely that incumbents will trust leaders from other communities to honour their promises. As a result, the politicization of ethnicity and religion reduces the costs of repression while increasing the costs of reform, making autocratization more likely than democratization.

In summary, incumbents are least likely to embark on reform in countries with great natural resource wealth, a weak institutional landscape, and a deeply divided society. Africa's democratic difficulties stem from three key developments in the first half of the twentieth century, the combined impact of which brought about precisely this worst-case scenario.

Neo-Patrimonial Rule

It has become a cliché to note that one of the barriers to establishing democracy and strong states in Africa is the prevalence of neo-patrimonial rule. Yet the term is often misunderstood and misapplied. Neo-patrimonialism is not simply a synonym for corruption. Rather, it refers to the collision between pre-existing "patrimonial" forms of political organization and the "modern" colonial state. Patrimonialism refers to political systems in which leaders derived their authority from their position at the apex of a family or an ethnic community. In such "traditional" forms of government, those in power were able to treat state resources as their personal largesse, and were only constrained by local norms and expectations in the absence of effective formal institutions. When such forms of political organization were fused with modern state structures, both were radically transformed, which in turn made it necessary to develop a new theoretical framework: *neo*-patrimonialism. The upshot of this symbiotic reshaping of the old and the new was a set of political systems that had the outward appearance of modern states – legislature, judiciary, an extensive bureaucracy – but the internal dynamics of personal rule. Consequently, the story of postcolonial Africa quickly became one of strong presidents and weak institutions – significantly reducing the costs of repression.

Of course, this is a broad generalization: both pre-colonial authority structures and the organization of colonial rule varied markedly across the continent. Whether the outcome of the colonial moment was shaped more by pre-existing practices or the imposition of a modern bureaucracy depended on the strength of existing power structures and the depth of colonial engagement. In the parts of Africa that already featured a system of hierarchical authority capable of maintaining political order, colonial powers typically followed the path of least resistance and co-opted established leadership structures. This process was epitomized by the relationship that developed between the British colonial government and the Hausa-Fulani in the north of what is now Nigeria under the policy of indirect rule pursued by Frederick Lugard, the governor-general of the territory between 1914 and 1919. Lacking the number of officers required to effectively police a vast territory, the British moved to co-opt and then maintain the Hausa-Fulani emirs who enjoyed effective control of the region due to their ability to wield both spiritual and political power.

By contrast, in many parts of pre-colonial Africa such extensive authority structures did not exist. In these areas, patrimonial rule often took the form of highly decentralized political systems in which leaders wielded power not over centralized states, but over relatively small communities or groups of villages. In such cases, colonial governments often went beyond simply reifying existing leaders and engaged in processes of social engineering. Consider the fate of the Igbo in the eastern part of Nigeria. In the pre-colonial period the Igbo were a largely stateless people and the localized nature of political authority placed limits on the abuse of power. This is not to say that pre-colonial Igbo societies were democratic. Leadership was still determined by lineage and exercised by men, and this distribution of power served to protect a highly unequal social system in which older men dominated economic and political opportunities. But for all this, Igbo authority structures remained highly decentralized. Thus, while Lugard was able to rule through an existing hierarchy in the North, he was forced to create a new one in the East. This centralization of power undermined some of the more democratic currents within pre-colonial social structures, and was often resisted by communities who considered chiefs anointed by colonial rule to lack legitimacy.

Although the degree of social transformation effected by colonial rule varied markedly across Africa, in general it left the continent with a tier of Big Men with enhanced coercive capacity and territorial control. The colonial era also had an important impact on gender relations, because the Big Men promoted through indirect and direct rule were just that: without exception, colonial regimes understood power to be a male domain and rarely co-opted women into positions of authority. The promotion of the male chief placed further distance between women and the exercise of power, and as a result the patron-client structures that evolved in the 1960s and 1970s were rarely headed by women (see Chapter 2).

The collision of pre-colonial authority structures and colonial rule also served to embed the logic of traditional forms of rule into the architecture of the state. This was significant because patrimonial rule typically recognized no distinction between a public and a private realm; as a result, the integration of such systems into colonial governments laid the foundation for later corruption and abuse of power. The ability of leaders to construct personal networks within the state enabled them to undermine important checks and balances institutions such as the judiciary and the legislature in order to bypass constitutional and legal constraints. Consequently, postcolonial bureaucracies did not evolve into meritocratic organizations dedicated to serving the national interest. Instead, they typically became vehicles for the advancement of certain sections of the population with a claim on the executive.

Because many leaders derived their authority from their influence over a particular community, the types of patronage networks that evolved were often rooted in ethnicity or other forms of communal identity. In turn, the willingness of presidents to divert the lion's share of the state's resources to their own supporters undermined the notion that the government should rule in the interests of all. Taken together, these developments led to the emergence of a set of states characterized by weak institutions and a winner-takes-all political dynamic that exacerbated the intensity of ethnic identities. It was precisely this combination of factors that rendered democratization so problematic because it exaggerated the benefits of office for the incumbent, made it less likely that deals struck between rival leaders would be honoured, and so reduced the barriers to the maintenance of authoritarian rule.

But while this account helps to explain the lack of reform in many states, it is important to keep in mind that not all African polities were (or are) equally neo-patrimonial. Given this, it is essential that we do not assume the existence of neo-patrimonialism, but rather think about the way in the presence or absence of patrimonial politics shapes the prospects for reform. For example, Namibia, South Africa, and Zimbabwe (up to the late 1990s) are often said to have avoided neo-patrimonial rule, and this is one of the factors that enabled these states to achieve smoother and more successful processes of democratization. In a further group of countries, corruption and the personalization of power has been a significant barrier to reform, but institutions have nonetheless played an important role in shaping political processes. For example, the one-party states of Benin and Senegal retained significantly more checks on the abuse of power than was the case in the continent's personal dictatorships and military regimes. As a result, these political systems never experienced the rampant misuse of state resources that was characteristic of Nigeria and Togo. More impressively, Botswana managed to both maintain multipartyism and, on the back of a strong tradition of respecting property rights, to establish a distinction between the public and private realms. As a result it has effectively managed its diamond wealth, consistently ranking as one of the fifty least corrupt countries in the world (see Chapter 1).[5]

In places such as Botswana and Senegal, stronger institutions, viable states, and a history of relatively inclusive politics meant that leaders found the costs of reform to be more acceptable than the costs of repression. Consequently, like many of Africa's less neo-patrimonial regimes, they remained relatively open during the 1970s and 1980s and made more meaningful and stable transitions to democracy in the 1990s.

---

[5] According to the Corruption Perception Index (CPI) run by Transparency International, see: www.transparency.org/policy_research/surveys_indices/cpi.

The Gatekeeper State

In addition to the emergence of neo-patrimonialism, the creation of centralized state structures with greater coercive control and a monopoly over economic opportunities undermined the potential for a more democratic politics to emerge. In the pre-colonial era, relatively little of the continent was governed by what we would today think of as states. In general, leaders lacked the coercive capacity to broadcast power across large areas. Moreover, Africa then had a very low population density, and so the ability of individuals or ethnic groups to migrate in order to escape exploitation placed real constraints on the ability of leaders to abuse their own subjects. Of course, some cases bucked this trend. In southern Africa, Shaka Zulu became notorious for his attempt to enforce rigid discipline within the Zulu Kingdom, and in West Africa, the Ashanti kingdom established a multilayered system of administration headed by the Asantehene that lasted from the early 1700s to the late 1800s. But such cases were the exception rather than the norm.

With the advent of colonial rule this picture began to change. Although borders were frequently porous, the demarcation of state lines and the creation of centralized – if limited – systems of policing and administration placed greater barriers on the free movement of peoples. Over time, this has enhanced the ability of the continent's leaders to intimidate and monitor their people, lowering the costs of repression. But it is important not to overstate the coercive capacity of African rulers. As a number of commentators have observed, African states have typically been built from the inside out: the absence of inter-state conflict has meant that leaders have had little incentive to invest in the construction of strong borders, and so they have tended to focus their limited resources on fortifying their regimes around the seat of power. This form of state development generated a centre-periphery divide in which the coercive capacity of states was uneven – high in the capital cities (the centre), but declining with every step into the rural hinterland (the periphery). As a result, many authoritarian regimes lacked the power to establish anything close to a totalitarian regime. It was partly for this reason that fragments of democracy continued to live on in the dark days of the 1980s.

The economic foundations of African states also played a major role in shaping the practice of politics, because the dominant economic role played by the state exaggerated the impact of neo-patrimonial rule.

This phenomenon is perhaps best illustrated by Frederick Cooper's notion of the gatekeeper state.[6] African states were gatekeepers in two important ways. First, they typically relied on their control of the national gate – of borders, ports, and airports – to sustain themselves via taxes and levies on the flow of goods, finance, and people. Again, this process has historical roots. Throughout the colonial period the main preoccupation of the occupying powers was to export African natural resources such as gold, cotton, copper, and coffee, in order to make the colonies pay for themselves. Although a wave of more progressive "welfare colonialism" spread across the continent following the Second World War, there was little attempt to construct balanced economies. As a result, most African economies were dependent on one or two main exports, and lacked the manufacturing sector, skills, or infrastructure needed for economic diversification, making them vulnerable to fluctuations in world prices for primary commodities. Along with poor economic decisions, corruption, and the protectionist policies of developed nations, this historical legacy hindered the development of a profitable private sector. Consequently, African states relied heavily on trade taxes to sustain government expenditure in the absence of revenue from income (direct) taxes (Figure I.2).

As noted previously, some governments were forced to enter into domestic bargains with organized labour in order to maintain production levels of key exports, and hence government revenues. Where this process of negotiation occurred, as in Zambia, it often supported the evolution of a more balanced state-society relationship (see Chapter 2). However, the majority of African regimes managed to survive on the proceeds of export and import duties, bypassing influential social groups. Of course, governments could only rely on trade taxes so long as control of the gate was sufficiently lucrative. When the value of coffee, copper, cocoa, peanuts, and tea fell on world markets early in the independence era, African leaders were forced to look elsewhere for additional revenue streams. If these governments had failed to secure resources from international lenders and donors, they might have been forced to take the failings of their economies more seriously and to build more effective systems of domestic taxation. Instead, this imperative was typically blunted, either by the identification of large finds of oil or gas, or by the availability of foreign aid and loans.

[6] Cooper, Frederick. *Africa Since 1940: The Past of the Present*. Cambridge: Cambridge University Press, 2002.

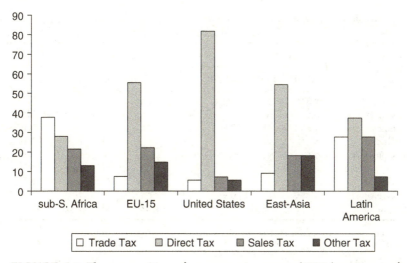

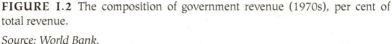

FIGURE I.2 The composition of government revenue (1970s), per cent of total revenue.

Source: World Bank.

Oil, loans, and international aid had a similar effect, in that they left African governments dependent for their survival not upon domestic factors (the quality of governance and the approval of the people) but upon a set of external factors (the price of oil and the favour of donors). Oil revenues and the economic support offered by the IMF and the World Bank to African states, along with the aid money provided by former colonial powers and new donors, enabled regimes that had little domestic legitimacy to survive. So long as donors failed to make democracy promotion a priority – and this was the case for the first thirty years of independence – foreign aid and loans effectively enabled African leaders to fund authoritarian rule (see Chapter 5). The impact of oil wealth was even more dramatic: no major sub-Saharan oil producer has ever been a democracy (Table I.2). Nigeria has perhaps the strongest claim to be counted as a multiparty success story, but although it has rejected military rule the government has consistently refused to allow fully free and fair elections. As a result, the political system remains stuck in the murky middle ground between democracy and authoritarianism. It is too early to tell what the effect of oil will be on Ghana, where commercially viable deposits were only discovered after stable democratic institutions and a comparatively effective auditing system had developed. The stronger checks and

TABLE I.2 *Major oil producers and the quality of democracy (1980–2010), oil revenue as % of GDP*

	1980		1990		2000		2010	
	% GDP	FH*	% GDP	FH	% GDP	FH	% GDP	FH
Angola	25.8**	NF	29.3	NF	63.3	NF	45.7	NF
C. d'Ivoire	0.2	PF	0.1	PF	0.6	PF	4.2	NF
Cameroon	13.6	NF	8.8	NF	11.0	NF	7.2	NF
Chad	0	NF	0	NF	0	NF	29.3	NF
Congo, R.	50.6	NF	41.3	NF	72.5	PF	64.1	NF
Eq. Guinea	0	NF	0	NF	95.8	NF	53.2	NF
Gabon	52.1	NF	32.6	PF	48.1	PF	42.6	NF
Nigeria	40.7	F	39.9	PF	41.4	PF	15.7	PF
Sudan	0	PF	0	NF	12.8	NF	17.2	NF

Notes: *FH = Freedom House overall rating, which categorizes countries into three groups: NF = Not Free, PF = Partly Free, F = Free. **First recorded amount from 1985.
Source: *World Bank and Freedom House.*

balances already in place in such countries may insulate them from the worst effects of the resource curse, but even if this is the case governments will be less reliant on taxing their own people to fund expenditure, and as a result may become harder to hold to account over time.

Over time, the combination of externally financed governments and weak domestic economies led to the development of a distinctive form of socio-economic relations that enabled African governments to become gatekeepers in a second way. Instead of the government being dependent upon the people to fund the bureaucracy and public services, the people became dependent on the government for hand-outs in the absence of formal sector employment. This relationship supported the pervasive spread of patron-client relationships rooted in the state, and empowered governments to manipulate economic opportunities to punish opponents and reward supporters. The exten-sion of patronage through neo-patrimonial networks is only the most obvious manifestation of this much wider process.

Economic centralization had already begun in earnest during the colonial period, when the colonial powers, driven by the need to increase production for the war effort, established marketing boards to secure greater control over the exchange of goods. By setting the colonial government up as sole purchaser, marketing boards curtailed private economic relationships and empowered colonial regimes to set prices. Although the willingness of Africans and low-level administrators to ignore some of the rules some of the time meant that colonial edicts were not always fully enforced, this nonetheless set a blueprint for the postcolonial era. After independence, marketing boards were retained in countries such as Côte d'Ivoire because they enabled governments to protect producing communities from the effects of large price fluctuations, and because they empowered governments to set prices, and thus generate a profit that could be used to sustain public spending. Indeed, postcolonial regimes often went further than their colonial predecessors, consolidating the position of the state as a gatekeeper of the means of accumulation. This is easiest to see in the case of countries that pursued the path of African socialism, such as Benin, Tanzania, and Zambia. In these states, the creation of parastatals and the practice of nationalizing successful private companies had negative economic consequences because it deterred entrepreneurialism, but was often retained because it also prevented the emergence of wealthy individuals capable of leading and funding the opposition.

A similar process occurred in many of the economies that at first sight appeared to be more open and capitalist. In Kenya and Nigeria, for example, governments paid greater lip service to the importance of economic competition, but their markets were anything but free. Instead, access to the market was tightly regulated through the creation of laborious bureaucratic processes. The number of barriers to the conduct of business escalated for two reasons. First, every new hurdle – such as the need to secure multiple licenses to set up a street stall – created fresh opportunities for bribery and so enabled civil servants to supplement their meagre wages. Second, the same regulations enabled the government to give its supporters preferential access to the credit, licenses, and permits needed to set up successful companies. Of course, many governments lacked the capacity to fully regulate all economic transactions, but even so, the scarcity of economic opportunities outside of the state meant that there was little opportunity for people to pursue their ambitions outside of politics. Through this process, the emergence of gatekeeper states on the continent made incumbent leaders less willing to give up their privileged positions, and encouraged those excluded from power to take great risks in their efforts to gain control of the state. This development was significant, because it helps to explain why democracy has so often become characterized by winner-takes-all politics and civil conflict (Chapter 5).

Freedom and Unity in the Nationalist Struggle

The third main development that shaped the prospects for democracy for African states was the mixed legacy of the nationalist struggle. The fight against colonial rule is often remembered on the continent as a moment of great national unity. To a certain extent this was true. People united against a common enemy and campaigned for the independence of a given territory – and in doing so tacitly accepted the artificial borders drawn by foreign powers. In turn, the anti-colonial struggle helped to encourage a sense of national identity in states that were often younger than some of their citizens. National identities were also brought to life by the way that liberation movements came to express their demand for self-government. While some leaders, such as Amílcar Cabral – who led the nationalist movements in Guinea-Bissau and Cape Verde – demanded a revolutionary transformation of both colonial boundaries and economic relations, many leaders focused on the more attainable goal of replacing white colonial governments with African ones. In this more modest formulation of anti-colonial ambitions, African political organizations typically campaigned first for African representation within the legislative arena, then for the right for Africans to run for office, and subsequently for the extension of the mass franchise, all the time seeking not to dismantle the existing political landscape, but rather to take it over.

Yet the notion that the late colonial period was a time of African unity was also a necessary myth, valuable to those in power because it enabled them to gloss over internal schisms and to obscure competing visions of how power should be distributed. In fact, nationalist movements were often deeply divided. The boundaries of African states had been drawn not with respect to the location and history of different ethnic groups but according to a geo-strategic logic. Even if European cartographers had been more sensitive to local context, they would have struggled to design states that made economic and cultural sense. The average African country is more diverse than Greater London, and the number of small ethnic groups in countries such as the DRC, Nigeria, and Uganda would have made it impossible to design polities that would have been both ethnically homogenous and large enough to be practicable. As a result, ethnic tensions complicated the formation of a unified nationalism movement.

To understand how and why ethnic tensions contributed to periods of political instability and civil conflict in a number of African states it is essential to consider the way in which ethnic identities were further entrenched, and politicized, under colonial rule. Although tremendously varied in their approach to ethnicity and citizenship, colonial governments tended to classify communities into clearly demarcated ethnic groups that could be mapped onto specific pieces of land – ignoring the complexity and fluidity that often characterized African societies and their patterns of migration. Once such groups had been identified, the colonial powers often strengthened the control of Big Men over their communities in order to create clear lines of authority through which potentially rebellious groups could be co-opted. In the process, they enhanced the capacity of their allies to centralize power over their communities, which facilitated the emergence of more politically unified ethnic groups.

The willingness of colonial governments to employ divide-and-rule politics, in which different communities were played off against each other in order to stymie the emergence of a united nationalist movement, further served to solidify group identities. Taken together, these policies worked to institutionalize identities and connect them to specific pieces of land. The reification of the "tribe" also provided Africans with incentives to organize as ethnic communities, because this was the most effective way in which they could press their demands on the colonial regime. Following Ranger, one might say that colonial governments believed in tribes, and Africans gave them tribes to believe in.[7] In turn, more politically salient ethnic identities made it less likely that political movements would remain united – a major problem for nationalist leaders, but a boon for authoritarian incumbents seeking to defend their position after independence.

Inter-ethnic tensions were also fostered by the varied impact of the colonial era on local political economies. The communities that lived

[7] See Ranger, Terence. "The Invention of Tradition in Colonial Africa" in Eric Hobsbawm and Terence Ranger (eds.), *The Invention of Tradition*. Cambridge: Cambridge University Press, 1983, pp. 211–262 and Ranger, Terence. "The Invention of Tradition Revisited: The Case of Colonial Africa" in Terence Ranger and Olufemi Vaughan (eds.), *Legitimacy and the State in Twentieth Century Africa*. Basingstoke: Palgrave Macmillan, 1993, pp. 62–111.

near sites of colonial settlement usually suffered the greatest disruption as a result of occupation and land alienation, but were also the groups that benefited the most from the opportunities colonial rule had to offer. Mission education may have provided a basis for self-advancement, but it was proximity to wage labour and positions in the colonial administration that facilitated the emergence of a new elite. Because the communities that suffered the most painful consequences of colonial rule typically also enjoyed higher levels of education, know-how, and capital, their leaders had both the motivation and the confidence required to campaign for a rapid transition to independence.

The Kikuyu of Kenya illustrate this pattern well. The demarcation of land in the most fertile parts of the country for white settlers helped to radicalize the Kikuyu community, ultimately leading to the violent Mau Mau rebellion of the 1950s. Simultaneously, high levels of missionary education and the greater employment options available in Nairobi ensured that the Kikuyu community assumed an economically privileged position. Moreover, many Kikuyu did not join the Mau Mau, but rather became "loyalists" and worked for the colonial regime. As a result, the Kikuyu were strongly represented within both the colonial administration and the nationalist movement, and it was predominantly leaders from the Kikuyu and Luo communities that established the Kenyan African National Union (KANU) in 1960 to push for the speedy end of colonial rule, confident that they had the necessary skills and opportunity to reap the benefits of independence.

By contrast, economically and politically marginal communities faced a more uncertain future. For such groups, independence promised not a new set of freedoms, but rather the prospect of being dominated by their rivals. In Kenya, the Kalenjin, Maasai, and coastal communities were numerically smaller and less economically advanced than the Luo and Kikuyu. They thus established their own nationalist organization, the Kenya African Democratic Union (KADU), which advocated a more conservative agenda. Encouraged by European settlers – who also had good reason to fear majority rule – KADU campaigned for a more gradual transition to independence and for the introduction of a *majimbo* ("regionalist") constitution that would allow Kenya's communities a degree of local self-government. This campaign split the nationalist movement in two and resulted in considerable inter-party violence.

Although a small number of relatively homogenous countries such as Botswana did not have to face these challenges, many more struggled to manage the tension between the need for national unity and the determination of minority groups to escape the tyranny of the majority. In both the DRC and Nigeria, for example, the end of colonial rule was shortly followed by the attempted secession of resource-rich areas controlled by disgruntled ethnic groups, precipitating a rapid descent into civil war (see Chapter 1).

As well as increasing the prospects of political instability, the political salience of ethno-regional identities intensified the power of leaders over their communities. Indeed, it was the cauldron of inter-ethnic political competition that brought neo-patrimonialism to life. Patrons proved able to play on their community's fear of marginalization in order to mobilize support without reference to any democratic credentials. For example, unscrupulous leaders could manipulate ethnic tensions in order to legitimate the suppression of dissent and cement their own hegemony by arguing that more unified ethnic rivals would take advantage of any internal divisions. By pursuing these strategies in addition to classic divide-and-rule tactics, incumbents such as Togo's Gnassingbé Eyadema and Kenya's Daniel arap Moi were able to mute criticism of their poor economic performance from within their own support base, and prevent the emergence of a united opposition (Chapter 2). But although these methods enabled authoritarian leaders to maintain control in the short-term, in the long-term the politicization of ethnicity often had disastrous consequences for national unity (Chapter 5).

The nationalist period also shaped the way that democracy, and the strains it can induce within diverse societies, came to be discussed and managed. This was not simply an issue of semantic importance; ideas also played a key role in shaping the costs of repression and reform. While African nationalists phrased their demands in very different ways across the continent, they shared two primary aims, summed up by the title of Julius Nyerere's famous article of 1964: "Freedom and Unity".[8] The cry of freedom resonated everywhere. In East Africa, the nationalist struggle was known as the battle for *uhuru* ("freedom"). In South Africa, the ANC's famous statement of principles was called the Freedom Charter. Freedom was a particularly effective rallying call because it could mean all things to all people: freedom from colonial oppression, freedom from poverty and unemployment, freedom to fulfil one's aspirations.

---

[8] Nyerere, Julius. "Freedom and Unity". *Transition* 14 (1964), pp. 40–45.

But the demand for freedom went hand in hand with a call to unity. In the eyes of philosopher-kings such as Leopold Senghor of Senegal, unity had both instrumental and intrinsic value. Instrumental, because internal divisions would weaken the effectiveness of African nationalism. Intrinsic, because it reflected a common African heritage and culture that needed to be preserved against the challenges that would come from within and without. The call to unity took a variety of forms. In the hands of Kwame Nkrumah, Ghana's influential independence leader, it became a message of pan-Africanism, a call to move beyond colonial borders and to celebrate the continent's common history and needs. Other founding fathers, such as Jomo Kenyatta in Kenya, were rhetorically supportive of pan-Africanism but in practice were more concerned with ensuring domestic unity, which they saw as being necessary first to secure independence and later to meet the challenge of nation-building.

The ideals of freedom and unity continue to exert a great hold over the African political imagination, yet they have existed in perpetual tension. Postcolonial regimes typically viewed disunity as the forerunner of civil conflict and responded by promoting unity at any cost, even when this meant imposing significant constraints on the rights of ordinary people to speak and act freely. During the 1960s, leaders drew on the nationalist rhetoric of unity to justify the extension of political control, paving the way for the marginalization of rival parties and the steady erosion of political space. In part, the call to unity was so effective because few nationalist parties had articulated or communicated a clear vision of a democratic future that might have acted as a bulwark against the descent into authoritarianism. The stated attachment of many nationalists to the pursuit of freedom did not imply a commitment, either by party leaders or by their followers, to the introduction of checks and balances on the exercise of power.

Especially where the liberation struggle was longer and more violent, as in Angola, Mozambique, Zimbabwe, and to a lesser extent Namibia and South Africa, African governments have tended to obsess over unity, recognizing that it is central to their ability to establish and sustain political hegemony. Parties such as the Zimbabwe African National Union (ZANU), for example, proved adept at manipulating the memory of the liberation struggle in order to depict opposition groups or dissenting individuals as "traitors", and thus legitimate targets of state violence (Chapter 6). In most cases the

quest to maintain political order did not lead to such extreme consequences, but when freedom and unity came into tension it was typically the latter that won out.

The appeal to unity was also effective because, following the civil
wars in the DRC and Nigeria, it resonated with the fears of domestic
populations and international observers. From the 1960s on, the fear
of instability, the assumed importance of unity to the maintenance
of order, and the notion that forced consensus was compatible with
"African" values, have combined to weaken international and domestic demand for democracy in Africa. In turn, this lack of demand has
reduced the pressure on African leaders to reform, making it easier to
sustain authoritarian rule. It was in part fear of civil strife that encouraged donors to initially endorse President Museveni's "no-party" system in Uganda in the mid-1990s, contrary to the general push for
political liberalization on the continent. Similarly, Western governments began to question the wisdom of promoting multiparty politics in Africa following the 2007/2008 electoral crisis in Kenya and the
resumption of civil war in Côte d'Ivoire following elections in 2010.

Of course, the nature of nationalist discourse and practice was also
shaped by the experience that African leaders and parties had of par-
ticipating in government under colonial rule. In Senegal, the French
authorities allowed for a far more open and participatory form of
politics, albeit in a small part of the country. In the four colonial
towns known as the Four Communes, African residents were able to
vote in elections to select a deputy to represent Senegal in the French
national assembly as early as 1848, although it was not until 1914 that
an African was elected to the post. As a result of the extension of
full voting rights to the African population of the Four Communes
in 1916, the Senegalese political elite gained far greater experience
of plural politics and self-rule than their counterparts elsewhere on
the continent, and this helps to explain why it has been one of the
most stable and democratic African states ever since (see Chapters 2
and 6).

However, the Senegalese experience was rare. In most cases the first
mass-franchise elections were typically not held until the late 1950s,
while in the DRC the Belgian colonial government denied Africans
meaningful political participation in national-level government until
the very eve of independence. African politicians were often able to
enter sham legislative bodies much earlier than this, but these were
largely talking shops: when the British colonial government created

urban advisory councils in the 1920s and 1930s to provide an outlet for African opinion, real power continued to reside with appointed, rather than elected, individuals. It is therefore hardly surprising that democratic practices did not become ingrained.

The Second Liberation?

The combination of neo-patrimonial rule, gatekeeper states, and the mixed legacy of African nationalism made it more likely that leaders would choose repression over reform. Although individual countries varied greatly in the extent to which they exhibited these features, for the first thirty years of independence conditions were rarely favourable to the construction and maintenance of democracy. Yet the flame of freedom was never fully extinguished. Like people everywhere, Africans have consistently sought to resist violations of their basic human rights and to play a role in shaping the decisions that affect their lives. This can be seen in the bravery of journalists who have exposed corruption at great risk to their personal safety, lawyers who have rejected lucrative jobs to defend pro-democracy activists, and ordinary people across the continent who have consistently taken the rare opportunities that they have been given to participate in the political process (see Chapter 2). Anyone who doubts this need only observe a voting queue in a country like Kenya or South Africa, where people wait patiently for hours in the baking sun just to cast their ballots, in stark contrast to the voter apathy so often documented in Western democracies.

From the late 1980s onward, a number of fundamental changes to the domestic and international environment undermined the position of African incumbents and increasingly exposed them to domestic pressure to reform. The remaining chapters of this book demonstrate the way in which economic decline, generational change, and the end of the Cold War – which encouraged the United States and a number of other Western governments to focus on democracy promotion – combined to intensify the opposition to authoritarian rule. When donors decided to use their leverage over economically fragile African governments to push for political liberalization, the costs of reform became more acceptable than the costs of repression for the first time since independence. Over the next ten years, multiparty elections were reintroduced across the continent (see Chapter 4).

But it is important not to make the mistake of assuming that just because countries held elections they were democracies. That a country has a multiparty constitution tells us remarkably little about how open the broader political system actually is. In 2010, Cape Verde received the best possible score from Freedom House, while Sudan received the worst: both had held elections in the previous twelve months. If the value of democracy is that it allows all individuals within a polity to have an equal say over the decisions that affect their lives, then elections do not lead to democratic government if citizens are prevented from registering support for their choice of candidate as a result of intimidation, or election rigging, or because their candidate is not actually allowed to stand. This lesson is perhaps better understood in Africa than anywhere else on earth. In countries such as Cameroon and Togo, incumbents with little respect for democratic norms reintroduced elections to appease domestic and international critics, but had no intention of allowing power to be transferred to the opposition. In such cases, the political systems that emerged were electoral-authoritarian: they formally allowed political competition but in reality denied citizens the political rights and civil liberties necessary to render elections meaningful (see Chapter 5). By the turn of the century the vast majority of African states were multiparty political systems, but only a few could claim to be full democracies.

To become consolidated democracies, these states must go through two separate but related processes. First, deepening the quality of democracy requires the evolution of institutions that are not controlled by the executive, enabling opposition parties to compete on a level playing field. In addition to reducing the advantages that incumbency confers on ruling parties, historically marginalized groups – including women – must be able to effectively communicate their own needs and desires. At present, even some of Africa's "success stories" such as Botswana and Namibia suffer major democratic deficits because although all citizens of voting age enjoy the formal right to participate in the political process, certain groups such as San Bushmen have faced significant barriers to their full participation in mainstream politics. Second, securing democratic gains requires the strengthening of democratic norms, practices, and procedures within political institutions, political parties, and society at-large. We can only speak of a consolidated democracy when plural politics has become the only game in town.[9]

[9] Przeworski, Adam. *Democracy and the Market: Political and Economic Reforms in Eastern Europe and Latin America.* Cambridge: Cambridge University Press, 1991, p. 26.

It is worth separating out these two dimensions of democratic consolidation because, following the reintroduction of multiparty politics, African countries occupied a variety of positions on both scales. In some countries, such as Benin and Cape Verde, open political systems emerged so rapidly that there was little time to entrench democratic gains, resulting in the creation of high quality but vulnerable democracies. By contrast, in countries such as Angola, governments utilized high levels of repression and censorship to maintain control, establishing poor quality but stable multiparty systems. In both contexts, the prospects for further reform will be improved by developments that increase the costs of repression and decrease the costs of reform, such as the evolution of a vibrant media and more autonomous democratic institutions.

But this is only one part of the equation. It is also important to ensure that opposition leaders invest their energies in strengthening the democratic system rather than undermining it. To understand how groups can be persuaded to buy-into the democratic process, and to eschew chauvinistic and exclusionary appeals, we must move beyond the framework developed in this chapter, which has considered democracy in Africa through the lens of incumbent leaders. Instead, we must shift focus to consider how political institutions can be designed to encourage opposition and rebel groups can be persuaded to invest in multiparty politics. This is the subject of the final part of the book.

To date, constitution writers have shown a remarkable lack of imagination when thinking about how to design democracies that last in Africa. Yet a closer look at Africa's success stories suggests that more inclusive institutional arrangements adapted to local circumstances may give competitive political systems stronger foundations. Consider Ghana, where the creation of a house of chiefs has ensured an ongoing role for traditional leaders, or Mauritius, where under-represented ethnic groups are appointed to the legislature so that parliament always more or less reflects the wider population. By reducing the cost of losing an election, such measures encourage incumbents and opposition parties to accept defeat and continue to play by the rules of the democratic game. This is not to suggest that we should apply different (i.e., lower) democratic standards when dealing with African countries. Although multiparty systems in the West are often highly majoritarian in that they give little power to losing candidates – as in the United Kingdom where the first-past-the-post system tends to exaggerate the winning margin of the largest party – democracy need not be. After all, we do not assume that the presence of federalism in the United States, the need for coalitions governments in Germany, or a rotating three-member presidency in Bosnia-Herzegovina automatically renders these countries undemocratic. Rather, we recognize that these variations in institutional design reflect different historical pathways to democracy and have played an important role in promoting more stable and open political systems. History suggests that similar compromises will serve to enhance, rather than hinder, democratic consolidation in Africa (see Conclusion).

Select Bibliography

Cooper, Frederick. *Africa Since 1940: The Past of the Present.* Cambridge: Cambridge University Press, 2002.

Dahl, Robert Alan. *Polyarchy: Participation and Opposition.* New Haven & London: Yale University Press, 1971.

Erdmann, Gero. "Neopatrimonialism and Political Regimes" in Nic Cheeseman, David Anderson, and Andrea Scheibler (eds) *The Routledge Handbook of African Politics.* Oxford: Routledge, 2013.

Herbst, Jeffrey. *States and Power in Africa: Comparative Lessons in Authority and Control.* Chichester: Princeton University Press, 2000.

Przeworski, Adam. *Democracy and the Market.* Cambridge: Cambridge University Press, 1991.

For a bibliography for this chapter go to www.democracyinafrica.org

CHAPTER 1

Fragments of Democracy: Participation and Control in Authoritarian Africa

The dominant story of the first decade of independence was the collapse of Africa's democratic experiment. Having experienced a wave of euphoria following the overthrow of colonial rule, the continent rapidly descended into a political and economic depression characterized by the emergence of repressive and corrupt regimes. If we exclude the cases of white minority rule in southern Africa, by the end of the 1970s only Botswana, Gambia, Mauritius, and – to a lesser degree – Senegal continued to practice multipartyism. As a result, for most Africans independence did not mean freedom from authoritarian rule. In many countries, the foundations of this process were laid in the colonial period. As we saw in the Introduction, the emergence of Big Men, the problematic legacy of African nationalism, and the creation of undeveloped economies directly under state control did not represent a strong foundation on which to build a stable and successful democracy.

Against this most unpromising of backdrops, it was the catastrophic failure of the continent's new political systems to manage competition over power and resources that put the final nails in the coffin of representative government. Bloody civil wars in what is now the DRC and Nigeria persuaded many commentators that ethnic diversity, multipartyism, and political stability were not compatible in the African context. The Cold War also undermined international

The title of this chapter draws on many conversations with Gavin Williams as well as his *Fragments of Democracy*. Cape Town: HSRC Publishers, 2003.

support for democratization, as both the United States and the Soviet Union proved willing to sacrifice democracy on the altar of their own national security. Together, these two trends made it easier for incumbent leaders to centralize power and to downgrade representative institutions. But even during the dark days of the 1970s a democratic light continued to shine, because the limited coercive capacity of state structures meant that governments were rarely in a position to rule through force alone. Instead, authoritarian leaders experimented with different combinations of participation and control in order to confer legitimacy on their regimes and so stave off the threat of popular uprising or military coup. Thus, while democracy was relegated to the backbenches after independence, it remained an important reference point for even the most authoritarian regimes.

The First Crisis of Democracy

Perhaps the most notorious crisis of African democracy occurred in Congo-Kinshasa (previously known as the Belgian Congo, later renamed Zaire, and now known as the Democratic Republic of the Congo). A particularly poisonous colonial legacy ensured that the Congo was a singularly difficult environment in which to experiment with multiparty politics. Under the brutal rule of King Leopold II of Belgium, millions died as the territory was turned into a personal fiefdom dedicated to the exploitation of rubber. The callous brutality of Leopold's tyranny, famously depicted in Joseph Conrad's novella, *Heart of Darkness*, was shocking even by the standards of the colonial era. However, even after Leopold's excesses had been exposed and the Congo had been annexed by the Belgian state in 1908, little was done to develop an effective national infrastructure or to prepare the country for independence, and there was no attempt to introduce representative government until the late 1950s. Africans were not allowed to vote until 1957, and even then municipal elections were limited to the urban centres of Léopoldville, Elisabethville, and Jadotville. As a result, the Congo's small and fragmented political elite – of, at most, 5,000 high school graduates – entered independence with virtually no experience of running one of the largest and most diverse countries in the world.

Into this most unpromising of contexts stepped Patrice Lumumba. Now remembered as the most tragic of Africa's independence leaders, Lumumba was born into a Catholic family and received a religious education before moving on to the government post office training school. A bright and hard-working student, he quickly joined the ranks of the Congolese elite as a postal clerk, and by 1955 had begun to show the leadership qualities that would make him famous, joining the Liberal Party of Belgium and editing party literature. Just six years later he was dead, killed by Congolese soldiers after a tumultuous period as his country's first prime minister. Lumumba's legend is one of the most revealing and controversial stories of African independence. It remains relevant today because his rise and fall have much to tell us about the way in which ethnic and regional divisions, manipulated by domestic and international actors, can undermine the prospects for democratization.

Having been promoted as the regional head of a Congolese trade union in 1955, Lumumba was subsequently arrested on charges of embezzling post office funds, but released a year later. His time in prison, combined with the rise of African nationalism across the continent, inspired him to adopt a more radical stance, and he subsequently developed a fierce critique of the inequalities of colonial rule that won him a new set of supporters. In turn, Lumumba's newfound political prominence brought him into contact with pan-Africanist leaders such as Ghana's Kwame Nkrumah, with whom he discussed the need for African unity and rapid independence, consolidating his commitment to the creation of a united nationalist movement in the Congo. Less than two years later he became one of the founding members – and ultimately the president – of the Congolese National Movement (MNC), which he intended to be a "non-tribal" party. The MNC subsequently became the platform through which Lumumba communicated his vision of a socially just Congolese state. Tall and thin, with engaging eyes, he spoke with authority and passion. His rhetorical ability, forthright tone, and concern for equality led his opponents to accuse him of being a communist. With typical force and candour, he replied: "I am not a Communist. The colonialists have campaigned against me throughout the country because I am a revolutionary and demand the abolition of the colonial regime, which ignored our human dignity. They look upon me as a Communist because I refused to be bribed by the imperialists."

The main barrier to Lumumba's dream of a united and radical nationalist movement was the deeply fragmented political landscape within which he operated. The late introduction of multiparty politics led to chronic infrastructural weaknesses within the government and individual political parties, and a political elite that lacked the experience of holding and sharing power. In turn, the lack of established political organizations in the Congo, combined with the difficulty of mobilizing colony-wide support in such a diverse polity, encouraged political leaders to focus on strengthening their own ethno-regional base rather than building effective national organizations. Not only did Lumumba fail to integrate other parties such as the Alliance of Bakongo (ABAKO) led by Joseph Kasa-Vubu; he struggled to maintain the unity of his own party, which split into two groups: Lumumba's MNC-L, and the MNC-K led by Albert Kalonji. Elections on the eve of independence in 1960 confirmed just how fractured the political system had become. Of the 13 parties that won legislative seats, many failed to stand candidates outside of their own province, and although the MNC-L emerged as the largest party, it won just 33 of 137 parliamentary seats. This left Lumumba in a weak bargaining position, and he was only able to secure the position of prime minister after agreeing to share executive power with his more conservative rival, Kasa-Vubu, who became the Congo's first president.

As prime minister, Lumumba faced a new set of challenges in his mission to unite the Congolese people. The likes of Kasa-Vubu and Moise Tshombe of the Confederation of Tribal Associations of Katanga (CONAKAT) sought to undermine his vision because they had a very different understanding of how independent Congo should be structured. Most significantly, they hoped to keep the central government weak in order to protect their own provincial bases of power, safe in the knowledge that their regions were sufficiently resource rich to survive without support from the centre. The rising tension between Lumumba, Kasa-Vubu, and Tshombe also reflected a wider desire for self-government that was keenly felt by many Congolese communities, which feared that leaders from rival groups would not govern in the interests of all. Just months after winning power, Lumumba found that his authority was being undermined by the combination of strong sectional interests and the absence of an effective state through which to exert control. As political stalemate quickly gave rise to an oppressive atmosphere of unease, Lumumba began to lose his grip on power.

Amidst rising instability, a military mutiny in July 1960 provided the excuse that the Belgian government had been looking for to deploy troops in the country against Lumumba's wishes. Although Belgium officially justified the operation on the basis of the need to protect Belgian citizens that had been caught up in the turmoil, Lumumba feared that its real purpose was to replace him with a leader who would make the Congo's vast natural resources more readily available. His fears were subsequently confirmed when Moise Tshombe declared Katangan secession, backed by more than 6,000 Belgian troops. Tshombe had brokered a deal in which Belgian companies were given privileged access to Katanga's reserves of mining copper, gold, and uranium in return for assistance in the creation of a viable Katangan military force.

Tshombe's declaration and Lumumba's determination to prevent Katangan secession led to outright conflict and the disintegration of what was left of the Congolese state. As clashes on a smaller scale broke out in the east and central parts of the country, the Congo descended into a brutal civil war in which more than 100,000 people lost their lives. In desperation, Lumumba requested the assistance of the United Nations (UN) to reassert his authority. But although the UN established the United Nations Operation in the Congo (ONUC), the limited mandate of the mission and the subsequent refusal of UN troops to restore central control over Katanga left him frustrated. Lumumba subsequently approached the Soviet Union in the hope that it would be a more effective international ally. But this decision proved fateful, for it confirmed U.S. fears regarding his "radical" politics, and encouraged the Central Intelligence Agency (CIA), which had already been cultivating relationships with some of Lumumba's main rivals including Kasa-Vubu and the chief of staff to the army, Joseph Mobutu, to move against him.

Emboldened by U.S. support, Mobutu took advantage of the political paralysis to launch a military coup, placing Lumumba under house arrest. In a final bid to regain control, Lumumba attempted to escape and reach his supporters in Stanleyville, but was captured by Mobutu's troops on 1 December 1960 and transported to Katanga. According to a Belgian inquiry in 2001, he was tortured and killed by Katangan gendarmes in the presence of Belgian officers, most likely with the full knowledge of the CIA, on 17 January 1961 – just six months after he was sworn in as prime minister.

Participation and Control

The "Congo crisis" had two major consequences for the development of African democracy. First, the disastrous impact of international engagement demonstrated the limited ability of international actors to keep the peace and broker political settlements in complex African states that they poorly understood. As a result, UN officials and foreign ministries became more hesitant to engage in peacekeeping work or the active defence of democracy in Africa. Instead, foreign governments increasingly found ways to work with authoritarian leaders, prioritizing stability and access to resources over the democratic rights of ordinary Africans. In turn, African leaders manipulated Cold War tensions between the United States and the Soviet Union for their own ends. Following Lumumba's death, Mobutu played on U.S. fears that communism would spread across the continent to secure almost continuous access to American funds and military support. This, and his willingness to act as a conduit for U.S. policy, enabled him to maintain one of the world's most violent and corrupt authoritarian regimes for more than thirty-five years. In this way, the international community played its own part in the rise of authoritarian Africa.

The second key legacy of the Congo crisis was that it raised deep concerns about the feasibility of democracy in Africa. These anxieties were soon reinforced by events in Nigeria, where the breakdown of civilian government also culminated in a secession attempt – in this case by the eastern part of the country that sought to gain independence as the Republic of Biafra – and civil war. Images of the hardships that the people of Biafra suffered as a result of a siege and subsequent military defeat were carried throughout the world, leaving an indelible impression of the high costs of democratic failure. Of course, by the mid-1960s, authoritarian regimes were already well established in some African countries. But in the wake of events in the Congo and Nigeria it became increasingly feasible for leaders to justify democratic backsliding on the grounds that their countries were too large, or too diverse, for multipartyism to work effectively. If Nigeria, why not Kenya? If Congo, why not Uganda, or Ethiopia, or Zambia? Despite considerable domestic resistance, African governments also had ways of legitimating the return to authoritarian rule to their own people. In many countries, leaders were able to sell the idea that political control should trump competition by arguing that this approach was little more than a continuation of the call to unity and consensus that had underpinned the anti-colonial struggle (see the Introduction).

It quickly became apparent that not all authoritarian regimes were the same. The two most common types of regime that emerged in postcolonial Africa were military rule and the one-party state. As in the Congo, the failure of multiparty politics typically generated a power vacuum that facilitated the entrance of the military onto the political stage. In the first decade of independence, military coups in Benin (1963), Congo-Brazzaville (1963), Togo (1963), Central African Republic (1966), and Ghana (1966) showed the capacity of even a relatively small group of coup plotters to gain and retain control of the state. By 1980, more than two-thirds of sub-Saharan African states had experienced some form of military rule. Although supporting undemocratic governments was at times embarrassing for international actors, this did not prevent such regimes from securing arms and resources from abroad.

One-party states were easier to justify than military regimes because it was less obvious that these political systems relied on coercion to maintain control, and there were already numerous examples of (seemingly) stable and effective single-party systems outside the continent, including Cuba, Mexico, and the Soviet Union. This was particularly true of countries in which one-party rule was introduced by the same nationalist parties that had secured vast majorities at the ballot box toward the end of colonial rule. In the immediate post-independence period, leaders such as Felix Houphouët-Boigny in Côte d'Ivoire and Ahmed Sékou Touré in Guinea were well placed to argue that in their countries the one-party state represented not authoritarian demagoguery, but the will of the people. Over the next thirty years, one-party states proved to be one of the most common and stable forms of government in Africa. At one point or another Angola, Benin, Burkina Faso, Burundi, Cameroon, Cape Verde, the Central African Republic, Chad, Comoros, Congo-Brazzaville, Congo-Kinshasa, Djibouti, Equatorial Guinea, Ethiopia, Gabon, Ghana, Guinea-Bissau, Liberia, Malawi, Mali, Mauritania, Mozambique, Niger, Rwanda, Sao Tome and Principle, Seychelles, Sierra Leone, Somalia, Sudan, and Togo all claimed single-party status.

But despite the curtailment of competition across the continent, the limited coercive capacity enjoyed by many African states meant that governments typically struggled to fully control political activity. Nationalist leaders also came under considerable pressure to maintain some element of representative government from their own supporters. Ordinary people did not forget that they had been promised freedom as well as unity, and many communities retained a strong desire to be able to have a say in the decisions that affected their lives. Consequently, most of Africa's presidents and prime ministers faced strong incentives to buttress coercive control with other mechanisms that enabled ordinary people to feel that they had a stake in government.

In addition to the distribution of patronage (discussed in Chapter 2), it was common for postcolonial governments to maintain some form of political participation, however superficial. This was most obvious in the continent's single-party systems. Although some authoritarian leaders created parties simply to try and legitimate brutal military dictatorships, this was not always true of the civilian regimes that had initially come to power through competitive elections. For example, in countries such as Côte d'Ivoire, Kenya, Senegal, and Tanzania, one-party governments continued to hold localized elections that allowed for a degree of accountability between local communities and their representatives.

Perhaps more surprisingly, many military leaders also sought to tap into forms of democratic legitimacy, despite the authoritarian foundations of their rule. In some countries, the invocation of elections or party structures was nothing more than mendacious political theatre – a sleight of hand designed to conceal the true nature of the regime. But in others, such as Benin and Ghana, the parties that military leaders created developed real roots. Thus, while power was progressively centralized across the continent, elements of representative government lived on, albeit in varying degrees. This point is of both historical and contemporary importance, because the balance between participation and control in a given country shaped the political landscape within which the transition to multiparty politics in the 1990s took place, and the prospects for democratic consolidation thereafter. In general, it was the states that maintained more inclusive and accountable political structures in the 1980s that emerged as Africa's most open and stable democracies in the 1990s (see Chapter 3).

Semi-Competitive Elections in the One-Party State

Perhaps the most eloquent and effective advocate of the one-party state was Tanzanian President Julius Nyerere, whose influence helped to promote the proliferation of single-party systems across the continent. When President Kenneth Kaunda of Zambia was informed that his former friend and right-hand man, Simon Kapwepwe, had decided to quit the ruling party – dividing the government and empowering the opposition – he flew to Tanzania to ask Nyerere how to go about establishing a one-party government. Nyerere was glad to help, because in his eyes multiparty politics was not just politically dangerous; it was unnecessary, and "un-African".

One of twenty-six children born to Nyerere Burito, one of several chiefs of the Zanaki, Nyerere was highly educated, first at government schools and later at Makerere University in Kampala and the University of Edinburgh. Like Lumumba, he was motivated by concerns of equality and unity, and it was in Edinburgh that he encountered the Fabian Society – a British organization that sought to advance the principle of socialism by gradual means – and began to think seriously about how he could integrate socialist principles with African political and economic realities.

Upon returning from his studies, Nyerere taught history, English, and Swahili at St. Francis's College, and subsequently became known as *Mwalimu* ("teacher"). Having been elected president of the Tanganyika African Association (TAA) in 1953, he set about transforming what had been a mainly civic organization dominated by civil servants into a more dynamic political movement. In 1954, the Tanganyika African National Unity (TANU) was born, and rapidly propelled Nyerere to political prominence. He was elected chief minister in 1960, and subsequently became the country's first prime minister upon independence in 1961. After Tanganyika became a republic in 1962, Nyerere was elected president with 98 per cent of the vote. Less than a year later, he moved to complete the first part of his political project, proposing legal changes to turn the country into a one-party state – although it had effectively been a single-party system since independence because TANU (or TANU-aligned) candidates had won all of the seats in the 1960 legislative council elections. Following the merger of Tanganyika and the island of Zanzibar in 1964 to form what would become the United Republic of Tanzania, this restriction was relaxed in order to allow the Afro Shirazi Party (ASP) to represent the island. However, after TANU and the ASP agreed to merge to form the Chama cha Mapinduzi (CCM) in 1977, the "Party of the Revolution" was proclaimed to be the only legal party.

Nyerere chose to limit the rights of his people to choose their own government because of his intellectual heritage and the challenges that he faced after independence. Given the lack of organized opposition to TANU, the main threat to Nyerere's authority came from within his party, not from without. TANU, like most nationalist governments, was a coalition of diverse interests that began to unravel once the unifying struggle against colonial rule was over. Shortly after independence, rival leaders challenged both Nyerere's policies and his political authority. A shrewd political operator, Nyerere understood that by banning opposition parties and so making it impossible for his rivals within TANU to establish rival political movements, he could undermine their ability to blackmail him into meeting their demands.

But Mwalimu's decision to rule through a one-party state was not simply motivated by self-preservation – Nyerere also believed that a single-party system was the best way to rapidly develop his country, which had entered independence with little infrastructure and a low skills base. As a leading anti-colonial figure in charge of a predominantly rural economy, Nyerere was reluctant to look west in his search for economic or political models. Instead he looked east to the Soviet Union, which had criticized British and U.S. imperialism in Africa and appeared to have achieved exactly what Tanzania needed to do: develop a self-sustainable economy from an agricultural base. In particular, Nyerere's vision reflected the communist preoccupation with equality and belief that the party – in this case TANU – was the vehicle through which development could be achieved. As Nyerere put it in the Arusha Declaration of 1967, "A committed member of TANU will be a socialist. ... The first duty of a TANU member, and especially of a TANU leader, is to accept these socialist principles, and to live his own life in accordance with them." But Nyerere understood that this would not be possible if TANU leaders were diverted from their task as a result of ethnic or political divisions. Recognizing that such distractions would be more likely under multipartyism, he concluded that a one-party state was essential to preserve the unity that nation-building and development demanded.

While the model of the Soviet Union was an important touchstone for many African leaders, a closer look at the period suggests that Nyerere's efforts to restructure society into an egalitarian system of large cooperative villages owed less to Soviet-style communism than to the more cautious socialist ideals that he had engaged with in the United Kingdom and his own interpretation of Tanzanian history and culture. Nyerere did not immediately move towards collectivization and nationalization. In fact, he initially presided over a relatively mixed economy that featured elements of capitalism and socialism, and only moved towards more extensive government intervention once this had begun to fail. His motivations for establishing a one-party state were similarly complex. Nyerere did not unthinkingly copy the model employed in the Soviet Union; rather, he came to the conclusion that an inclusive single-party system was perfectly suited to African norms and values. His views in this regard were profoundly shaped by his childhood experience of watching his father arbitrate disputes in rural Tanganyika, which imbued in him a somewhat idealized understanding of African traditional life in which decision-making was characterized not by competition between different leaders and ideas but by the slow evolution of consensus – literally talking out an issue under a tree until an agreement had been forged. On this basis, Nyerere argued that the one-party state could be seen as a manifestation of African democracy: it was simply a modern vehicle through which to bring about the consensus that elders had always sought. This part of his justification was later appropriated by other leaders, such as Kaunda, who claimed that while Western democracy only allowed citizens to participate in government every four years the one-party state would allow for constant participation.

Although their governments failed to live up to this promise, this was not just empty talk. Civilian one-party states proved to be the most stable form of government in Africa after independence precisely because they combined tight control with political participation. In Tanzania, Nyerere instituted regular one-party elections in which voters could choose between a set of TANU candidates. Although it is impossible to be certain, the outcomes of these elections appear to have largely reflected the will of the voters, at least in the first decade of independence. This meant that the electorate in countries such as Kenya, Tanzania, and Zambia were able to use the polls to register their discontent with their local representatives – and they did, with around 50 per cent of Members of Parliament (MPs) losing their seats in every election. This kept legislators on their toes and facilitated elite rotation, enabling younger leaders with new ideas to enter parliament. It also encouraged ordinary people to feel that they had a say in the decisions that affected their lives, which in turn helped Nyerere to legitimate a political system that in many ways was actually failing his people: although Tanzania achieved remarkably high literacy levels in the 1970s, per capita GDP fell in the early 1980s, so that on average people were poorer in 1986 than they had been in 1981.

Unsurprisingly, single-party elections developed their own distinctive dynamics. Because voters rejected candidates who paid them insufficient attention, legislators were forced to focus on constituency service and to raise locally sensitive issues on the floor of the house. Moreover, because all of the candidates belonged to the same party, and elections focused were held at constituency level, they became obsessively local. This reduced the potential for divisive open competition between larger ethnic and regional communities, aiding Nyerere's efforts to construct a coherent Tanzanian identity (for more on which, see the Conclusion to this book). And because many rural constituencies were fairly ethnically homogenous in countries like Kenya, voters had to choose between individuals on a different basis, and so a candidate's record and personal qualities became of central importance (see Chapter 2). Where they worked best, one-party elections empowered communities to hold their leaders accountable on the issues closest to their hearts.

While participation was an important source of legitimacy, Nyerere's authority was also underpinned by the extension of political control. Power was centralized under the presidency, representative institutions such as the legislature were downgraded, and, following the example of the Soviet Union, trade union leaders and youth leaders were co-opted into the party hierarchy through the creation of a party-sponsored youth league and trade union congress. Centralization was buttressed by overt coercion when required. When it transpired that many Tanzanians did not share Nyerere's understanding of their culture and traditions, and were reluctant to uproot their families in order to move into the large villages that were a central element of his *Ujamaa* ("unity"/"familyhood") project, force was used to ensure compliance. Coercion was also deployed to deter political opposition. In 1962, Nyerere introduced the Preventative Detention Act, which was subsequently used to imprison opposition leaders who could not otherwise be contained. It is thought that by 1979 there were more political prisoners in Tanzania than in apartheid South Africa, and Amnesty International identified (and supported) almost 150 "prisoners of conscience" in the 1970s alone.

Ironically, most civilian one-party states were ultimately undermined not by external opposition but by the atrophy of the ruling party itself. Nyerere found that the absence of multiparty competition blunted the enthusiasm of party members, while a chronic lack of resources had resulted in the deterioration of the party's organizational capacity shortly after independence. His response was to extend the party's life by fusing it with the state, so that state resources could be used to fund the ruling party, and party activists could be used to radicalize the bureaucracy to socialist ends. But while the conflation of party and state structures kept the CCM from collapse it was not without costs. What Nyerere had not anticipated was that the fusion of party and state would create bloated committees, unclear authority structures, and institutional blockages, as technocrats and party officials competed for supremacy. Although in principle his new system generated more avenues through which people could engage with their rulers, in reality the labyrinthine world of committee systems was so unresponsive that ordinary Tanzanians began to lose faith in the party-state and in many cases chose to disengage from the formal political system.

For all of the economic and political limitations of the one-party state, Nyerere is still regarded by many as a hero, and for good reasons. By promoting a shared set of cultural values and symbols he defused inter-communal tensions and built a Tanzanian national identity that has stood the test of time. By emphasizing equality and discipline he prevented – or at least postponed – the emergence of the venal corruption that proved so destructive in nearby Kenya. And by ultimately recognizing the limitations of the policies that he introduced, he also facilitated change, first when he resigned his office in 1985 in order to let others introduce desperately needed economic reforms – becoming one of the only African leaders to leave power voluntarily in the 1980s – and later, when he intervened to persuade his successors within the CCM to abandon the one-party state and reintroduce multiparty politics in the early 1990s (see Chapter 3).

Military Rule and Politics Without Politicians

Like the creation of one-party states, military rule came about through a variety of different pathways. In many cases, coups were driven by the desire of military personnel to improve, or at least maintain, their position. The infamous Idi Amin claimed that he had overthrown Milton Obote's government in Uganda in order to defend freedom of speech and the right to free and fair elections. In reality, he was more concerned with self-protection: Amin most likely knew that Obote planned to replace him as commander of the army, which would have left him vulnerable to prosecution for the murder of one of his main rivals within the military, Brigadier P.Y. Okoya. But while self-advancement motivated many coup plotters, military intervention was often facilitated by the political instability generated by the failure of civilian regimes themselves. This was the case with the coup that brought Yakubu Gowon to power in Nigeria, which occurred amidst a period of chronic instability in the mid 1960s.

Gowon had joined the army in 1954 and attended the Royal Military Academy at Sandhurst in England, but although he was promoted to lieutenant colonel in 1963 he remained largely unknown. It was a series of unpredictable events, and his particular ethnic and religious identity, that thrust Gowon into the political limelight and conferred on him one of the most important roles in Nigeria's postcolonial history: holding the country together during the civil war, and stabilizing it thereafter.

The way Gowon undertook this most difficult of tasks owed much to the lessons that he drew from the Congo crisis, where he served as part of a Nigerian peacekeeping force in the early 1960s. What he gained from this experience was a keen awareness of the capacity of political competition to destabilize fragile societies, and the potential for federal political systems to exacerbate demands for secession. Both points were pertinent to the political situation in Nigeria. Long before Gowon came on the scene, the civilian regime of Prime Minister Sir Abubakar Tafawa Balewa had begun to fragment under the weight of its own internal contradictions. The federal system bequeathed by the British served to encourage tension between the country's three regions, each of which was dominated by a different ethnic group: the Housa-Fulani in the north, the Yoruba in the west, and the Igbo in the east. On the one hand, leaders from each community sought to monopolize the regional governments as their personal fiefdoms, rigging elections and attacking their rivals in the process. On the other, they fought bitterly over national power and how it should be distributed. Taken together, these two trends made for a violent, volatile, and dangerous political atmosphere. As ethnic tensions escalated, a group of mostly Igbo military officers overthrew the civilian government on 15 January 1966, killing the prime minister and the premier of the Northern Region, Samuel Akintola, in the process. Rightly or wrongly, Northern military leaders interpreted the coup as an Igbo power grab, and responded with a counter-coup on 29 July.

The second coup was led by Murtula Mohammed, who desired the position of supreme commander for himself. However, he ultimately lost out to Gowon, even though his rival had not played a significant role in the coup itself. Gowon owed his ascendency more to luck than judgment. Despite being just thirty-two years of age, he outranked

Mohammed. Moreover, while Mohammed was a Hausa-Fulani Muslim from the North, Gowon was unusual in being a Northerner who was neither Hausa-Fulani, nor a Muslim. Given this, a government led by Gowon appeared to be less likely to exacerbate ethnic and religious tension with the mostly Christian south. However, despite this small advantage Gowon failed to reconcile the Igbo east to the new political arrangement, and his plan to redraw the country's federal system to reduce the power of the largest ethnic groups further antagonized Eastern leaders. Combined with a number of attacks on Igbo communities living in the north of the country, this hastened the attempted secession of the Eastern region as the self-proclaimed Republic of Biafra and the subsequent onset of civil war. As a result, Gowon spent three of his first four years in power fighting a conflict that cost the lives of an estimated 100,000 military personnel and between 500,000 and 2 million civilians.

Despite the recent discovery of oil, which was predominantly located in the east of the country, Biafra lacked the resources or technical capacity to defeat the Nigerian army and was ultimately forced to announce an unconditional ceasefire, bringing the war to an end on 13 January 1970. Gowon now faced his second major challenge: how to unify and rebuild the country. He began in a spirit of reconciliation, stating that there had been "no victor, no vanquished", and initiating a reconciliation, reconstruction and rehabilitation program to rebuild the Eastern Region – although the latter policy met with limited success. But this left the question of how to actually govern Nigeria in peacetime. Like his civilian counterparts who established one-party states, Gowon associated multiparty competition with inter-communal tension. But unlike single-party states in which the ruling party lived on as a vehicle of popular participation – at least in theory – Gowon was distrustful of the political class and so restricted their presence in his government. He was also reluctant to allow for any kind of elections to be held because competition, even at the local level, was unpredictable and had the potential to exacerbate pre-existing tensions.

In particular, Gowon feared that reengaging with political leaders even at the regional level might intensify the existing divisions within the military that had initially pushed the country towards civil war. But practicing politics without politicians brought its own problems; most notably, it made it harder for the military government to legitimate itself and to anticipate shifts in public opinion. Gowon therefore faced a difficult choice between banning politicians and elections at the risk of not being able to anticipate the public mood on the one hand, and endangering the unity of the armed forces by engaging in representative government on the other.

As Henry Bienen's research in Western State reveals, the need to maintain the legitimacy of the regime in the wake of the civil war ultimately encouraged Gowon to give a greater role to civilian leaders within the government than he had at first envisaged. To this end, he announced that a civilian Federal Executive Council (FEC) would be established to share executive authority with the Supreme Military Council (SMC) in June 1967. Civilian appointees were called commissioners because Gowon believed that his countrymen "were not anxious to see those who in recent years participated in politics back in ministerial seats".[1] Similar reforms were introduced with some variations at the state level. However, this technocratic hybrid failed to resolve the main problems facing Gowon. For one thing, the attempt to generate a more responsive political system without engaging with politicians was largely unsuccessful because many of the "civilians" appointed to the FEC (and its regional equivalents) had previously been political leaders. They therefore saw themselves as representing specific parties and interests, whether these officially existed or not. Consequently, civilian commissioners began to engage in a disorganized form of party politics that undermined the ability of the government to claim political neutrality and so threatened to introduce broader social tensions into the very heart of the military.

But although the civilian representatives operated very much as political animals, they failed to effectively connect the government to local communities. The small number of commissioners and their lack of an effective party machine rendered it almost impossible to reach out to the grassroots. This failure had significant consequences in Western State, where the lack of information on public opinion meant that the government failed to anticipate a widespread wave of riots in 1968 and 1969 in which farmers refused to pay taxes. Once the riots had started, the absence of effective political structures further hampered attempts to identify the source of the dispute and broker a resolution. Consequently, the military was forced to

---

[1] Bienen, Henry "Military Rule and Political Process: Nigerian Example". *Comparative Politics* 10, 2 (1978), p. 211.

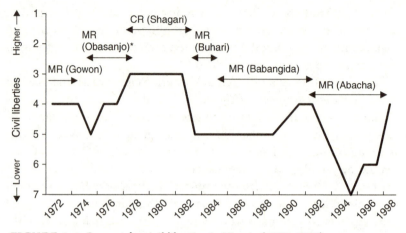

FIGURE 1.1 Respect for civil liberties in Nigeria (1972–1998).

Freedom House Index 1–7, lower scores = more respect for civil liberties. MR = military rule, CR = civilian regime. (Name) = president.
Note: *Murtala Mohammed came to power after Gowon was overthrown in 1975, but was assassinated in 1976.
Source: Freedom House.

utilize increasingly coercive strategies. Subsequent Nigerian military regimes struggled with the same conundrum, and it was in part the need to compensate for inadequate mechanisms of representation, along with the paranoia of military leaders – which increased with each and every coup attempt – that resulted in a series of increasingly repressive regimes (Figure 1.1).

Gowon's time in power was short lived. In 1975, he was overthrown in a coup that briefly saw Murtula Mohammed installed as president. The limitations that Gowon had recognized subsequently troubled other leaders, both within Nigeria and without. Many military presidents responded by trying to have their cake and eat it, erecting shell parties that they could entirely control in order to confer a veneer of democratic respectability on what remained authoritarian regimes. Even Mobutu, one of Africa's least democratically inclined leaders, sought to build popular acceptance of his rule by forming the Popular Movement of the Revolution (MPR), which became the sole legal party in the Congo under the 1967 constitution. He also attempted to tap into the legitimacy of the ballot box, putting the 1967 constitution to a referendum and standing for election in 1970 and 1977, demonstrating that even the most capricious of leaders is susceptible to the lure of democratic respectability (although, of course, not democratic uncertainty: Mobutu never won less than 98 per cent of the vote).

In other cases reforms were less superficial, as leaders attempted a kind of political alchemy, transforming weak military regimes into coercive one-party states. Take Benin, for example. The capture of power by Major Mathieu Kérékou in 1972 ended a destabilizing cycle of coup and counter-coup that had threatened to tear the country apart. Kérékou immediately set about consolidating his position, creating the People's Revolutionary Party of Benin (PRPB) in 1975, complete with a central committee, party congress, and, at the grassroots, Committees for the Defence of the Revolution (CDRs). Although some key decisions continued to be made by the military, under the PRPB government Benin developed a political system that was similar in some respects to the one-party states of Tanzania and Zambia. As in those systems, a left-leaning government presided over a political structure that offered party activists little opportunity to shape national policy, but held regular elections. However, the system established in Benin did not engage the local population to the extent that one-party polls did in countries such as Kenya (chapter 2), because the input of citizens was restricted to voting "yes" or "no" to a list of candidates put forward by the ruling party, and so voters were not able to select their own representatives. Yet despite the clear constraints that this system placed on the political engagement or ordinary people, the balance between participation and control struck by Kérékou proved to be remarkably stable, surviving for nineteen years in a county in which the life expectancy of previous military regimes had been counted in months.

Botswana: The Diamond in the Rough?

Not all of Africa's independent states gave up on multipartyism. Mauritius, Gambia, and Botswana ploughed a lonely furrow as examples of more democratic governments on a largely authoritarian continent. Botswana's success is particularly notable because of the country's vast diamond wealth. In developing an open and stable political economy, Botswana therefore avoided two major continental trends: the collapse of multipartyism and the resource curse (see Introduction). But on closer inspection it becomes clear that Botswana's political stability depended less on the institutionalization of competitive party politics, and more on a combination of deference to traditional leaders, ethnic homogeneity, and a self-restraining political elite. Indeed, the formula for Botswana's success deployed by the first president, Seretse Khama, relied on a combination of participation and control reminiscent of the continent's civilian one-party states.

Khama was a British-trained lawyer who had been born into one of the royal families of the Bechuanaland Protectorate (as it was then known), and later ruled the country from 1965 until his death in 1980. Botswana's status as one of Africa's most open and well-managed states owes much to his vision of how the country could best navigate the challenges of independence. Despite his very public role as a traditional leader, Khama entered the national political scene relatively late, founding the Botswana Democratic Party (BDP) in 1962, in opposition to the more radical Botswana People's Party (BPP). The BDP brought together a broadly conservative coalition that included chiefs and rural commoners, as well as civil servants and teachers who had used their salary to become respectable cattle owners, and it was this powerful and well-resourced alliance that powered Khama to a landslide election victory in 1965. Motivated by his distrust of radical politics and his high regard for the rule of law, Khama set about building a conservative government in which the rights of citizens – and opposition parties – would be respected.

First and foremost, Khama recognized that BDP hegemony would be strongest if it was constructed on the basis of the social and economic dominance of the party leadership and their allies. The close relationship between chiefs and the BDP, and the ability of traditional leaders to use their control over land and labour to maintain their political and cultural relevance, empowered Khama to dominate political life, especially in rural areas. Moreover, Botswana's hierarchical social structure and the deference of Tswana communities towards royal or traditional leaders meant that many ordinary Batswana were unwilling to criticize Khama, at least in public.

The BDP's ability to use the social standing of its leaders to ensure the compliance of citizens was facilitated by the country's tiny and relatively homogenous population. Just over 500,000 people lived in Botswana at the point of independence, and the eight main Tswana-speaking communities comprised more than three-quarters of the population. The existence of a common set of cultural symbols and a common language made it easier for Khama to construct a viable national identity and ensured that the political system never fragmented in the way that it did in the Congo. Helped by an opposition that was often hamstrung by internal power struggles and personal disputes, Bostwana's more homogenous and deferential political culture enabled the BDP to secure its hold on power: to date, the party has never won less than a two-thirds majority of the seats in a parliamentary election.

But to leave the story here would be unfair to Khama, because popular support for the BDP also owed much to the party's remarkable track record in office. In stark contrast to Africa's neo-patrimonial states (see Introduction), in which those in public office treated the states resources as their own, Khama maintained a professional bureaucracy and a clear division between the public and private sphere. As a result, Botswana has consistently ranked as the least corrupt country in Africa. In turn, this allowed the government and its bureaucracy to focus on effectively investing the $3 billion a year the country received in diamond revenues in a way that would sustain long-term economic growth. It did so with considerable success: having been one of the world's poorest countries at the point of independence, Botswana achieved an average economic growth rate of 7.7 per cent for the next thirty years and is now classified by the World Bank as an upper middle income country.

For the most part, Botswana has also maintained a remarkably open political landscape. Although BDP dominance meant that the government faced little formal resistance to its policies, Khama promoted dialogue between his regime and the people. Most significantly, he harnessed mechanisms of political participation that had been used to facilitate debate and consultation in the pre-colonial era. The roots of popular participation in Botswana run deep. To understand why, it is important to appreciate that before and during colonial rule the country developed one of Africa's most unequal societies. "Chiefs" controlled land, labour, and cattle, and enjoyed considerable leeway to direct and control the lives of "commoners". The need to build a broader sense of political community and to legitimate the unequal distribution of wealth encouraged chiefs to sustain and promote an indigenous mechanism of public consultation known as *kgotlas*. These meetings could be attended by both men and women and were intended to allow ordinary people to say whether or not they agreed with the chiefs decisions. Maintaining kgotlas into the independence era enabled the BDP to get a feel for the popularity, or otherwise, of its proposals. And just as in Kenya and Tanzania, the ability of people to participate in the decisions that affected their lives conferred legitimacy on the regime.

But although many of Khama's achievements sparkle, and the successful adoption of kgotlas is a powerful demonstration of the value of
allowing African democracies to draw upon socially embedded norms
and customs, Botswana is a misleading poster boy for multipartyism
in Africa. Not only has party politics been largely uncompetitive, but
many of Botswana's democratic gains have yet to be institutionalized
in ways that place tight constraints on those in power. In the absence
of a strong opposition, postcolonial leaders were understandably
reluctant to place constraints on their own activities: Khama was a
good leader, but not a saint.

Given the lack of a vigilant, active, and robust civil society, the
continued existence of an open political system rests on the volun-
tary compliance of the political elite. For this reason, Kenneth Good
has referred to Botswana as an "elite democracy".[2] Allegations of
democratic backsliding under the government of third president Ian
Khama – Seretse Khama's son – demonstrate the weaknesses of such a
system. According to his critics, Ian Khama, previously commander of
the Botswana Defence Force, has militarized the government, favour-
ing hierarchy over discussion and prioritizing order at the expense of
human rights – a tendency epitomised by his support of legislation
such as the Security and Intelligence Bill of 2006, which consolidated
the growing influence of the security forces while making no provisions for parliamentary oversight.

Moreover, although kgotlas helped to legitimate the regime, they
did not represent a system of direct or discursive democracy. Leaders
were not bound by the verdict of the people and although in principle women could speak, they rarely did. Instead, discussions tended
to be dominated by a small, wealthy, male elite. Moreover, because it
was the government that controlled kgotla meetings and determined
their content, the BDP was gifted a monopoly over one of the primary
mechanisms of mass communication. This is important, because there
is evidence that for all Seretse Khama's qualities, the party's elite, perhaps too accustomed to deference from the masses, has taken its poorest supporters for granted.

Despite all of the positive headlines, over the last thirty years
Botswana's score on the Human Development Index (HDI) – a comparative measure of life expectancy, literacy, education, and standard

---

[2] Good, Kenneth. "Enduring Elite Democracy in Botswana". *Democratization* 6, 1
(1999), pp. 50–66.

of living – has shown little improvement (0.155 on a 0 to 1 scale). While the lack of movement on key development indicators is partly related to the devastating impact of HIV/AIDS, which is carried by almost one-quarter of the population, it also reflects the failure of the government to fully share the benefits of economic growth. As a result, Botswana remains one of the world's most unequal societies: around half of the population survive on less than $1 a day, and urban areas face an acute housing problem with overcrowded squatter settlements. This means that if, like Alexis de Tocqueville, we value democracy because it improves the lot of the worse off, Botswana still has some way to go.

The Past of the Present

The political systems and ideas developed in the immediate post-independence period continue to reverberate in Africa today. Most notably, the perception that multiparty competition represents a grave danger to social harmony, and that inter-communal conflict is best managed by curtailing political competition, is still popular among political elites and some donors. Indeed, recent attempts to end political crises in countries such as Kenya and Zimbabwe through the creation of power-sharing "unity" governments all but reintroduced the one-party state into a number of African countries, if only temporarily (see the Conclusion to this volume).

Variations in the institutional structure of authoritarian rule in the 1970s and 1980s also shaped the different pathways that countries took to multipartyism in the 1990s. Bratton and van de Walle have argued that the more participation and competition there was in the ancien régime, the better the prospects for democratic consolidation.[3] The logic underpinning their argument is that participatory forms of authoritarian rule were more likely to have fostered strong civil society groups, inculcated norms of electoral representation, and to have produced active and democratically conscious societies. Moreover, competitive forms of authoritarian rule were more likely to have developed norms in favour of representative government and institutions capable of maintaining their independence from the executive.

[3] Bratton, Michael, and Nicolas Van de Walle. *Democratic Experiments in Africa: Regime Transitions in Comparative Perspective.* Cambridge: Cambridge University Press, 1997.

Given this, Bratton and van de Walle predicted that former one-party states would enjoy a smoother transition to multipartyism than cases of military rule and personal dictatorship.

The experience of the 1990s provides some support for this intuition. In countries such as Benin, Senegal, Tanzania, and Zambia, the existence of norms of accountability, electoral systems, and judiciaries with at least some capacity for independent action had an important double effect. On the one hand, more effective checks and balances made it more costly for presidents to engage in repression. On the other, stronger institutions and higher levels of political trust made it less threatening for presidents to introduce democratic reforms. As a result, when the leaders of one-party states came under pressure to democratize in the late 1980s they were more likely to respond positively than their counterparts who were operating under military rule.

The legacy bequeathed by less participatory and more coercive military regimes was more problematic. Take the example of Colonel Bokassa's military government in the Central African Republic (CAR). After seizing power in 1965 Bokassa dismantled the state, eviscerated the bureaucracy, and progressively undermined the space for dissenting voices to be heard. Fearful of losing power following a series of coup attempts between 1974 and 1976, he systematically purged his administration of talented individuals and factions that he feared could pose a potential threat to his own position. By the time he was overthrown in 1979, Bokassa had effectively destroyed the country's representative institutions and civil society, and had laid the foundations of a political landscape in which power was understood not to derive from the popular will, but from the barrel of a gun. Ever since, the CAR has struggled to overcome the twin challenge of establishing representative government and sending the military back to the barracks. Despite relatively open elections in 1993 and 1998/9, attempted transitions to multipartyism have ultimately been curtailed by coups.

The experience of the CAR reflects the struggles of many military regimes to re-civilianize politics. Indeed, even where civilian rule has been established, the armed forces have typically remained close to power, with the past lives of military leaders thinly disguised by democratic titles and civilian clothes (Table 1.1). Of the ninety-one presidents and prime ministers that have held office on the continent in civilian regimes since 1989, fully 45 per cent had considerable experience either in the state military or in rebel groups prior to holding political office.

TABLE 1.1 *Civilian African presidents with prior military/rebel experience*
(as of July 2014)

Country*	Leader	Rebel/ non-state army	State military
Angola	José dos Santos	Y	–
Botswana	Ian Khama	–	Y
Burkina Faso	Blaise Compaoré	–	Y
Burundi	Pierre Nkurunziza	Y	–
DRC	Joseph Kabila	Y	Y
Equatorial Guinea	Teodoro Obiang	–	Y
Ethiopia	Mulatu Teshome**	–	Y
Guinea-Bissau	Manuel Serifo Nhamadjo	–	Y
Mozambique	Armando Emílio Guebuza	Y	–
Namibia	Hifikepunye Pohamba	Y	–
Nigeria	Goodluck Jonathan	–	Y
Rep. of Congo	Denis Sassou-Nguesso	–	Y
Rwanda	Paul Kagame	Y	–
South Africa	Jacob Zuma	Y	–
Tanzania	Jakaya Kikwete	–	Y
South Sudan	Salva Kiir Mayardit	Y	Y
Sudan	Omar al-Bashir	–	Y
Uganda	Yoweri Museveni	Y	–
Zimbabwe	Robert Mugabe	Y	–

* Only civilian regimes holding multiparty elections are included in this table. Only rebel/military experience accrued before securing the presidency is included.
** Mulatu Teshome is the president of Ethiopia, but under the Ethiopian political system power resides with the prime minister. Following the death of Meles Zenawi in August 2012, he was succeeded as prime minister by Hailemariam Desalegn, who has no prior military or rebel experience.

But although the institutional legacy of a country plays an important role in shaping its future, the categories of one-party state and military-rule are not coherent or distinct enough to represent a hard and fast guide to the process of democratic consolidation. For example, the impact of military rule on future developments depended on the way in which leaders went about consolidating their authority. Regimes that opted for more coercive governments, such as Cameroon and the Congo, or who cloaked themselves in the imagery of democracy but had no interest in constructing more representative political structures, as in the CAR, generated significant barriers to democratization. But in countries where the government was progressively civilianized and power was at least partly transferred to new party structures, as in Benin and Ghana, the legacy of military rule was not that dissimilar to that of the one-party state.

At the same time, the long and contingent nature of processes of democratization, in which political trajectories may be radically altered by unanticipated crises and the idiosyncratic decisions of individual leaders, means that the hold of institutional legacies fades over time. It is therefore not surprising that while former one-party states such as Senegal, Tanzania, and Zambia have remained stable under multiparty rule, some have also witnessed the emergence of civil strife and political disorder, as in Côte d'Ivoire and Kenya (see Chapter 5). Moreover, while military regimes in the CAR and the DRC have made little progress towards democracy, in Liberia and Sierra Leone periods of civil conflict and military rule subsequently gave way to relatively free and fair elections. These varied pathways can only be understood if we consider the full range of factors that shaped whether leaders responded to the winds of change that blew across the continent in the late 1980s and early 1990 with repression or reform, a question that is taken up in chapter three Chapter 3.

Select Bibliography

Bienen, Henry. *Kenya: The Politics of Participation and Control.* Princeton: Princeton University Press, 1977.

Diamond, Larry, Anthony Kirk-Green, and Oyeleye Oyediran (eds.). *Transition Without End: Nigerian Politics and Civil Society under Babangida.* Boulder and London: Lynne Rienner, 1997.

Good, Kenneth. "Enduring Elite Democracy in Botswana". *Democratization* 6, 1 (1999), pp. 50–66.

Jackson, Robert H., and Carl G. Rosberg. *Personal Rule in Black Africa: Prince, Autocrat, Prophet, Tyrant.* Berkeley: University of California Press, 1982.

Nyerere, Julius. "One Party Government". *Transition* 2 (1961), pp. 9–11.

For a bibliography for this chapter go to www.democracyinafrica.org

CHAPTER 2

Cultures of Resistance: Civil Society and the Limits of Power

The downgrading of democratic institutions and the emergence of one-party, military, and dictatorial rule strengthened the position of African leaders in the 1970s. But most African governments lacked the coercive capacity to govern through repression alone. Rulers therefore faced strong incentives to build and maintain a support base. Of course, nationalist heroes could fall back on the glory of the anti-colonial struggle and their role as founding fathers to generate personal loyalty, but on its own this was rarely enough. Consider the fall from grace of Kwame Nkrumah, perhaps Africa's most iconic nationalist leader. Having first come to prominence as the general secretary of the United Gold Coast Convention (UGCC), he soon became impatient with the UGCC's moderate stance and the slow pace of change.

A period of imprisonment in 1948 at the hands of the colonial government intensified Nkrumah's conviction that the Gold Coast (now Ghana) needed "self government now" and he subsequently left the UGCC to lead the more radical Convention People's Party (CPP). Thereafter he became one of the most passionate critics of colonial rule, and one of the most eloquent advocates of African unity. Indeed, Nkrumah's invocation to "Seek ye first the political Kingdom and all else will be added to you" became the defining statement of the nationalist belief that once the colonial state had been transferred to African hands, all else would follow. It certainly resonated in the Gold Coast, where the CPP rapidly emerged as the dominant political party, enabling Nkrumah to secure the position of prime minister in 1952.

But Nkrumah's confidence that his control of the state would enable him to effect far-reaching social, political, and economic transformation was also his undoing. Having declared Ghanaian independence in 1957, the CPP overreached itself. Government control over economic activity was tightened in order to channel resources towards industrialization, which Nkrumah believed was necessary for Ghana to establish economic autonomy – and hence "true" independence – from Western powers. But the policy frustrated business leaders and farmers, whose surpluses were taken by the government, while the cost of Nkrumah's projects soon plunged the country into debt. In an attempt to maintain social order, the CPP introduced the Trade Union Act of 1958, which made strikes illegal. However, this came at the cost of alienating precisely those labour groups that had supported Nkrumah's rise to power. Efforts to establish authority over rural areas by placing chiefs under tighter political control also had a detrimental effect on the government's reputation, while the abuses committed under the Preventative Detention Act, which allowed Nkrumah to detain people without trial for up to five years, increased public dissatisfaction with his regime. Amidst mounting criticism and opposition, Nkrumah was overthrown in a coup in February 1966 – less than a decade after the end of colonial rule.

The downfall of one of Africa's most effective and high-profile founding fathers sent shockwaves throughout the continent. It demonstrated that simply being a nationalist leader and centralizing control under the presidency was not enough. Authoritarian rule threatened to be highly unstable unless regimes could maintain some degree of public support. As a result, Africa's autocrats spent the next thirty years co-opting those groups within their societies that were too important, or too dangerous, to exclude. But while this process was designed to insulate undemocratic regimes from public criticism, it also placed leaders under considerable pressure to respond to the needs of at least some of their supporters. As a result, political intermediaries and the communities that they represented were not wholly impotent in the face of authoritarian rule.

Most commonly, leaders sought to give their regimes social roots by deploying "clientelism" – the exchange of resources, jobs, or gifts for political support. When they could afford it, governments used state resources to buy the loyalty – or at least the acquiescence – of diverse communities. In other words, the dispersal of patronage came to be one of the main strategies through which African leaders pursued the demanding task of nation-building. The organization and currency of clientelism varied case by case but usually revolved around the creation of highly personalized patron-client networks and the expansion of state employment to reward supporters. Sometimes the disbursement of funds was brash and ostentatious: Kenya's second president, Daniel arap Moi, became known for throwing money out of the window as he was driven from Nairobi to his home in the Rift Valley. In other cases it was more careful and considered. In Botswana, Tanzania, and Zambia, members of the ruling party were discouraged from excessively exploiting their positions and from public displays of wealth, but government jobs were nonetheless distributed to reward loyalty and punish opposition. While these networks strengthened the position of those in power, they also placed them under a serious obligation. Patron-client relationships implied duties and responsibilities for patrons as well as clients. Once established, local expectations of the appropriate role of the state and the political class had to be fulfilled if the government was to survive. As a result, patron-client networks simultaneously mobilized support for the government and exposed leaders to a degree of pressure from below.

Less commonly, civilian one-party states often allowed communities to select their own representatives and tolerated a degree of criticism of policies from intellectuals, playwrights, and journalists, in order to bolster their legitimacy, as we saw in Chapter 1. Although attacks on the president and his closest advisors were always out of bounds, this left open avenues through which the failings of the political class could be exposed and, through satire, made fun of. The fragility of power also encouraged leaders to enter into marriages of convenience with non-governmental organizations such as churches and trade unions in order to secure their compliance. In turn, these delicate alliances conferred on these groups a degree of influence over the areas of government policy of greatest concern to their members. As a result, what is now known as "civil society" played a role in mediating authoritarian rule, even in some of the continent's more repressive countries.

Patronage, Poverty, and Inequality

The way in which patronage was dispensed shaped the kinds of politics that emerged in the 1970s. In southern Africa, the greater salience of urban identities and trade union movements meant that funds were more likely to be channelled through – and to enhance the significance of – institutions such as political parties and labour organizations. In a number of West African countries, political structures also had deep roots. In Ghana, for example, they reached back to organizations such as the Aborigines Rights Protection Society, which was formed in 1898 to contest colonial legislation that threatened traditional land tenure, and subsequently emerged as one of the main sources of opposition to colonial rule. But in the rest of West Africa and most of East Africa, the absence or weakness of such institutions meant that patronage was more likely to be distributed through heavily personalized networks, giving rise to new generations of Big Men capable of manipulating the flow of resources in order to develop followings of their own.

Because clientelism helped authoritarian governments to maintain public support, it is tempting to think that it improved the position of ordinary people. In fact, patron-client networks were rooted in economic inequality and increased the gap between the "haves" and the "have-nots" over time. Corruption sometimes served to "redistribute" resources, facilitating handouts to those who might have otherwise gone without, but corrupt leaders rarely shared more than a tiny proportion of what they stole. Consider Nigeria, where the collection of billions of dollars of oil revenues has gone hand in hand with endemic poverty. The value of oil rents, combined with the vast gap between rich and poor, empowered otherwise unpopular leaders to placate important parts of political society. While the extensive use of repression kept military regimes in power, patronage was the glue that – for a short while at least – held them together.

Over time, such practices not only exacerbated inequalities between the rich and the poor, but also between those communities with strong representation in government and those that found themselves at the margins of power, exacerbating inter-communal tensions. Because resources passed through a number of different tiers before they reached ordinary citizens, and everyone along the way took their cut, the relatively small number of people at the top of the pyramid benefited most. By contrast, one-third of the population continued to live in extreme poverty. Consequently, Nigeria quickly became characterized by a grotesquely wealthy elite and a destitute poor, reflecting a broader continental trend (Tables 2.1 and 2.2). The impact of such iniquitous economic systems was reinforced by the failure of most governments to maintain investment in health and

TABLE 2.1 *Inequality in selected African countries*

Country	Rich/poor ratio*	Gini (year)**	
South Africa	44.2	63.1 (2009)	Most unequal
Botswana	40.0	61.0 (1994)	↑
Zambia	31.8	57.5 (2010)	
Lesotho	48.9	52.5 (2003)	
Nigeria	21.8	48.8 (2010)	
Kenya	19.4	47.7 (2005)	
Ghana	16.2	42.8 (2006)	
Côte d'Ivoire	14.3	41.5 (2008)	
USA	15.9	40.8 (2000)	
Senegal	12.5	40.3 (2011)	
Tanzania	10.5	37.6 (2007)	
UK	28.5	36.0 (1999)	
Ethiopia	8.6	33.6 (2011)	
Poland	7.8	32.7 (2011)	↓
Japan	4.5	24.9 (1993)	Least unequal

* The ratio of the average income of the richest 10 per cent as compared to the poorest 10 per cent, higher ratios = more unequal.
** 0 = maximal equality, 100 = maximal inequality.
Source: World Bank.

TABLE 2.2 *Poverty levels in developing countries (2005)*

Region	People living on less than $1.25 a day (%)
East Asia and Pacific	16.8
Latin America and the Caribbean	8.2
South Asia	40.4
sub-Saharan Africa	50.9
Middle East and North Africa	0.04

Source: World Bank.

education, which in turn made it harder for the children of poor families to compete with those from wealthy backgrounds.

At the same time, the expansion of state employment created a bureaucratic bourgeoisie, as those with jobs in the public sector became steadily wealthier than the people they served. In the process, much of Africa's new middle-class gained a vested interest in preserving, rather than challenging, the status quo. But while it is easy to understand why people fortunate enough to have direct access to state resources saw value in the system, it is harder to explain why the poorest members of society accepted such a disadvantageous arrangement. One reason is that media censorship and low levels of education meant that many Africans did not fully appreciate the extent to which they were being exploited. Another is that they had little choice: authoritarian rule was often arbitrary and brutal. A more disturbing explanation is that because patron-client systems drew on established moral and political norms, they were often perceived as being legitimate even though they promoted inequality and poverty. The ability of leaders to escape censure for inequality and corruption is important, because it is one of the main reasons that efforts to promote "good governance" have made little progress in much of the continent.

The Politics of Reciprocity

Following independence in 1963, Kenya's first president, Jomo Kenyatta, established a classic model of Big Man rule that relied heavily on personalized patronage networks. In large part, Kenyatta adopted this strategy because he distrusted his own party and did not want to have to rely on it as the foundation of his power. During the anti-colonial struggle, Kenyatta had been detained on trumped up charges of leading the anti-colonial Mau Mau rebellion (see Introduction). As a result, he was absent from the political scene during the critical phase in which the party that he would later lead – the Kenya African National Union (KANU) – was established. Thus, in contrast to the leaders of other one-party states such as Kaunda in Zambia and Nyerere in Tanzania, who were able to build their parties in their own image (see Chapter 1), Kenyatta inherited an organization led by figures whose loyalty he did not fully trust and whose values he did not share. Significantly, although the British government had identified him as a dangerous subversive, Kenyatta's political and social views were decidedly conservative, and thus stood in sharp contrast to the African socialism advocated by the likes of KANU's prominent Luo leader, Oginga Odinga.

Kenyatta's disposition towards KANU improved little after the dissolution of the opposition in 1964 turned Kenya into a one-party state. Instead, the absence of formal opposition encouraged deep ideological and ethnic divisions to come to the fore within the government. In the mid 1960s, members of a more radical faction headed by Oginga

Odinga directly and publicly challenged the more conservative group around Kenyatta, causing a major rift in the party. The two groups became known as KANU A and KANU B, and the radicals even sat on the "opposition" benches within parliament to emphasise their rejection of key elements of government policy.

Faced with such internal opposition, Kenyatta saw little attraction in the Tanzanian model of nation building, in which the party was reified as the vehicle of social and economic transformation. Instead, he allowed the formal party apparatus to wither and die, choosing to maintain control through the established colonial bureaucracy, the Provincial Administration, which the British had expanded into one of the most effective state institutions on the continent as part of the effort to contain the Mau Mau rebellion. But this solution left Kenyatta with the problem of how to facilitate participation, promote development, and hence legitimate his government among the wider public. The Provincial Administration was effective, but not popular. Kenyatta's solution was to establish one of Africa's most effective, and responsive, patron-client networks. He began by harnessing an established local custom know as *harambee* (literally "all pull together" in Swahili), in which communities pooled labour and resources in order to meet locally defined needs. In contrast to the continent's African socialists, who encouraged their citizens to look to the state for development, Kenyatta told Kenyans that development was their own responsibility. Rejecting notions of a deserving poor, he argued that wealth would come to those who worked hard.

Kenyans were not left entirely to their own devices, though. Kenyatta announced that KANU Members of Parliament (MPs) – who continued to be elected on a constituency basis throughout the one-party period – would be responsible for leading harambee initiatives. Once local communities had constructed schools and hospitals, the state would reward them by taking on the running costs. This proved to be a stroke of genius. The desperate need for development meant that communities responded with great energy and ingenuity to the opportunity to access state resources. And by maintaining elections and making MPs responsible for development, Kenyatta empowered communities to hold their leaders accountable on the issues that they cared most about. This both enhanced the legitimacy of the regime and forced MPs to focus on fundraising and local issues, rather than national policy and the performance of the executive. Moreover, because the popularity of MPs depended on their access to state resources, which were in turn controlled by Kenyatta, the system of clientelism enabled the president to make or break political careers. As a result, Kenyan legislators became increasingly dependent on senior political figures for finance.

Kenyatta's patron-client network simultaneously drew on established practices and transformed them. Most notably, the patronage networks that emerged in Kenya institutionalized a particular form of local accountability. Because MPs faced regular elections, they went to great lengths to demonstrate their commitment to their constituencies, continually travelling home to hold meetings with local notables, and exchanging cash or other economic favours for political support. Constituents were therefore empowered to make demands on their representatives. This was one of the main reasons that Kenyatta's vision proved so effective: it resonated with a moral economy, most pronounced among the Kikuyu community, in which leaders' accumulation of wealth was seen to be legitimate so long as it led to benefits for the community.[1] Because Kenyatta's policies encouraged Kenyans to evaluate their MPs on the basis of their personal contribution to local development, it solidified the impression that the suitability of a leader was related to their wealth. One consequence of the desire of communities to tap into avenues of economic and political influence was that voters increasingly spurned chiefs and teachers in favour of businessmen who were better placed to satisfy local demands. Indeed, MPs quickly came to play all of the functions abdicated by the central government, as they were expected to help out with school fees, medicine, and hospital expenses. This quickly turned them into classic Big Men; part representative, part local celebrity, part welfare state.

The form of accountability that emerged through this reciprocal relationship had real limits. Precisely because patronage became institutionalized as a form of political legitimation, voters were encouraged to turn a blind eye to the question of how MPs sourced their resources so long as funds were channelled back home. At the same time, the practice of restricting competition to the constituency level reinforced the notion that politicians were primarily responsible to their own bailiwick, rather than to the broader national interest. This localism, combined with Kenyatta's willingness to favour his

---

[1] Lonsdale, John. "Moral and Political Argument in Kenya" in Bruce Berman, Dickson Eyoh, and Will Kymlicka (eds), *Ethnicity and Democracy in Africa*. Oxford: James Currey, 2004, pp. 73–95.

Kikuyu ethnic group, encouraged a winner-takes-all mentality within the single-party framework that retarded the evolution of important democratic ideals such as the principle that leaders should be equally responsible to all citizens, and that public resources should not be used for private ends.

Perhaps the most striking feature of this system of ethnic favouritism and patronage politics was that it persuaded ordinary Kenyans to willingly participate in a process that increased the gap between rich and poor over time. When Kenyans rejected their constituency MPs, they were not demanding a change in the rules of the game, but rather a new patron better able to deliver within the patron-client system. In other words, political frustrations on the ground were often expressed in a way that reinforced, rather than undermined, the status quo. Kenyatta's system of Big Man rule was thus particularly prone to abuse, and to public toleration of that abuse. During the tenure of the second president, Daniel arap Moi (1982–2002), the harambee system spun out of control. Senior political figures stole vast amounts of state resources, some of which they channelled to their constituents in order to shore up their ailing legitimacy. The rapid increase in harambee donations meant that leaders increasingly found that they could only meet their constituents' expectations by borrowing large amounts from Moi and his aides, which in turn increased their dependence on the president. As MPs became enmeshed in a corrupt financial framework, they developed a shared interest in maintaining the system on which their privileged positions depended. Moreover, because patronage networks and constituency elections focused voters' attentions on their individual representatives instead of the wider political system, it prevented the poor from recognizing their common exploitation. In turn, this reduced the pressure on the political class to implement genuine reform, undermining the prospects for democratic consolidation.

The Politics of Evil

That Big Men were sometimes able to legitimate their wealth and power does not mean that inequality and poverty went without comment. Instead, popular frustration with the difficulties of everyday life infused novels, music, plays, and witchcraft folklore. At first sight, witchcraft appears to be exactly the sort of "irrational" belief system that makes building democracy so difficult in Africa. But in the same way that patron-client relationships simultaneously allowed elements of accountability and exploitation, so witchcraft has been used both as a mechanism of political control and as a "weapon of the weak".[2]

From the pre-colonial period onward, the widespread belief in an invisible spiritual realm – which exists in parallel to the visible world and can act upon it – has conferred considerable power on those thought to be capable of wielding occult power. As a result, witchcraft accusations were particularly potent political weapons in the decades after independence, for good or for ill. Consider the Njang Njang movement in Guinea-Bissau. Following the rise to power of the African Party for the Independence of Guinea and Cape Verde (PAIGC), female party activists became frustrated by the monopolization of power and economic resources by senior male leaders. In the months that followed, popular dissent among young people came to be fused with a healing cult that developed among women from the Balanta community who were unable to conceive or whose children had died, resulting in a movement that harnessed witchcraft as a way of coping with socio-economic insecurity and responding to gender hierarchies and generational tensions. The movement was ultimately suppressed by the government, who feared its subversive potential, but not before it had shaken Balanta society to its core.

While witchcraft accusations and parables were usually not so politically entwined, it is possible to read them as implicit critiques of inequality and injustice. Like satire, witchcraft was an attractive medium through which to question the status quo because it allowed individuals to speak the truth to power through stories that, precisely because they could be understood in multiple ways, protected the storyteller from retribution. Interpreted in a particular way, tales about evil forces accumulating great power and wealth at the expense of ordinary people could easily be interpreted as a commentary on poverty and inequality. But as with the patron-client networks described previously, the reach of such critiques was limited.

For one thing, witchcraft accusations were typically made against people personally known to the accuser, rather than against senior government figures. For example, Geschiere and Nyamnjoh record witchcraft accusations made by rural dwellers against relatives who had moved to the city and were perceived to have failed in their duty to share their good fortune with their kin. Writing about Cameroon,

---

[2] Ferguson, James. *Weapons of the Weak: Everyday Forms of Peasant Resistance*. New Haven: Yale University Press, 1985.

they describe a spate of accusations of "Zombie witchcraft" in the early 1990s in which black magic was alleged to have been perpetrated by the nouveaux riche, who instead of eating their victims sought to possess them and put them to work. These narratives of spiritual cum economic exploitation caught the public imagination because they spoke to the concerns of many poor rural communities who felt they had missed out on the benefits of globalization and modernity because of the actions of urban elites. And like the patron-client relationships discussed earlier, the fact that they tapped into a shared moral economy regarding the obligations of wealthier family or community members gave them greater resonance. Similar critiques have been identified across the continent, from Benin to South Africa, and from Côte d'Ivoire to Zambia, which makes it tempting to see witchcraft as a metaphorical rallying cry against the unfair distribution of economic opportunities. But the fact that most accusations documented in Benin and Cameroon focused on the failings of family members or local notables to maintain their personal commitments to those they had close relationships with, rather than on the failings of the wealthy or the political class to consider the needs of the whole population, suggests that they are more likely to reinforce existing patron-client ties, than to challenge them – much like the politics of reciprocity in Kenya.

Even more problematically, witchcraft accusations were often intended not to advocate for social justice, but to settle scores and to legitimate violence. Despite the difficulty of finding hard evidence in such cases, those found guilty of practicing witchcraft were frequently "sentenced" to severe beatings and even death. In light of this, the fact that a majority of accusations were made against women is an important reminder that the strategies deployed by the politically marginalized may be just as cruel and arbitrary as the ones utilized by those in power.

Witchcraft was also vulnerable to manipulation by political leaders, some of whom sought to harness occult power in order to construct an image of invincibility and omniscience, and thus intimidate rivals. From the pre-colonial era onward, authority structures in Africa have tended to be most durable when they fused political and religious power. Leaders typically found that they were more likely to receive compliance from their subjects if their positions appeared to be ordained by some higher power. The most notorious purveyor of such practices in the postcolonial period was Idi Amin, the brutal Ugandan dictator who kept a store of shrunken heads and body parts to protect him from his enemies, both real and imagined. But the power of witchcraft was also harnessed in more subtle ways. In Togo, President Eyadema threatened to use his "powers" to strike down opponents, while simultaneously manipulating witchcraft accusations to legitimate the persecution of his rivals. Similarly, Mobutu employed the Senegalese marabout "witchdoctor", El Hadji Babacar Kébé, and an influential Malian marabout, Serigne Babacar Cissé, to demonstrate his spiritual power. As a result, while the threat of witchcraft accusations keeps many wealthy Africans up at night, the battle over occult power is just as likely to reinforce the status quo as to challenge it.

Mediating Authoritarian Rule

Authoritarian rule also inspired a range of critiques with less problematic democratic foundations. Lawyers such as Bram Fischer, the Afrikaner who defended Nelson Mandela at the Rivonia Trial, sought, where possible, to use the rule of law to protect dissidents. Writers, actors, and musicians offered cutting critiques of the abuse of power, from Chinua Achebe's seminal novel *When Things Fall Apart* (1974), to Ngũgĩ wa Thiong'o's recent magnus opus the *Wizard of the Crow* (2006). University lecturers and students were also a frequent thorn in the side of the continent's autocrats, even in the highly repressive atmosphere of the 1980s. Similarly, a number of brave journalists have risked their livelihoods and in some cases their lives to expose the hypocrisy of ruling parties. In 2011, the Golden Pen of Freedom Award was given to Dawit Isaak, the founder of the Eritrean newspaper *Setit*, who was jailed in 2001 for publishing letters demanding democratic reform.

But although individuals were able to inspire episodes of opposition to authoritarian rule, protests were typically more effective when embedded within a durable organizational framework. This raises the tricky question of what counts as such a framework and how they come about. It is often assumed that a stronger "civil society" – a term that is usually used to refer to non-state organizations such as churches, trade unions and human rights groups – would help to promote democratic consolidation. However, it is not clear whether it makes sense to place so much faith in such groups in the African context. The idea that civil society will act as a check on the government is based on the rather hopeful assumption that these organizations are in some way separate from, and willing to act against, the state. But in postcolonial Africa, the groups that survived authoritarian rule usually did so because they had been co-opted by the government, or forced to enter into an uneasy alliance with authoritarian leaders. Their ability to criticize authoritarian rule was therefore compromised. At the same time, where clientelist networks were effective, as in Kenya, they tended to integrate members of the middle class into the regime, undermining their willingness to provide leadership to campaigns for democratic reform.

However, while the compromised nature of many civil society groups limited their potential to check the abuse of power, it did not render them wholly impotent. Few governments were strong enough to wholly subordinate the most powerful non-state actors, and so while smaller associations were typically harassed out of existence or assimilated into the regime, this was not always true of larger religious organizations and trade unions. Because Africa has the highest rates of religious activity of any continent in the world (Figure 2.1), religious leaders enjoyed considerable social and political influence. Where trade unions were strong, union leaders also came to play an equally important role. In predominantly rural African states, low levels of industrialization, urbanization, and formal employment, along with low population density, meant that textile workers, agricultural cooperatives, and manual labourers often found it difficult to mobilize strong and effective trade unions at the national level. By contrast, in parts of southern Africa vast quantities of copper, gold, and diamonds resulted in an explosion of mining that conferred real influence on trade unions, which often enjoyed a membership base to rival the ruling party.

The ability of church and trade union groups to control religious and economic power rendered them particularly dangerous opponents for authoritarian leaders. Where such organizations existed, ruling parties thus faced strong incentives to negotiate with them to secure their support – tacit or otherwise. Because few governments could afford to simply repress larger religious organizations and unions, which in turn could not operate freely without the acquiescence of the government, uneasy marriages of convenience emerged. There was nothing new about this. In the colonial period, governments established health and education services by co-opting missionary institutions. Today, NGOs and charities provide many essential services, once more blurring the dividing line between the state and civil society.

The relationship between civil society and the state is therefore best conceptualized as a two-way valve that enabled authoritarian regimes

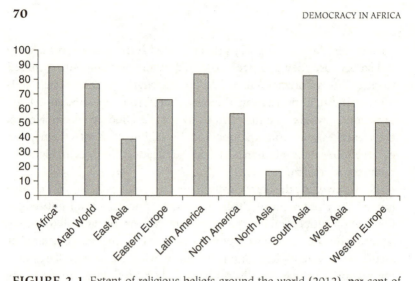

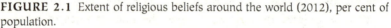

FIGURE 2.1 Extent of religious beliefs around the world (2012), per cent of population.

The question was: "Irrespective of whether you attend a place of worship or not, would you say you are a religious person, not a religious persons or a convinced atheist?"

* Africa includes North Africa.
Source: *Gallup*.

to maintain social control, but at times empowered non-state actors to exert leverage on the government. In some cases, this prevented the worst excesses of authoritarian rule and supported the emergence of an important, if limited, form of social contract between the governments and its citizens (see Introduction). However, such relationships typically changed over time. In the 1960s and early 1970s, when African governments had sufficient resources to both invest in their patronage networks and maintain the wages of trade unionists, leaders found these relationships relatively easy to manage. But when economic decline undermined the finances of African states from the mid-1970s onward, sections of civil society became increasingly willing to use their influence to push for more reform. This was important, because in those countries where religious organizations and trade union groups had managed to maintain some degree of independence from the state, they often emerged as leading players in the campaign for democracy.

Striking for Democracy?

Nowhere were unions more significant to political developments than in Zambia, where copper mining began in the 1920s and accelerated rapidly in the late colonial period. By 1953, the mines employed around 270,000 workers and urbanization increased at a pace that terrified the colonial authorities. British officials feared that "detribalized" Africans would overcome ethnic differences and find common cause against imperialism. Their concern was not without foundation: in March 1953 the Northern Rhodesian Zambian Mineworker's Union, frustrated by the limitations of the tribal councils established by the colonial government, voted to elect their own leaders. From this point on, Zambian unions proved able and willing to resist co-optation, ultimately emerging as unlikely political kingmakers.

In the late colonial period, the success of the United National Independence Party (UNIP) – the more radical branch of the nationalist movement led by Kenneth Kaunda – was founded on the support of urban labour. A fearful colonial government made it illegal for trade unions to take an active role in politics, but this did not prevent UNIP from establishing itself as the dominant political party by recruiting union activists with valuable experience of political organization in high-density urban areas. Once independence had been achieved, Kaunda's left-leaning government attempted to harness the power of organized labour by establishing the Zambian Congress of Trade Unions (ZCTU) and affiliating it to the party, but the unions would not be tamed. In large part, this was because they were well financed and thus not dependent on government funds. In the 1960s, the Mineworker's Union of Zambia (MUZ) automatically received contributions from the wages of its 40,000 members, and by the early 1970s its finances were considerably healthier than UNIP's. Of course, some individual union leaders were susceptible to the ruling party's advances, but even in these cases the vigilance of rank-and-file members kept their representatives in check. Leaders seen to have "sold out" to UNIP were rejected, and workers engaged in wildcat strikes if the outcomes of official negotiations were not to their liking.

UNIP could ill afford to ignore workers' demands because the copper that miners dug out of the ground accounted for the vast majority of the country's export revenue, and so industrial disputes undermined the nation's finances. Frustrated, Kaunda sought to shackle the unions by introducing the Industrial Relations Act of 1971, which undermined the right to strike. However, the act had little effect on labour relations in practice, and the number of workers involved in industrial disputes remained high throughout the 1970s (Table 2.3). By the end of the decade it had become clear that neither the government nor the unions could effectively pursue their goals without the

TABLE 2.3 *Industrial disputes in Zambia (1970–1978)*

Year	Reported disputes	Workers involved	Days lost
1970	12	32,300	123,000
1971	127	15,000	18,900
1972	74	10,500	20,900
1973	65	7,000	5,700
1974	55	7,400	38,700
1975	78	17,000	51,000
1976	59	5,600	6,500
1977	51	10,700	15,900
1978	56	43,100	301,600

Source: Munyonzwe Hamalengwa, *Class Struggles in Zambia, 1889–1989,* and *The Fall of Kenneth Kaunda, 1990–1991.* London: University Press of America, 1992, p. 9.

cooperation of the other. As a result, an uneasy alliance emerged. The MUZ and other unions accepted the curtailment of multiparty politics and the creation of a one-party state in 1972. For its part, UNIP made concessions on issues such as wages and living conditions. Such compromises significantly constrained the options available to Kaunda, because they made it difficult for the government to divert copper revenues to support agricultural development in order to share the nation's wealth and diversify the Zambian economy, which was essential for the country's long-term prospects.

Although the unions were primarily motivated by the needs of union members rather than by the national interest writ large, their position as key intermediaries between UNIP and urban labour meant that they effectively constrained the ruling party's ability to dominate the political environment in towns and cities, and so checked the consolidation of authoritarian rule. In the 1980s, the continued failure of Kaunda to deliver economic recovery, along with the mounting evidence of the inefficient and ineffective nature of his regime, further undermined UNIP's ability to manage the alliance.

Under the outspoken and intransigent leadership of Frederick Chiluba, the ZCTU adopted an increasingly critical attitude to the ruling party, resulting in the arrest of Chiluba and other union leaders in 1981. Yet even in the mid-1980s, UNIP's willingness to concede ground on key union demands prevented the ZCTU from fully breaking ranks with the government. Despite a prolonged period of negative economic growth, the unions only declared their formal opposition to Kaunda's one-party state in the late 1980s, after UNIP had attempted to appoint party loyalists to key union positions and agreed to a hugely unpopular financial arrangement with the IMF. This proved to be a critical turning point. Demonstrating the political significance of the unions, Chiluba became the first major public figure to openly advocate the end of the one-party state – a role that was typically performed by church leaders. His rallying cry met with widespread support.

Largely as a result of Chiluba's ability to deliver the organizational capacity of the union movement, he was selected to lead the MMD, a broad opposition alliance that demanded the reintroduction of multi-party politics and, when Kaunda obliged, defeated UNIP at the ballot box, giving rise to one of the continent's first transfers of power (see Chapter 3). In this way the unions that had for so long sustained UNIP ultimately played a central role in its demise, demonstrating the fragility of the marriages of convenience that emerged between governments and organized labour after independence.

Praying for Democracy?

Where authoritarian rule was at its most fierce and capricious, the repression of civil society often meant that religious organizations were often the only national organizations to survive. Let us return to the DRC (then called Zaire) under the brutal reign of Mobutu Sese Seko Kuku Ngbendu waza Banga – an adopted name that translates roughly as "the all-powerful warrior who, because of his endurance and inflexible will to win, will go from conquest to conquest leaving fire in his wake". As we saw in Chapter 1, Mobutus's time in office is associated with the worst excesses of authoritarian rule. Yet during his tenure the Catholic Church not only survived, but also became more important in people's lives. As the public services provided by the regime collapsed, the Church's network of schools and hospitals effectively became a default welfare state.

Mobutu was deeply suspicious of the Church, its organizational capacity, and its lasting spiritual authority over his people. However, the MPR government was not prepared to simply eliminate the Church because a majority of the population were practicing members and Mobutu was wary of alienating such a large constituency. For its part, the Catholic Church strove to retain a degree of independence from the regime, and at times Bishops made brave criticisms of the government. However, the story of the Church in Zaire is not a proud one, because it was never a straightforward bulwark against the abuse of power. Instead, what emerged was a different kind of marriage of convenience, in which for long periods the Catholic Church tacitly accepted the status quo in return for being allowed to practice and to recruit followers.

This pattern did not start at independence but had its roots in the colonial era, when the Catholic Church provided spiritual cover for the abuses of Belgian rule, and in return was granted a religious monopoly within the territory. This willing collaboration undermined the legitimacy of the Church in the eyes of many nationalists. Perhaps because Church leaders understood that the end of colonial rule had left them vulnerable, the Church remained unwilling to speak truth to power after independence. When the army killed a number of demonstrating students in the spring of 1968, a group of liberal Catholic intellectuals went to see Joseph-Albert Malula, the Archbishop of Kinshasa, and demanded that he speak out against the atrocities. Malula responded by telling them to mind their own business because only he had the authority to decide what to say to government; ultimately, although Malula intervened to insist on individual Catholic burials – the army had proposed mass graves – he stopped short of denouncing the regime.

This incident reflects a broader pattern in which lower-ranking officials who were more exposed to the everyday brutality of the government advocated radical strategies of resistance, but were overruled by senior clergy who feared that a more confrontational approach would inspire a crackdown on Church activities. Such a development would have both undermined the social and economic status of Church leaders and hampered the Church's ability to compete in an increasingly competitive spiritual marketplace. In particular, Catholic leaders feared losing ground to the Protestant and African Independent Churches. These organizations had been more critical of colonial rule and quicker to side with Mobutu; they were therefore well placed to access the state patronage they required to challenge the predominance of the Catholic Church. Moreover, the MPR government explicitly welcomed religious competition and actively fostered rival religious movements that it hoped would reduce the Church's influence.

Following the pattern just described in Zambia, the uneasy compromise between Church and state began to break down in the

1980s as the regime employed evermore-repressive strategies to contain public dissatisfaction. Following a series of increasingly critical Episcopal letters from Catholic bishops, the Church publicly called on Mobutu to open up the political system. After the president agreed to establish a Sovereign National Conference (SNC), during which representatives of the country's different social groups would discuss how to take the country forward, the Church maintained the pressure for change. Following the announcement that the SNC would be suspended in January 1992, Catholic leaders called people to the streets for a "March of Hope". Tragically, the protest did not reach its destination, because government forces fired indiscriminately at the protestors, killing more than forty and wounding many more. Following this atrocity, the Church became increasingly critical of the regime, inspired by the visits to the continent of Pope John Paul II in September 1988 and April 1989, and his call for Catholics to "step forward and play a role in their societies".

The role played by the Catholic Church in Zaire was not dissimilar to the way that Catholic, Protestant, Anglican, and Presbyterian Churches engaged with authoritarian rule across the continent. With some important exceptions, these organizations generally tolerated democratic backsliding in the 1970s, but later spoke out bravely in defence of human rights. The legitimacy and organizational capacity of these churches, along with their international connections, made it safer for religious leaders to openly advocate political liberalization. In the process, they broke long-kept silences and paved the way for an outpouring of public criticism. Moreover, by allowing opposition leaders to meet and discuss tactics at funerals and weddings, some churches also provided much-needed shelter for the continent's nascent pro-democracy movements.

But not all religious organizations followed the same path. In the 1980s, Africa witnessed the rapid spread of Pentecostalism, a Christian renewal movement that places great emphasis on direct personal communication with God. The rise of Pentecostal Churches was partly inspired by the spread of the movement in the United States, but also owed much to the ability of Pentecostal leaders to speak to the main concerns of their congregations: poverty, witchcraft, and social dislocation. Of course, not all churches were the same, but the obsession of Pentecostal leaders with making new converts, combined with the religion's overt focus on wealth creation, meant that the movement was at times more willing to embrace authoritarian rule than the established churches. In Kenya, a leader of the Gospel Redeemed Church responded to criticism of Daniel arap Moi's corrupt and violent regime by Catholic and Anglican leaders by telling his congregation – which included the president – that "people should shut up, accept the present leadership and prepare to go to Heaven."[3] This was not an isolated case. Following widespread criticism of Ghana's presidential election in 1992, the winner, Jerry John Rawlings, sought to confer legitimacy on the process by asking Christian churches to hold a thanksgiving service. Only Pentecostal leaders agreed to attend.

Islam represented another dynamic altogether. But although Islam is often said to be less supportive of democratic norms and values than Christianity, the relationship between Muslim leaders and authoritarian rule was also complex. Indeed, in some countries the strength of Islam played an important role in limiting the extension of government control. Consider Senegal, which, along with Djibouti, Gambia, Guinea, Mali, Mauritania, Niger, Sierra Leone, and Somalia, entered the postcolonial period as a predominantly Muslim state (Figure 2.2). Islam has been present in Senegal for more than a millennium and today Muslims make up around 95 per cent of the population. Most of the Muslim majority are organized into hierarchical Sufi orders led by religious authorities known as marabouts. Around the time of independence in 1960, the Sufi brotherhoods exerted great influence in the political and economic sphere as a result of the religious authority they enjoyed over their disciples and their central economic role in the production of peanuts, which provided the majority of jobs in rural areas. Winning the support of the marabouts was therefore an important first step towards securing political power. This point was not lost on Leopold Senghor, the poet leader of the Union Progressiste Sénégalaise (UPS), who skilfully outmanoeuvred his main rival, Lamine Gueye, by constructing alliances with influential Sufi leaders in the 1950s.

After independence, the close relationship between the marabouts and the UPS continued, but Sufi leaders fiercely guarded their independence. Recognizing the spiritual and organizational power of the Sufi orders, the government realized that it made more sense to work with the marabouts, rather than to try and control them. In any case Senghor, who received a religious education in Senegal before

---

[3] Paul Gifford. "Some Recent Developments in African Christianity". *African Affairs* 93, 373 (1994), pp. 513–534, p. 529.

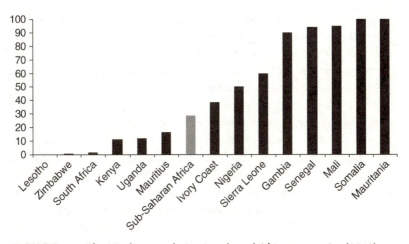

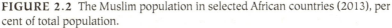

FIGURE 2.2 The Muslim population in selected African countries (2013), per cent of total population.
Source: CIA, except for sub-Saharan Africa, which comes from the Pew Research Centre (2010).

attending the Sorbonne in Paris, and who had already amassed a decade of legislative experience at the point of independence, preferred consensus to confrontation (see Introduction). The overall consequence of this arrangement was that the UPS recruited a significant portion of its popular base second hand, relying on the marabouts to deliver the support – or at least the acquiescence – of their followers.

While the UPS needed the Sufi brotherhood to mobilize support, the marabouts also relied on their political allies to help maintain their spiritual and economic monopoly. The vested interest of both parties in maintaining this relationship meant that the presence of powerful Islamic leaders did not undermine the secular Senegalese state; instead, the marabouts and the UPS formed a remarkably stable alliance. While many bureaucrats and party officials privately mocked the marabouts, they also recognized that the stability of the regime and the success of development projects rested on the cooperation of religious leaders. For their part, many marabout cared little for the polices pursued out by Senghor and his successor, Abdou Diouf, but they understood the value of avoiding unnecessary conflict and so accepted the political status quo.

In contrast to the DRC, Senegal did not become a violent and repressive state in the 1960s. Instead, when the UPS became the sole political party in 1966 the government followed the pattern of civilian one-party states elsewhere in Africa by maintaining avenues of political participation (see Chapter 1). Later, following criticism of his regime in the early 1970s, Senghor responded by liberalizing the political system, introducing a form of constrained multiparty competition at a time when most of his counterparts were cracking down on opposition. Senghor's decision was not prompted by the strength of religious leaders, who neither actively supported nor opposed multipartyism. Rather, it reflected the country's early exposure to representative government and his considerable experience of, and respect for, plural politics. But because Sufi leaders were determined to maintain their rural influence, they did play an important role in checking the power of the UPS – now rebranded as the Parti Socialiste du Sénégal (PS) – in other ways.

Immediately after independence, Senghor's government set about extending its influence into rural areas, taking over the marketing of peanuts and establishing a nationwide agricultural education service. Marabouts tolerated this extension of central control, but often complained about the way in which policies were administered. Most notably, in the early 1960s the Sufi brotherhoods successfully resisted efforts by then-Prime Minister Mamadou Dia to strengthen bureaucratic control in rural areas, which threatened to end the privileged position of religious leaders as the sole broker between the peasantry and the state. The episode contributed to Dia's political downfall. Tensions had already emerged between the prime minister and Senghor, who favoured very different models of political organization. Whereas Dia wanted to build a centralized party structure in which he had an intermediary in every jurisdiction, Senghor sought to sustain weaker factions so that he could play one group off against another. Following accusations that Dia was planning to overthrow Senghor in a coup, he was forced to resign as prime minister in 1962, and was subsequently imprisoned until 1974. As a result, Dia's reforms were never implemented and the marabouts won a small, but important, victory.

By placing limits on what political leaders could do, marabouts effectively sustained a degree of political space outside of the party's control. Moreover, because the Sufi brotherhoods always maintained a degree of independence from the state, they were able to remove their support from the PS when pressure for regime change began to build in the late 1980s and early 1990s. By this time, the Sufi brotherhood's political influence had been undercut by the same processes of urbanization and economic decline that eroded support for the PS government. Nonetheless, the refusal of many marabouts to publicly back the government boosted the momentum of the opposition and so contributed to Senegal's first transfer of power in 2000 (see Chapter 6). The impact of Christianity and Islam in countries such as the Congo and Senegal was therefore much more similar than contemporary debates about shari'a (Islamic) law would suggest. In these states, religious organizations did not fully defend democratic norms and values, but neither did they facilitate authoritarian excess.

Mobilizing for Democracy?

Even where trade unions or religious bodies were weak, presidents did not always find it easy to maintain control over social movements. At times, this enabled groups to advance their own agendas, occasionally promoting the cause of democracy in the process. Take Uganda in the 1980s. Following a period of chronic instability under Idi Amin, elections returned Milton Obote and his Uganda People's Congress (UPC) to power in 1980. However, this did little to stabilize the country, because rival leaders such as Yoweri Museveni rejected the results. Although Museveni had previously worked for Obote's intelligence services, and had fought by his side against Amin, he quickly resolved to take power through force. Over the next five years, his National Resistance Army (NRA) fought a successful bush war that severely weakened the UPC regime.

Despite this progress, it was not Museveni that ultimately toppled Obote, but a coup led by Lieutenant-General Tito Okello, who aimed to replace the country's ailing multiparty system with military rule. Museveni refused to recognize Okello's authority, arguing that he had been complicit in the UPC's failings and that, having fought against the regime for four long years, the NRA had won the right to lead. After attempts to negotiate an end to the conflict met with failure, Museveni took his forces back to the bush, confident in the superiority of his troops. Just over a month later, on 26 January 1986, he declared victory after watching the NRA overrun the capital city.

As president, Museveni, who had studied economics and political science at the University of Dar es Salaam in Tanzania, began to turn Uganda around. Having reconsidered his early support for Marxism, he embraced the reform agenda of the IMF and World Bank. A period of economic and political stabilization followed, which led Western donors to identify him as one of a "new generation" of reform-minded African leaders. But despite the lavish praise from foreign governments, Museveni was never a democrat. He recognized the need for political participation to legitimate his government, but at heart Museveni was a military man who valued hierarchy and control over competition and free speech. At the same time, he feared that reintroducing multiparty politics would lead to further instability and ethnic tension. As a result, his National Resistance Movement (NRM) government consistently resisted calls for political liberalization, which Museveni feared would exacerbate the ethnic and regional fault lines that had come to the fore during the violence and instability of the previous decade. Instead, the new president promoted a system of "no-party democracy" in which individuals were allowed to compete for office but only on a non-partisan basis.[4]

This form of government was much like a one-party state, but with the important difference that Museveni claimed that in Uganda there were no parties at all. Although this message resonated with many Ugandans, who associated political parties with division and instability, such a description was somewhat disingenuous. While Museveni liked to depict the NRM as an inclusive social force, in reality it was a ruling party in all but name. However, the ideological justification for "Movement democracy" suggested that legislators and activists were not bound by the need to follow the party line, and many took advantage of this to maintain a degree of independence from the executive. As a result, the Ugandan parliament became one of the liveliest legislatures on the continent.

The greater space for debate also created opportunities for civil society groups, facilitating the rise of one of Africa's most effective women's movements. Under the government of Idi Amin, women's groups had been centralized and co-opted under the National Council of Women in Uganda, which was located in the office of the prime minister. But as Aili Mari Tripp's research has shown, the UN Nairobi women's conference in 1985 inspired a resurgence of women's organizations across the continent.[5] Frustrated that they had not been able to fully participate in the conference due to what they described as the

---

[4] Nelson Kasfir. "'No-Party Democracy' in Uganda". *Journal of Democracy* 9, 2 (1998), pp. 49–63.

[5] This section draws on Tripp, Aili. "Women's Movements and Challenges to Neopatrimonial Rule: Preliminary Observations from Africa". *Development and Change* 32, 1 (2001), pp. 33–54.

"political control that was in Uganda at the time", a group of women led by Dr Hilda Tadria decided to establish an organization to provide an independent voice for Ugandan women. Later that year, Action for Development (ACFODE) was born.

Representing women in Uganda was not an easy task. Male economic and political dominance had been gradually consolidated during the colonial period, and exacerbated by decades of violent conflict. By the 1980s, most female rights were either not legally recognized or not enforced. Reflecting broader continental trends, Ugandan women typically found it difficult to exercise free political choices, inherit land, or secure state protection from violence and rape. But despite this most challenging of contexts, ACFODE was able to take advantage of the new openings created by the no-party system to raise the profile of women's issues and to encourage the government to enhance women's representation in predominantly male arenas. Their efforts were not without success. Most notably, in 1987 Museveni acknowledged the complaints of the women's movement by creating the post of minister for women and development. Although many of the initiatives taken by the ministry – such as the drafting of a progressive domestic relations bill – were not effectively implemented because they lacked full government support, the creation of the post demonstrated that groups such as ACFODE had become too influential for the NRM to simply ignore. But official recognition by the NRM created challenges as well as opportunities, and activists debated whether they could achieve more by working within the regime or by resisting co-optation – after all, ACFODE had been explicitly established as an independent organization.

Some women's groups ultimately entered into a different kind of uneasy alliance, limiting their criticism of the president and the wider political system so that they could build a relationship with the NRM in order to push for progress on gender issues. Although this strategy involved implicitly endorsing an undemocratic regime, it also enabled the women's movement to secure some important successes, most notably the agreement of the 1995 constituent assembly – which had been tasked with agreeing a new constitution – that at least one-third of local government seats should be reserved for women. Moreover, because some influential women's groups refused to be fully incorporated into the ruling party, they retained the capacity to push messages that contradicted the NRM's own agenda. For example, following the reintroduction of multiparty politics in 2005, the Uganda Women's

Network (UWONET), one of the bodies that emerged in the wake of ACFODE, pressured the government to act against the harassment of women voters by their husbands and other males with differing political views. As part of these efforts, UWONET and other organizations such as the Coalition for Political Accountability to Women threw their weight behind a broader campaign to increase the professionalism and capacity of the electoral commission. In this way, the women's movement contributed to the pressure on Museveni to allow for a more inclusive and responsive form of government, even if it did not fundamentally change the way that the political game was played at the national level. As with trade unions in Zambia and the Catholic Church in the Congo, women's groups in Uganda walked a fine line between support and opposition, reflecting the inconsistent political role of African civil society in the 1980s.

Democratizing Civil Society?

The reintroduction of multipartyism in the 1990s did not simply democratize civil-society. Rather, it transformed Africa's formal and informal institutions in ways that reinforced the ambiguous relationship between civil society and democracy. Most obviously, the resumption of political competition increased the pressure on leaders to secure votes and so they devoted even more time and resources to maintaining their patron-client networks, co-opting journalists, academics, and non-governmental organizations (NGOs) in the process. This trend was perhaps most obvious in Kenya, where the transition from authoritarian rule in 1992 exacerbated the willingness of government figures to engage in harambee activities. Before the elections in 1992 and 1997, Moi appeared at an average of one harambee meeting every two weeks, expanding and deepening the networks that he had developed during the one-party state. In addition to widespread intimidation, state-sponsored ethnic clashes, and opposition disunity, the continued flow of resources to a broad coalition of constituencies enabled Moi to hang onto power in 1992 and 1997 (Chapter 5). In turn, this intensified the significance of patronage within Kenyan political life, transforming many "non-governmental" actors into agents of one party or another.

Similarly, the reintroduction of multipartyism did not erode the significance of "traditional" belief systems such as witchcraft, but rather gave them a new lease of life. During the one-party state in Benin, President

Kerekou employed the Malian marabout Serigne Babacar Cissé to bolster his regime's spiritual credentials. Cissé rose to become a minister and was said to use his powers to attack Kerekou's enemies. Following the reintroduction of multipartyism, Cissé's reputation became even more important to Kerekou as he sought to intimidate the opposition with tales of his spiritual hegemony. In the run-up to the "founding" elections of 1991, the main opposition candidate, Nicephore Soglo, was struck down by an illness that, according to popular rumour, had been concocted by Kerekou's occult army. Although Soglo subsequently won the election, he quickly moved to address his perceived inferiority in the spiritual realm, organizing his own international *vodun* ("voodoo") festival, Ouidah 92, and officially recognizing vodun as one of Benin's "great religions" alongside Islam and Christianity.

At a more mundane level, competition in legislative and local elections created new business for witchdoctors, as a small but significant number of candidates sought to bewitch rivals and to intimidate opposition supporters. One important consequence of this process was that witchcraft accusations became increasingly bound up with political disputes and inter-communal disagreements. According to Adam Ashcroft, after the end of apartheid in South Africa the ubiquity of witchcraft accusations gave rise to a "presumption of malice" between different communities. Especially in multi-ethnic parts of the country, allegations of witchcraft by members of one community against the leader of another heightened inter-communal suspicion and contributed to the rise of ethnic chauvinism.[6] As a result, the resurgence of the politics of evil made for less harmonious social relations, increasing the prospects of civil strife.

In the early 1990s the role of many formal civil society actors was also transformed in new and often problematic ways. The combination of economic decline and an over-reliance on international funds meant that many elected governments had little choice but to at least partially implement IMF and World Bank policies. This typically resulted in a reduction in government spending and the privatization of key industries and parastatals, leading to a fall in the level of state employment. Together with high levels of background unemployment, this reduced the number of people working in the formal economy and so undermined the bargaining position of trade unions (see Chapter 3).

---

[6] Ashcroft, Adam. *Witchcraft, Violence, and Democracy in South Africa*. Chicago: University of Chicago Press, 2005.

Religious organizations suffered no such decline, but their role also changed. In countries such as Côte d'Ivoire, Nigeria, and Kenya, the reintroduction of multiparty politics served to intensify religious cleavages. In the run-up to the 2007 Kenyan elections, established churches that had previously portrayed themselves as impartial defenders of human rights adopted explicitly partisan positions. Amidst false rumours that opposition leader Raila Odinga had signed an MOU with Muslim voters to turn Kenya into a shari'a state – a form of government that locates political authority in the interpretation of Muslim religious texts – traditional Christian churches became increasingly willing to support candidates sympathetic to their cause. Some evangelical clergy went further and ran for public office themselves. The result was a divisive politicization of religion to the extent that, following the outbreak of electoral violence in 2008, religious leaders were not seen to be sufficiently neutral to lead mediation efforts.

Political competition also accelerated the expansion of more radical strains of Islam. In the 1990s, the combination of multiparty elections, rising expenditure on religious education in Africa by countries such as Iran and Saudi Arabia, and the polemical activities of al-Qaeda and Osama bin Laden led to a new set of debates regarding the introduction of shari'a law in Nigeria. In the international media, these debates were often depicted as being driven by international conspiracies, but in reality they owed more to domestic political struggles. The northern part of Nigeria is mostly Muslim while the southern part is mostly Christian, and so the role of religion is hard to separate from that of region and ethnicity (on which see chapter 1). The decision of a group of Nigerian Muslim leaders to campaign for the introduction of shari'a law in the 1990s was motivated by a complex combination of religious belief, fear of losing adherents to aggressive and increasingly successful Pentecostal Churches, and displeasure that Nigeria was led by Olusegun Obasanjo, a devout Christian. The issue of shari'a was particularly attractive to these leaders not because they sympathized with the aims of Osama bin Laden, but because it made it easier to exacerbate religious cleavages and mobilize supporters, and thus to consolidate their hold over their own communities at a time of great political uncertainty.

The implementation of shari'a law was facilitated by the country's federal status, which enabled Governor Ahmad Rufai San to introduce shari'a in the north-western state of Zamfara in 1999, arguing that this was perfectly compatible with Nigeria's status as a secular state at the national level. But although shari'a was introduced alongside a multiparty political system, some of the decisions subsequently made under shari'a rule clearly violated the human rights of defendants, including Christians living in the north of the country. In 2002, a shari'a court in Katsina State sentenced a woman found guilty of adultery to death by stoning, sparking outrage throughout the largely Christian south. Although the decision was later overturned on appeal, the episode led to a heated debate about whether regional shari'a rule and national democratic rule could peacefully coexist.

The continent's women's organizations have also been transformed in complex ways by the reintroduction of multiparty politics. Although elections brought higher levels of female representation in countries willing to employ gender quotas, such as Rwanda (see Chapter 6), many women's organizations struggled to retain their original focus. In Nigeria and Zambia, for example, the wives of civilian presidents publicly declared an interest in "women's issues" and pledged to promote women-friendly policies within government. But while such high-profile endorsements increased the salience of the women's movement, their incorporation into the ruling party also compromised their independence and credibility. Returning to Zambia, President Chiluba's wife, Vera, used her Hope Foundation to distribute much-needed food, clothes, and drugs to poor Zambians – but then also used her foundation to launch scathing attacks on the opposition.

Thus, while women's groups, churches, and unions continued to play an important role in shaping the balance of power between states and societies, the transition to multiparty politics did not automatically make civil society any more civil, or any more democratic.

Select Bibliography

Chabal, Patrick. *Political Domination in Africa: Reflections on the Limits of Power.* Cambridge: Cambridge University Press, 1986.

Ellis, Stephen, and Gerrie ter Haar. *Worlds of Power: Religious Thought and Political Practice in Africa.* Oxford: Oxford University Press, 2004.

Haynes, Jeffrey. *Religion and Politics in Africa.* Nairobi: East African Educational Publishers, 1996.

Tripp, Aili. "Women's Movements and Challenges to Neopatrimonial Rule: Preliminary Observations from Africa". *Development and Change* 32, 1 (2001), pp. 33–54.

For a bibliography for this chapter go to www.democracyinafrica.org

CHAPTER 3

The Second Liberation: Economic Decline, the End of the Cold War, and the Struggle for Democracy

From the late 1980s onward, the African political landscape was transformed as one-party states, personal dictatorships, and military rule gave way to multiparty politics. If independence was the continent's first liberation, many saw the 1990s as democracy's second coming. Between 1989 and 1994, thirty-five sub-Saharan African countries reintroduced multiparty elections, bringing political openings to around 500 million people. By 2010, only Eritrea and Swaziland had failed to hold multiparty polls of some kind. The timing of this second liberation makes it tempting to interpret political change in Africa as a by-product of the collapse of the Soviet Union and the end of the Cold War; an aftershock of the seismic changes in the international landscape which, for a short while, alleviated the security concerns of Western governments, making them more willing to promote democracy abroad. However, democracy was never simply granted by international actors: it had to be won through the blood and sweat of domestic opposition groups and the sacrifices of ordinary people.

The extent of democratization in a given country was thus shaped by both international pressure and the domestic context. But these two factors did not operate independently of each other, because the success of international efforts depended on the presence of a strong domestic pro-reform constituency, and vice versa. It was more legitimate, and hence easier, for foreign governments to intervene when they could point to an active and large pro-democracy movement. Conversely, civil society campaigns, strikes, and the like were more effective when foreign actors used their influence to protect protestors from repression. Genuine democratization was therefore most likely to occur when a united and effective domestic opposition met with a supportive international community.

The Roots of the Third Wave

The collapse of authoritarian rule in Africa began years before protestors took to the streets in Benin, with the financial meltdown of the 1980s. Falling government revenue undermined the ability of incumbents to satisfy their support base and rendered them dependent on the financial support of interactional actors. In turn, this left African governments increasingly vulnerable to domestic and international criticism, and so facilitated later processes of democratization.

The economic crisis of the 1980s had many roots. Colonial rule left a set of economies that were overly reliant on one or two exports for income and foreign exchange. After the end of the 1960s, a sharp decline in the value of commodities such as coffee and copper, combined with rising oil prices following the shocks of 1973 and 1979, led to rising import costs and falling export revenue. With the exception of oil-exporting countries such as Angola and Nigeria, which benefitted from higher prices, this pushed government balance sheets into the red. But Africa's economic malaise was not simply a case of bad luck: the unfavourable international context was exacerbated by poor economic management. Those governments committed to African socialism often pursued policies of nationalization and social reorganization that proved to be costly, inefficient, and unpopular – think back to the failings of the Ujamaa experiment of forced villagization in Tanzania described in Chapter 1. From Benin to Zambia, the extension of state control over the economy created bureaucratic blockages and opportunities for corruption that alienated foreign investors.

Most capitalist regimes fared little better, however, because nominally "free market" governments nonetheless manipulated their control over licenses, permits, and credit – and hence entry into the market – to reward supporters. In doing so, they created a set of economic distortions that were different, but no less problematic, than their socialist counterparts. At the same time, the patronage networks constructed by leaders to consolidate their power diverted resources away from more profitable investment, whatever the political leanings of the regime (see Chapter 2).

Even those states that benefited from considerable holdings of gas, gold, and oil struggled to grow their economies in the 1980s. Instead, countries such as Nigeria became textbook illustrations of the resource curse. Because high export earnings from oil drove up the value of the Nigerian currency (the Naira), they made exports more expensive, and as a result other industries became less internationally competitive. Nigeria thus failed to reduce its dependence on oil revenues by diversifying its economy, and as a result its economic fortunes remained vulnerable to fluctuations in the value of oil on world markets. The negative impact of this process might have been alleviated had the revenue from the sale of natural resources been invested in supporting the development of new industries. But instead, a significant proportion of export revenues were either stolen or squandered on white elephant projects. At the same time, the centralization of economic opportunities under "gatekeeper" states in which access to wealth depended on control of the government encouraged heated competition for political control (see Introduction). In turn, this increased the likelihood of civil conflict, leading to further economic decline in countries such as Liberia and Sierra Leone. With the exception of Botswana and possibly South Africa, the proceeds from natural resources did not support sustainable economic growth.

In the early 1980s, the situation was so bad that Africa actually got poorer every year (Figure 3.1). As a result, African governments began to approach the IMF and the World Bank in desperate need of international assistance. Over the next decade, what started as a trickle became a flood. The number of IMF agreements signed with African countries increased from two in 1978 to twenty-one in 1981. In just a few years, the continent's debt spiralled out of all control. Between 1970 and 1984 the cost of debt servicing increased from $449 million to $7.4 billion. Failure to keep up payments was an ever-present concern: by 1981 the IMF had already reported twenty-three countries for being in arrears. Thus began Africa's financial dependence on Western governments (Figure 3.2).

The IMF and World Bank responded to the continent's economic collapse by imposing increasingly stringent conditions on economic assistance. Both institutions had been established with a conditionality clause that empowered them to require countries to implement certain reforms in order to secure their support. Conditionality was necessary because the future of the IMF and the World Bank depended on loans being paid back, and so the sustainability of the entire system rested on debtor governments pursuing sound economic policies.

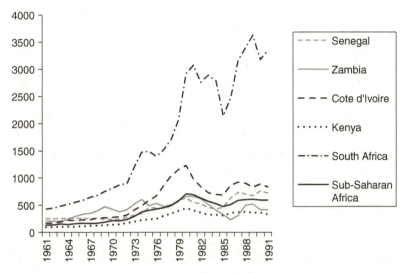

FIGURE 3.1 GDP per capita in selected African countries (1961–1981), current US$.
Source: World Bank.

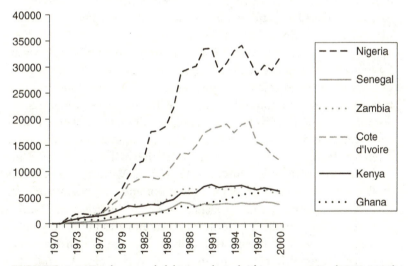

FIGURE 3.2 Total external debt in selected African countries (1970–2000), millions in current US$.
Source: World Bank.

However, exactly what conditions could reasonably be demanded of client states proved to be something of a moving target. Following an era of minimal conditionality in the 1960s and early 1970s, the IMF and the World Bank began to adopt a far more invasive approach in the

1980s. The failure of many African governments to keep up their debt repayments both discredited their economic policies and empowered the two institutions to argue that reform was essential. Significantly, at the same time that the World Bank was becoming increasingly powerful, its officials were becoming evermore confident that they could identify – and resolve – the causes of Africa's economic failings. The World Bank's now infamous Berg Report of 1981 argued that the main factor distorting the performance of African economies was African politics: the corrupt and inefficient nature of the African state was preventing the proper functioning of the market. The obvious solution was to scale back the state.

Over the next decade, the World Bank sought to reorder African economies through Structural Adjustment Programs (SAPs). The standard template of a Structural Adjustment Programme (SAP) included a reduction in government expenditure, the privatization of key assets, and the removal of subsidies and tariffs. Heavily indebted African governments were poorly placed to withstand this attack on the state, especially given the refusal of a slew of secondary lenders to engage with governments that did not already have an agreement with the IMF. But conditionality was nonetheless resisted both explicitly and covertly. Some left-leaning states were able to challenge IMF orthodoxy by sourcing financial support from China, Cuba, Norway, Sweden, and the USSR, as well as from international NGOs such as Oxfam, in order to reduce their reliance on the IMF. Governments that rhetorically committed themselves to the World Bank's SAPs also proved able to subvert its policies by failing to implement measures that would disadvantage key support groups and diverting funds intended for economic restructuring to the maintenance of ailing patronage networks. Because the IMF and the World Bank had very weak mechanisms through which to monitor and punish governments that failed to comply, countries such as Benin, Liberia, and Zambia were able to repeatedly secure new agreements despite having failed to meet previous conditions. Ironically, it was the nominally socialist governments of Rawlings in Ghana and Museveni in Uganda that implemented the SAP model most faithfully, despite their criticisms of Western economic formulae.

Because SAPs were patchily enforced, their impact was not always immediately felt, and so the onset of adjustment was not strongly correlated with the outbreak of political unrest. Over time, however, the continual erosion of state capacity, coupled with the failure of SAPs to actually inspire economic recovery, made it increasingly difficult for African leaders to maintain services and patron-client networks. In turn, this sowed the seeds of public discontent. In the 1960s and 1970s, patronage had been a critical tool of national integration. Leaders in countries such as Nigeria, Senegal, and Zambia consolidated their power by integrating a range of groups into their regimes through the distribution of economic opportunities. Typical strategies included the creation of jobs for university leaders, the appointment of allies to lucrative positions on the boards of state-owned companies and organizations, and the public dissemination of development funds and cold hard cash. However, from the 1970s onward most governments were forced to pare down these patronage networks, restricting access to state resources to an ever-decreasing circle of insiders, thus undermining their own support base. Especially in countries such as Kenya where conceptions of the right to lead was bound up with the ability of an individual to take care of the community, economic collapse hit a president's reputation hard (see Chapter 2).

The development of pro-democracy movements began well before the 1990s. Chapter 2 documented the various ways in which journalists, religious leaders, and trade unionists struggled to prevent the abuse of power after independence. And although some authoritarian governments enjoyed local legitimacy, such as the civilian one-party states described in Chapter 1, currents of resistance were always present. The formation of military dictatorships and one-party states, for example, was typically resisted by a range of actors including lawyers, rival political leaders, and minority communities who feared exclusion within the new political dispensation. From the 1970s onward, this opposition deepened as a result of both economic decline and the increasing centralization of power in the hands of unresponsive and increasingly unpopular presidents and prime ministers. Across the continent, Africans began to publicly express a common desire to have a say in the decisions that shaped their own lives.

Over time, generational change further weakened the hold of ruling parties over the popular imagination. Following the death or resignation of founding fathers such as Kenyatta (died 1978), Nyerere (resigned 1985), and Senghor (resigned 1980), their successors rarely enjoyed the personal standing required to sustain failing regimes. By the late 1980s, a generation was becoming politically active that had no memory of the liberation struggle and whose defining experience was not of the glorious defeat of colonial rule but of unemployment and repression. As population growth increased and economies stalled, governments were unable to find jobs for thousands of school leavers and university graduates, some of whom became lawyers or joined NGOs, leading to the emergence of a larger and more critical civil society. Precisely because such groups were not dependent on the government for their employment, they were often more critical of their government's economic and political failings.

As we saw in Chapter 2, when these civil organizations moved from criticizing individual policies to questioning the foundations of authoritarian rule itself, the pressure for democratization intensified dramatically. With the exception of a small number of countries such as Botswana, Mauritius, Senegal, and Tanzania, the first response of most African governments was to increase the level of repression. Many leaders also came to realize that while shrinking patronage networks were a political liability, economic exclusion could be turned into a political weapon. By purposefully cutting off the access of disloyal individuals and communities to state resources, incumbents could demonstrate the high cost of opposition and so frighten citizens into acquiescence.

Others moved straight to more violent strategies. President Ibrahim Babangida in Nigeria and General Gnassingbé Eyadéma in Togo, for example, resorted to increasingly brutal strategies in order to punish dissidents and maintain their grip on power. But repression also had to be paid for. During the height of the Cold War, a number of African dictators proved more than capable of taking advantage of the deep tensions between East and West to play America, the Soviet Union, China, Cuba, the United Kingdom, and France off against each other in order to access military aid that was the equal of funds distributed by the IMF or World Bank (see Chapter 4). This international support enabled autocrats to pay army salaries and police wages and so empowered them to ignore the wishes of their citizens. In the worst cases, international funds and arms contributed to the militarization of politics in Ethiopia and Somalia and the prolongation of civil conflict in Angola and Mozambique.

Against this backdrop, the end of the Cold War in the late 1980s acted as a trigger for African democratization. On the one hand, the overthrow of authoritarian rule in countries such as Czechoslovakia and Poland inspired and reinvigorated pro-democracy forces in Africa. Religious and trade union leaders invoked events in Romania, Poland, and East Germany as precedents for the type of political reform needed in Africa. And as organizations such as the United Democratic Front (UDF) in South Africa and FORD in Kenya grew in size and strength, they demonstrated just how unpopular and illegitimate their governments had become. In turn, evidence of democratic progress on the continent, such as the release of Nelson Mandela in South Africa in 1990 and the early victories of opposition parties in Benin and Zambia in 1991, instilled a newfound confidence in opposition groups across Africa.

On the other hand, the victory of America over the Soviet Union meant that Western governments faced less pressure to put security considerations ahead of human rights concerns. International donors thus became less willing to prop up authoritarian states at the precise moment when Africa's dictators most needed international financial support to help them contain dissent. Contrary to popular wisdom, this process did not begin with the Velvet Revolutions of 1989 but started earlier; Eastern support for left-leaning African governments declined from the early 1980s onward, and dropped sharply after Gorbachev became president of the Soviet Union in 1988. However, the disintegration of the USSR was nonetheless significant because it made it clear that there would be no resurgence of Soviet engagement. As a result, Africa's bankrupt regimes became increasingly reliant on American financial support and hence vulnerable to shifts in U.S. foreign policy. At the same time, the apparent victory of liberal democracy against all comers and the mounting evidence of mass support for political reform in Africa emboldened America and some European states to make democracy promotion a priority for the first time.

The combination of mounting domestic unrest and international criticism meant that it became increasingly unfeasible for African autocrats to block reform. Over the next decade, even the continent's most brutal dictators were forced to legalize opposition parties and reintroduce elections, empowering domestic actors to make their own history. For a brief moment, democracy appeared to be the only game in town.

Transition Trajectories

Although these general trends played out across the continent, there were significant variations in the capacity of different governments to manage the process of change. Some leaders presided over economies that were effectively bankrupt, as in Benin and Zambia, while others were able to survive on the export of oil and minerals, as in Sudan and Togo. In a minority of countries, a history of trade union mobilization helped to create a well-organized, cross-ethnic opposition, as in Zambia and later Zimbabwe, but in others decades of repression and pronounced ethnic cleavages meant that civil society movements were fragmented and vulnerable, as in Cameroon and the DRC. The impact of the international community also varied markedly: while international actors were willing to throw their weight behind democratization when little else was at stake, as in Benin, Ghana, and Malawi, they adopted far more ambiguous strategies with regards to key allies in areas of considerable geo-strategic importance, such as Nigeria. These variations help to explain the remarkably different pathways that African regimes followed during the 1990s.

Democratization involves three distinct but overlapping processes: the transition to multipartyism, the reconstitution of a new political order, and the later process of consolidating democratic gains. While almost all African countries embarked on the first phase of this journey, many stalled in the second stage and few became liberal democracies. How much liberalization a leader allowed depended on whether or not they saw repression or reform as the most acceptable response to the particular circumstances they faced (see Introduction). In part, this decision was shaped by personal morality, but it also had a lot to do with how much a leader stood to lose from leaving office and the feasibility of retaining power through undemocratic means.

In countries such as Benin and Zambia, presidents with little international support and failing economies faced strong opposition movements. Under these conditions there were clear limits to how long authoritarian control could be maintained. Together with the reluctance of Presidents Kérékou and Kaunda to retain power by any means necessary, this meant that the governments of Benin and Zambia came to view reform as being more acceptable than repression. As a result, they responded to the winds of change by opening up their political systems. In turn, political liberalization served to further embolden the opposition, which made the task of retaining control through repression increasingly unfeasible. Consequently, cases of *transition from below* often resulted in relatively free and fair elections that were dominated by the opposition.

By contrast, where opposition to the regime remained diffuse, and the intervention of international actors was weak or non-existent, incumbents were in a far stronger position to undertake reform at their own pace. In countries that had largely experienced stable civilian rule and in which the ruling party had less to fear from opening up the political system, such as Senegal and Tanzania, domestic elites proved more inclined to deal with criticism through compromise rather than coercion, resulting in *transition from above*. But precisely because incumbents retained significant control of the process, this form of transition rarely resulted in a rapid transfer of power.

In the largest set of cases, incumbents found the notion of full political liberalization unacceptable because of the benefits they received from being in power and the personal risks of losing power, but were unable to re-establish their hegemony. The period of stalemate that followed was typically resolved in one of four very different ways. In countries where institutions were stronger and sufficient trust and common ground could be established between rival parties, such as South Africa, moderate leaders from both sides entered talks that resulted in *negotiated transitions*. Because the deals brokered between the incumbent and the opposition protected their core interests, they typically delivered transitions that were relatively stable but also less radical than many rank-and-file opposition supporters had hoped. But few African countries featured the necessary institutions or trust for successful negotiations. Instead, decades of neo-patrimonial rule had bred cultures of distrust, and generated weak institutions incapable of enforcing deals made by rival leaders. It is for this reason that so many African transitions only occurred after a violent rupture of the political system.

In a small number of cases, such as Mali, stalemate was broken by a military coup that removed the incumbent and paved the way for multiparty elections. The fate of such *domestically triggered transitions* was highly variable because it remained dependent on the willingness of the military junta to go back to barracks and foster the emergence of a civilian regime. Although the Malian coup leaders did preside over a free and fair election in 1992, military governments in countries such as Mauritania found it impossible to resist the temptation to cling onto power (for a discussion of the legacy of military rule see Chapter 1). In other cases, the deadlock was broken by the intervention of donors who stepped in to halt financial transfers to the government and so forced presidents to hold elections. But because leaders

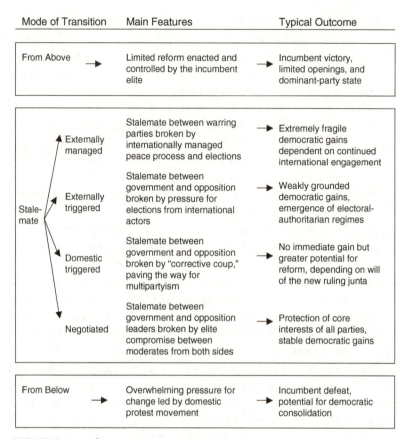

Mode of Transition	Main Features	Typical Outcome
From Above →	Limited reform enacted and controlled by the incumbent elite	→ Incumbent victory, limited openings, and dominant-party state
Stalemate — Externally managed	Stalemate between warring parties broken by internationally managed peace process and elections	→ Extremely fragile democratic gains dependent on continued international engagement
Externally triggered	Stalemate between government and opposition broken by pressure for elections from international actors	→ Weakly grounded democratic gains, emergence of electoral-authoritarian regimes
Domestic triggered	Stalemate between government and opposition broken by "corrective coup," paving the way for multipartyism	→ No immediate gain but greater potential for reform, depending on will of the new ruling junta
Negotiated	Stalemate between government and opposition leaders broken by elite compromise between moderates from both sides	→ Protection of core interests of all parties, stable democratic gains
From Below →	Overwhelming pressure for change led by domestic protest movement	→ Incumbent defeat, potential for democratic consolidation

FIGURE 3.3 African transition trajectories.

in countries such as Kenya and Togo lacked the will to reform, *externally triggered transitions* usually resulted in flawed elections that were almost always won by the ruling party.

The final set of stalemate cases were rather different and arose where countries had emerged from, or were in the middle of, civil war. In countries such as Angola and Liberia, transitions typically occurred following the breakdown of political order, in a situation in which competition was not between competing parties, but between rebel armies. Here, the reintroduction of multiparty politics owed much to the efforts of the international community to push for the use of elections as a mechanism of conflict resolution during protracted peace processes. In the absence of trust and strong institutions, such transitions were dependent on comprehensive international engagement to guarantee the peace and hence make the risks of engaging in genuine political dialogue acceptable to all. In turn, this dependency on foreign support presented real challenges to the sustainability of democratic gains, making *externally managed transitions* extremely fragile and prone to reversal. Discussion of this particularly problematic mode of transition is reserved for Chapter 4.

Transitions from Above

In contrast to most of Africa, the gradual opening up of the political system in Senegal and Tanzania began well before the end of the Cold War (see Chapter 6 for Senegal). Indeed, instead of being dragged kicking and screaming into a new multiparty era, incumbents in these countries led processes of "top-down democratization" that were driven not by opposition groups but by the ruling party itself.[1] They did so because they enjoyed a high level of control over the political environment and so had little to lose from encouraging greater competition. At the same time, they understood that reform could be used to enhance the democratic rights and liberties of their citizens and hence to renew the purpose and legitimacy of their governments.

Let us return to the case of Tanzania. As we saw in Chapter 1, following independence Julius Nyerere developed the archetypal African one-party state under the CCM. Nyerere became one of the first African leaders to voluntarily step down from power in 1985, in large part because he came to realise that his faith in African socialism had led to economic collapse and felt that fresh leadership was required to open up of the economy to greater competition. However, the quality of economic management improved little under Nyerere's successor. Instead, President Ali Hassan Mwinyi presided over a period of flagrant corruption that became popularly known as the era of *ruksa* ("do your own thing"). But although economic reform did little to revive the country's economic fortunes, pro-democracy sentiment remained limited. The effective co-optation of civil society groups into the ruling party, an ineffective trade union movement, and low population density represented effective barriers to the coordination of opposition to the ruling party. At the same time, Nyerere's powerful legacy, and his warnings about the need for unity in order to build a strong and

[1] Hydén, Goran. "Top-Down Democratization in Tanzania". *Journal of Democracy* 10, 4 (1999), pp. 142–155.

developed nation continued to exert a hold over the imagination of many Tanzanians, who remained skeptical of the need for opposition parties well into the 2000s.

Political liberalization was therefore not driven from below: there was no strong and unified pro-democracy campaign capable of rendering authoritarian rule unsustainable. Instead, CCM elites chose to open up the political system because they recognized that by doing so they could reap the benefits of greater domestic and international legitimacy without any real risk to their hegemony. Reformers argued that greater competition would provide fresh incentives for CCM leaders to respond to popular concerns, and so would breathe new life into the party, without undermining their hold on power. The benefits of reform therefore outweighed the risks. Nyerere himself continued to play a leading role in this process, arguing that Tanzania could not afford to ignore the significance of events in Eastern Europe and that only by moving towards democracy would the country be able to attract the international funds, loans, and investments that it needed to kick-start economic growth. President Mwinyi ultimately agreed, establishing a special commission to report on the legal changes that would be needed to legalize opposition parties. Although the government rejected many of the proposals of the commission and so retained some of the more authoritarian elements of the political system, it agreed to stage multiparty elections in 1995. The outcome of these polls demonstrated that the CCM had correctly read the lie of the land, as Benjamin Mkapa, the party's presidential candidate, was elected with around two-thirds of the vote. Over the next decade, the CCM continued to dominate politics on the mainland, as the former one-party state was carefully transformed into a dominant-party system.

Transition from Below

Transitions from below, in which ruling parties democratized because they came under great domestic and international pressure and had relatively little to fear from reform, were also relatively rare, but this was the pathway followed by both Benin and Zambia. In Benin, President Kérékou had come to power in 1972 and initially enjoyed considerable success, bringing a destabilizing period of coup and counter-coup to an end by transforming his military regime into a durable one-party state (see Chapter 1). Although he pledged that his regime would not follow any "foreign ideologies", after two years in office he declared that his regime would take a Marxist-Leninist approach. But Kérékou was more a military man than an ideologue and his PRPB government was concerned less with revolutionary ideals than with using its control over the economy to consolidate its hold on power. The proliferation of inefficient state-owned companies was a drain on public finances, while tight constraints on the private sector ensured that it never contributed significantly to government revenue. As a result, the level of national debt expanded to $1 billion, leaving the country with a $100 million a year bill just to service the interest. In response to mounting public disaffection, the PRPB engaged in a process of self-criticism from 1980 onward, but this was largely superficial and Kérékou refused to contemplate more far-reaching economic or political reforms.

Change could not be deferred forever, however. Over time, the government's failure to reverse the process of economic decline undermined its ability to meet its spending commitments. In 1986, a program that provided employment for university graduates was cut, creating a ready-made pool of potential recruits for the nascent pro-democracy movement. Falling health and education expenditure, combined with a freeze on the allowances received by public employees, further strengthened opposition to the regime – particularly among student groups and the illegal Communist Party of Dahomey (PCD). Despite government concessions, opposition to the regime continued to result in sporadic protests in the years that followed, each time revealing the steady erosion of the regime's authority. The protests escalated further in March 1989, when students were joined by employees from the Ministry of Finance, plantation workers, medical staff, and civil servants. As these groups compared their lists of complaints, a series of isolated demands for better pay or working conditions evolved into a unified demand for political reform.

The extent of opposition to the ruling party restricted Kérékou's options. Desperate for the resources needed to placate the protestors, he rushed to sign an agreement with the IMF to secure international financial assistance, but it proved to be too little, too late. On December 5, huge illegal demonstrations in Cotonou and the threat of a general strike forced Kérékou to abandon Marxism-Leninism and establish a national conference to discuss the country's political and economic future. Even at this late stage, Kérékou planned to broker a power-sharing deal that would have enabled him to retain the presidency. But instead of empowering the PRPB to regain control of the political agenda, the conference created new opportunities for unions, student groups, new religious movements, local development associations, and cultural bodies to push their own demands on the regime. Delegates successfully asserted the sovereignty of the conference and its right to dismiss the government and establish a new administration. Although Kérékou was allowed to remain as president, the conference announced a new cabinet against his wishes, and appointed Nicéphore Soglo, a former candidate for the presidency of the IMF, as prime minister.

Kérékou accepted these developments because he had no appetite to brutalize his own people, but also because he realized that it was not feasible to sustain power through force alone. Despite his military history, Kérékou had resigned his military position in 1987, and relations between the PRPB and the armed forces had subsequently deteriorated. Falling state revenue made it impossible to maintain military pay, undermining morale and paving the way for two coup attempts in 1988 that demonstrated that the security forces felt little loyalty for the regime. Moreover, unlike some of his counterparts in Francophone Africa, Kérékou could not bank on any financial or military assistance from France, the former colonial power. Following a deliberate attempt to divorce the country from French influence, relations between the two countries had soured. Moreover, Benin lacked natural resources and was of little geostrategic importance, and so Kérékou had little influence over international actors.

While the prospects of blocking reform were minimal, Kérékou also had fewer reasons to fear losing power than many of his counterparts. The offences he had committed in office had been relatively minor and the politics of the one-party state had been relatively peaceful. He therefore had no reason to expect persecution or prosecution from the nascent opposition, which meant that he did not feel compelled to maintain power at any cost. That said, Kérékou's willingness to pursue reform rather than repression may also have been underpinned by a certain naivety about his ability to win at the ballot box. By the time he agreed to reintroduce multipartyism no high-profile leaders had lost power as a result of the reintroduction of elections, and he may not have realized the extent of the challenge that he would face in the founding election of 1991. If so, then he significantly underestimated the threat posed by the new prime minister, Soglo, who polled 36 per cent of the vote in the first round, 9 per cent more than Kérékou. Because neither candidate secured more than 50 per cent, a run-off was held. Despite Kérékou's best efforts, the perception that the PRPB was a sinking ship encouraged the steady atrophy of leaders and activists to the opposition, enabling Soglo to dominate the second round, winning two-thirds of the poll. Faced with further proof of the weakness of his position, Kérékou quickly accepted defeat. Transition from below in Benin thus ended with one of Africa's first constitutional transfers of power. In turn, opposition victory paved the way for a period of open and competitive political competition: in the 1996 elections, Kérékou staged a remarkable comeback to defeat Soglo, at which point Benin became only the second African country to have experienced two transfers of power.

A similar story unfolded in Zambia, where the complete collapse of the economy eroded support for President Kaunda and his UNIP government, resulting in the emergence of a broad "anyone but UNIP" opposition under the banner of the MMD. The MMD successfully integrated marginalized businessmen, long-suffering farmers, and unemployed urbanites into a powerful coalition. Once the MMD had appointed union leader Frederick Chiluba as the party's president, the union's hard-won autonomy from UNIP meant that the opposition could effectively rally organized labour to its cause (see Chapter 2). Thereafter, the MMD was able to tap into the union's powerful organizational structures, and as a result the opposition quickly developed a greater capacity to mobilize support than the government.

Like Kérékou, Kaunda ultimately chose to reform the system rather than to repress the opposition. In charge of a relatively limited state structure, and denied international financial assistance, he lacked the means to co-opt or crush the MMD. And having spent his time in office attempting to build a cohesive national identity, Kaunda had no desire to turn his country into a police state or to use divide-and-rule politics to stay in power. As with the PRPB in Benin, the UNIP regime had detained and at times beaten opponents, but had not engaged in the kind of assassinations and ethnic cleansing likely to engender revenge attacks. At the same time, the yes-men that surrounded the president told him that he could win an election, which led him to view reform as a more acceptable strategy than repression. Kaunda therefore agreed to a constitutional amendment that reintroduced multiparty elections in August 1991. But once opposition political parties had been legalized, UNIP struggled to control the pace of change, and to prevent its MPs from defecting to the MMD. Although Kaunda sought to revitalize his regime by reengaging with traditional leaders and promising to give a large pay rise to public sector workers, the party had become a hollow shell, unable to penetrate and mobilize Zambian society. As a result, UNIP's collapse was humiliating: in a two-horse race, Kaunda polled just 20 per cent of the vote, one of the worst performances ever by an incumbent in an African election.

After Benin and Zambia, African leaders on the rest of the continent became much more aware – and concerned about – the danger posed by the reintroduction of multiparty elections.

Externally Triggered Transitions

African leaders were typically less willing to contemplate reform than Kaunda and Kérékou, but were also less able to retain control than the CCM in Tanzania. This resulted in periods of stalemate between the government and opposition that were resolved in a number of different ways. In countries such as Kenya, Malawi, and Togo, donors intervened to break the impasse by demanding the introduction of elections.

The stability of the Kenyan one-party state had been slowly eroding for years under the unpopular tenure of President Daniel arap Moi. Economic decline meant that Moi found it increasingly difficult to maintain his patronage networks, which was a major problem in a regime founded on patron-client relationships (see Chapter 2). Against this backdrop, the manipulation of one-party elections in 1988 proved to be a turning point because, by rigging out "disloyal" elements, Moi both alienated influential political leaders and undermined the last vestiges of his government's legitimacy. Many of those who lost out in national and party elections quickly concluded that it was no longer possible to pursue their personal ambitions within the one-party framework, and so spoke out in favour of democracy for the first time. Most significantly, two senior political figures that had previously been KANU ministers, Charles Rubia and Kenneth Matiba, launched a campaign to reintroduce multiparty politics in May 1992. In so doing, they provided a focal point for widespread frustration with the Moi state. The subsequent formation of FORD represented the greatest threat to KANU's hold on power since independence. The thousands of protestors who subsequently defied state bans and police brutality to attend pro-democracy rallies on 7 July, popularly known as *saba saba* ("seven seven"), demonstrated just how unpopular the ruling party had become. As church leaders spoke out against the rising tide of human rights abuses, the Law Society of Kenya mobilized to defend opposition activists brought before the courts.

Although the strength of the opposition meant that repression was a costly option, Moi was in a far stronger position than his counterparts in Benin and Zambia. For one thing, Kenya's economy had continued to grow throughout the one-party era, albeit slowly, and so he had more resources to co-opt support and fund the actions of the police and militias. Through the coercive capacity of the police, the paramilitary General Service Unit (GSU), and the prefectural structure of the provincial administration, Moi also retained a greater capacity to maintain control beyond the capital city than many of his counterparts elsewhere on the continent. Significantly, while repression remained a feasible option, Moi considered the potential cost of opening up the political system to be unacceptable. Throughout his time in office, he had deliberately weakened institutions so that he could steal from the state and remove any potential source of threat to his regime. The personal benefits that he enjoyed through the presidency made him particularly unwilling to give up the position. At the same time, his intimate knowledge of Kenya's compromised institutions meant that he was not prepared to do a deal with the opposition, because he knew that if his rivals took power there would be nothing to stop them from using their own neo-patrimonial networks to manipulate the judiciary and the electoral commission. Thus, the only way he could secure his interests and those of his supporters was by retaining the presidency.

But even though he was committed to resisting reform, Moi failed to crush the campaign to reintroduce multiparty elections due to the strength of domestic resistance. During a tense standoff between government and opposition, television images of the brutal repression of FORD activists encouraged international actors to intervene. Although some foreign governments continued to condone the Moi regime, U.S. Ambassador Smith Hempstone refused to keep quiet about the human rights abuses in his midst. His influence was considerable. In November 1991, the Paris Group announced that it was suspending balance of payment support and the rapid disbursement of aid pending economic and "good governance" reforms. Foreign aid only comprised around 9 per cent of GDP in Kenya and so the government was less dependent on donors than the average African state. However, Moi recognized that it did not make sense to limp on against the wishes of the U.S. government. He would need international assistance in the long-run, and came to realize that if he had to hold elections it made sense to be able to contest them from a position of strength – not years later when all of his funds had run out. Moi therefore agreed to legalize opposition parties, but resolved to do the bare minimum necessary to appease donors, gambling that if he could turn the taps of foreign aid back on, he could keep hold of the presidency. As we shall see in Chapter 5, this gambit paid off. Because Moi faced insufficient pressure to allow for meaningful constitutional reform he continued to enjoy great advantages over the opposition, which, together with his willingness to use violence and intimidation, enabled him to win multiparty elections in 1992 and 1997.

External intervention also played a role in the reintroduction of elections in Togo, where General Eyadéma had previously established himself as one of Africa's most distinctive and feared political leaders. Eyadéma initially became president following a military coup in 1967, and like Kérékou established a political party, the Rally of the Togolese People (RTP), in order to confer the image of a civilian government on his regime (see Chapter 1). In reality, however, his control was underpinned by brutal human rights abuses, a divide-and-rule strategy that privileged his Kabye ethnic group, and a bizarre personality cult that reached its nadir with the publication of a comic that depicted him as an invincible superhero. This was the kind of tyranny usually found not in Africa, but in Hollywood movies. Sadly for the people of Togo, Eyadéma's superpowers did not extend to the efficient management of the economy. Instead, the corrupt and partisan nature of RTP rule resulted in a steady erosion of support for the regime and by the late 1980s Eyadéma had begun to lose political and economic control.

In an attempt to restore the reputation of his government, Eyadéma created a National Human Rights Commission to investigate allegations of abuse. The Commission was widely expected to deliver a whitewash, but to everyone's surprise – including Eyadéma – it reported evidence of widespread brutality. Thereafter, international governments had little choice but to add their voices to the calls for reform. Having spoken out in favour of political liberalization at the seventeenth conference of French and African leaders in June 1990, President Mitterrand suggested that it was time to hold a national conference and to end restrictions on the freedom of speech. But Eyadéma had begun to believe his own theatre and had no intention of implementing reforms that might undermine his hold on power. Rather, he adopted a similar strategy to Moi, allowing cosmetic reforms to keep donors on-side while all the time looking for ways to re-establish authoritarian control.

Eyadéma's confidence that this could be achieved derived from a number of sources. Most significantly, revenue from mineral and phosphate exports kept the Togolese treasury afloat and enabled the RPT to keep party activists and the army on-side. At the same time, the greater coercive capacity of the regime, and Eyadéma's willingness to deploy it, meant that the opposition was both more fragmented and more cautious than in nearby Benin. Indeed, Eyadéma was able to retain the support of groups such as the Togolese National Movement of Students and Trainees (MONESTO) into the 1990s. The general also knew that despite all the fine rhetoric the French would be unlikely to cut off relations – Togolese exports were too valuable, and in any case he was well connected within the Palais de l'Elysee. In turn, the willingness of the French government to tolerate Eyadéma's half-hearted reforms, even when evidence emerged that the military had drowned thirty protestors in Bé Lagoon, undermined the position of the opposition.

Thus, while Togo's national conference initially appeared to be following the model established in Benin, it reached a radically different conclusion. The meeting started promisingly, as the early proceedings of the conference inspired an outpouring of anti-regime sentiment. Although Eyadéma remained as president, the conference chose a religious leader, Monsignor Kpodzro of Atakpamé, as chair, and a human rights lawyer, Joseph Koffigoh, as prime minister. But when the conference attempted to exert its sovereignty in order to introduce constitutional change – emulating the actions of its counterpart in Benin – the RPT counter-attacked with brute force. In December 1991, Koffigoh was arrested and forced to comply with Eyadéma's demands. Then, in October, forty of the high commissioners who had been appointed as an interim government were taken hostage by the army. The crackdown inspired widespread domestic criticism, but once an attempt to overthrow the regime by junior officers in March 1993 had failed, it became clear that the main danger to the

RPT had passed.[2] After the excitement of the national conference, the presidential elections of August 1993 were something of an anticlimax. The RPT controlled the process from start to finish, intimidating rival candidates into boycotting the polls and prohibiting any opposition leaders likely to perform well from standing. As a result, no opposition candidate secured more than 2 per cent of the official result. Having survived the third-wave, Eyadéma's tenure was only brought to an end by his death in 2005, demonstrating the fragile nature of externally-triggered transitions.

Negotiated Transitions

In contrast to Kenya and Togo, deadlock in South Africa was broken through compromise – perhaps the only example of a negotiated transition in Africa. That the apartheid government felt compelled to negotiate owed much to the size and strength of the domestic opposition. Organized and ideologically engaged African nationalism emerged comparatively early in South Africa, partly as a result of higher levels of industrialization, urbanization, and exposure to international intellectual currents. The first incarnation of the African National Congress (ANC) was formed in January 1912, well before the emergence of nationalist movements in the rest of the continent, although the organization only rose to political prominence in the 1940s when it was refashioned as a mass movement.

The ANC initially demanded reform rather than revolution, but the slow pace of change and the explicitly discriminatory policies of the National Party (NP) that came to power in 1948 encouraged a more militant approach. The apartheid regime quickly moved to strengthen its control over the location, education, and administration of black communities, while the Prohibition of Mixed Marriages Act and the Immorality Amendment Act criminalized interracial relationships. Despite the injustices of apartheid rule, the ANC waged a largely non-violent struggle until the Sharpeville massacre in 1960. Earlier that year, the ANC had begun to plan a peaceful demonstration against the Pass Laws that restricted the movement of blacks. However, that campaign had been pre-empted by the Pan African

---

[2] Nwajiaku, Kathryn. "The National Conferences in Benin and Togo Revisited". *The Journal of Modern African Studies* 32, 3 (1994), pp. 429–447.

Congress (PAC), which moved to organize its own protest in the township of Sharpeville.

On 21 March, thousands of people converged on a police station without the pass books that they were required to hold by law, and offered themselves for arrest. As more and more protestors arrived the atmosphere become increasingly antagonistic and tense. An attempt by the police to arrest one of the organizers resulted in scuffles and led some of the protestors to charge towards the police, who responded by firing into the crowd, killing sixty-nine people. The apartheid government subsequently declared a state of emergency and banned both the ANC and the PAC, forcing the liberation movement to go underground. In response to the failure of non-violent tactics and the brutality of NP rule, the ANC developed a military wing, Umkhonto we Sizwe (Spear of the Nation), and, along with factions of the PAC and the South African Communist Party (SACP), began to launch guerrilla attacks against the apartheid state.

This marked an important turning point in the struggle, but the ANC never came close to defeating the apartheid regime through force. Instead, it was non-violent forms of protest that demonstrated the real limitations of the state in the 1980s. In 1983, the NP announced plans to introduce a tricameral parliament that would have established a system of separate, and unequal, representation for whites, Indians, and coloureds. This blatant attempt at divide-and-rule politics fused many of the strands of resistance to apartheid rule, leading to the formation of the United Democratic Front (UDF). Although it was more of a loose confederation than an organization in its own right, the UDF followed in the footsteps of the ANC and gave direction to the anti-apartheid struggle at a crucial moment. By the time that the Congress of South African Trade Unions (COSATU) was established and joined the UDF in the mid-1980s, the movement had more than 3 million members and, through its affiliated unions, church organizations, and civil groups, the capacity to challenge the state.

The apartheid government attempted to undermine the efforts of the ANC and UDF by seeking to blunt the appeal of black nationalism. "Homelands" were created for different ethnic groups to create a false sense of self-government, and black Africans willing to work with the regime were helped to establish authority over their own communities. Meanwhile, coloureds and Indians were consistently treated differently to blacks. Neither strategy was sufficient to undermine the momentum of the liberation struggle, however, and so white minority rule had to be sustained through coercion. When black nationalism regained momentum in the mid- to late 1980s, the government of P.W. Botha responded by granting the security forces free reign to expand their activities in order to contain the insurgency. Yet while Botha's policies led to the progressive militarization of the South African state, they failed to extinguish organized opposition.

At the same time, there was little evidence that the apartheid regime was about to fall, despite four decades of struggle. For all the coordinating capacity of the UDF and the economic leverage of COSATU, the ANC remained an illegal organization and many ANC leaders remained in jail. Thus by the time that F.W. de Klerk rose to the leadership of the NP and the state presidency in 1989, the country was at an impasse. A man known for his conservative attitude, de Klerk was not an obvious candidate to be the architect of the end of apartheid. His father had been a president of the state senate and interim state president in 1975. For his part, de Klerk Jr. had been elected as an NP MP in 1969 and entered the cabinet in 1978, subsequently holding a host of ministries including Mineral and Energy Affairs (1980–1992) and National Education and Planning (1984–1989). This suggests that de Klerk did not decide to negotiate an end to apartheid because of a lifelong commitment to liberty and equality. Rather, he understood that economic decline and a changing international climate meant that the situation that he inherited was unsustainable. Like Moi in Kenya, de Klerk came to realize than in such a context, his best chance of protecting the interests of his supporters was to lead, rather than to resist, change.

The pressure for reform came from multiple sources. Political unrest and "disinvestment" campaigns placed multinational companies under pressure to break their links with South Africa, with considerable effect. The decision of Chase Manhattan and other banks not to extend new lines of credit in 1985 triggered a debt crisis that undermined confidence in the South African Rand, while the passage of the Comprehensive Anti-Apartheid Act by the U.S. Congress prohibited new U.S. investment. As a result of these developments, and the refusal of the government to properly educate and train black workers, the productivity of the economy declined, and the number of new jobs created per year fell. The thawing of relations between East and West, and the eventual collapse of the Soviet bloc, was also significant because it meant that the NP could no longer trade on its position as the U.S.'s anti-communist ally in Africa. Together with the process of economic decline, this undermined the NP's ability to meet the high costs of repression: in the 1980s the annual defence bill hovered around $3.5 billion and in 1982 represented some 22.7 per cent of the budget.

de Klerk was not the only one to realize that far from threatening the white economy, political reform was a prerequisite for its recovery. Increasing numbers of business leaders, media commentators, and NP members had already come to the same conclusion. When the apartheid economy began to seriously falter in the mid-1980s, some of the leading figures of South African industry and finance started to communicate with the ANC in exile, in violation of South African law. By positioning himself as one of the leaders of the *verligte* ("enlightened") movement within the party, de Klerk ensured that he was well placed to take advantage of this shifting sentiment, and to take over after Botha was forced out of power by ill health and criticism of his handling of Namibian independence.

At the same time, a different set of factors meant that ANC leaders were also becoming more willing to compromise. The collapse of the Soviet Union deprived the movement of much of its funding and leftist drive, which simultaneously strengthened the hand of those in the ANC who favoured negotiation, and made negotiations a more palatable proposition for the government. But a negotiated transition required more than just the recognition that compromise was needed – it also required figures such as de Klerk and ANC leader Nelson Mandela to believe that any deals that they entered into would be kept. The gradual increase in informal contact between white business leaders, moderate NP members, and the ANC leadership from the mid-1980s onward was therefore of great importance, because it helped to build trust between the main participants. More important still was the existence of a set of political institutions that retained a degree of independence from executive control.

In contrast to Kenya and Togo, the independence of political institutions in South Africa had not been wholly undermined by neo-patrimonial politics (see Chapter 2). Of course, power was abused under apartheid, and the regime was often closed and opaque, with the secretive Afrikaner Broederbond ("Afrikaner Brotherhood") wielding great influence behind the scenes. But South African leaders operated under real constraints. Consider the career of Balthazar Johannes Vorster, who was prime minister from 1966 until he retired from the position in 1978, at which point he was elected to the less powerful position of state president. The same year, Vorster was accused of colluding with a cabinet minister, Connie Mulder, to divert government resources to fund a propaganda war on behalf of his party. Although he was exonerated from some of the charges, a commission of enquire in 1979 found that Vorster "knew everything" and he was forced to resign, his political reputation seriously tarnished.

The presence of institutions capable of acting autonomously from the executive increased the faith of leaders on both sides that a negotiated settlement could deliver fair and reliable outcomes and was therefore worth their time and effort. Even so, the negotiations proved to be a long and difficult process. de Klerk moved to free Nelson Mandela and unban the ANC in 1990, leading to the start of formal negotiations to end apartheid through the Convention for a Democratic South Africa (CODESA) in December 1991. It took three long years for the parties to reach agreement on exactly how, and when, the country would return to majority rule. Despite this, the very process of forging a compromise through repeated discussions played an important role in legitimating the transition. Because both parties had been able to gain concessions on issues of major concern, they had a vested interest in making the agreement work. The NP, for example, was able to secure assurances that the land and wealth of whites would be protected, and was effectively guaranteed cabinet representation in a government of national unity after the elections. As a result of these concessions, NP leaders and supporters had less to fear from the prospect of an ANC victory in the elections of 1994 than would have otherwise been the case. In turn, the support of the two main political parties for the transition played an important role in reducing the threat of racial and ethnic conflict around the polls.

The remarkable political stability that resulted from South Africa's negotiated transition highlights the extent to which conflictual and unstable processes of democratization elsewhere on the continent were rooted in weak institutions and neo-patrimonial practices. Yet precisely because a negotiated transition required moderates to find areas of common agreement and to leave their own hardliners behind, the settlement frustrated more radical members of the ANC, SACP, and COSATU who had hoped that the political revolution would be followed by a social revolution. Instead, it quickly became clear that for the majority of South Africans, political emancipation would not be rapidly translated into economic opportunity.

Making and Remaking the Future

The types of transitions that states went through in the 1990s have much to tell us about the political landscape within which Africa's democratic experiments played out, and in this sense are useful for helping us to think through the prospects for democratic consolidation in different countries. However, political transitions are fluid and conditions on the ground are subject to rapid change. In countries with a history of conflict and instability, transitions are under constant risk from military coups, ethnic clashes, and renewed civil war (discussed at length in Chapter 4). Even in largely peaceful states, the factors that shaped the strategies adopted by political leaders varied over time. Socio-economic change often undermined the hold of once-powerful civil society groups, while the economic resources available to governments fluctuated with the global price of their main source of exports, and the enthusiasm of international actors for democracy soon waned. Moreover, in the small number of countries in which transfers of power took place, new leaders often had very different understandings of the best way to balance reform and repression, and so made different choices when they were faced with similar situations to their predecessors. As a result, many countries became derailed from the pathways suggested in Figure 3.3 (for a complete breakdown of the period 1990–2014 see Appendix 1).

Consider the contrasting fate of Benin and Zambia after the reintroduction of multiparty elections. In both countries, the overwhelming forces stacked against the ruling party meant that incumbents were forced to first legalize opposition parties and later to accept defeat at the ballot box. The transfer of power removed the old regime and disrupted established patronage networks, creating the opportunity for genuine democratic reform. But while Benin emerged as an open and stable democracy, the overthrow of Kaunda in Zambia led to the most venal and corrupt regime in the country's history under the presidency of Frederick Chiluba (Figure 3.4).

The failings of the new government were partly personal: Chiluba proved to be more interested in purchasing expensive monogrammed suits than in rebuilding his country. But the reason that Chiluba was able to escape censure and to erode Zambia's democratic gains was that the political landscape had undergone a dramatic transformation since the final years of Kaunda's rule. Despite being a former union leader, Chiluba followed the advice of the International Monetary

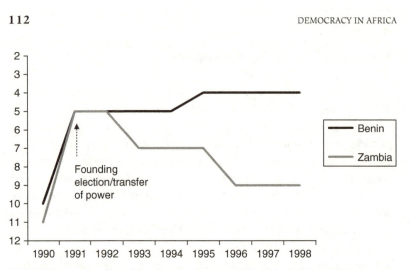

FIGURE 3.4 Quality of freedom in Benin and Zambia (1990–1998).

This is a summary score which is composed of the political rights score (1–7) added to the civil liberties score (1–7) for a given year, which generates a 2–14 scale on which lower scores = more free.
Source: Freedom House.

Fund (IMF) and World Bank to privatize the mines. Combined with rising unemployment, and splits over how to respond to privatization, this undercut the strategic position of organized labour within the Zambian economy and reduced the capacity of trade unions to check the power of the ruling party.

Moreover, while Chiluba did not enjoy any more constitutional power than Kaunda had done, he received stronger support from donors, who incorrectly interpreted privatization as a signal that the MMD was genuinely committed to political and economic reform. Zambia's second president was therefore placed under less domestic and international pressure than his predecessor. Unfortunately, this emboldened him to indulge his lust for wealth, and he subsequently established a highly personalized and corrupt regime that looted an estimated $46 million from the Zambian state.

The more that Chiluba came to enjoy the benefits of office and to fear prosecution for his crimes, the more determined he was to retain power. Ahead of the 1996 elections, just five years after campaigning for the reintroduction of multipartyism, he manipulated the electoral law to prohibit Kaunda from standing. Only in 2001, when his attempt to secure an unconstitutional third term was opposed by a broad alliance of religious groups, trade unions, rival parties, and a major faction of his own party, was he finally held to account. In Benin and Zambia, then, the past continues to shape the present, but not always in predictable ways.

Select Bibliography

Berg, Elliot. *Accelerated Development in Sub-Saharan Africa: An Agenda For Action.* Washington, DC: World Bank, 1981.

Bratton, Michael, and Nicolas Van de Walle. *Democratic Experiments in Africa: Regime Transitions in Comparative Perspective.* Cambridge: Cambridge University Press, 1997.

Huntington, Samuel P. *The Third Wave: Democratization in the Late Twentieth Century.* London: University of Oklahoma Press, 1993.

Van de Walle, Nicolas. *African Economies and the Politics of Permanent Crisis, 1979–1999.* New York: Cambridge University Press, 2001.

For a bibliography for this chapter go to www.democracyinafrica.org

CHAPTER 4

Exporting Elections: International Donors and the Era of Democratic Dependency

International efforts to reform Africa did not end with the reintroduction of multiparty politics in the early 1990s. Instead, a number of European and North American governments became frustrated with the slow pace of change and began to take a more active role in democracy promotion. The U.S. government sold these policies to its own citizens as both a moral imperative and a way to protect U.S. interests by exporting its own values. As John F. Kennedy put it in a Special Message to the Congress on Foreign Aid back in 1961: "There is no escaping our obligations: our moral obligations as a wise leader and good neighbor in the interdependent community of free nations ... and our political obligations as the single largest counter to the adversaries of freedom." Freed from Cold War pressures, the 1990s appeared to be America's moment to liberate the world by painting it in its own image.

By 1994, the growing salience of democracy promotion within the United States Agency for International Development (USAID) had led to the creation of the Centre for Democracy and Governance, which grew rapidly over the following five years and by 2009 had amassed a global annual budget in excess of $420 million. All told, USAID's spending on democracy promotion rose from $103 million in 1990 to more than $1 billion in 2005.[1] This was not all new money – in some cases existing projects were simply rebranded to fit

---

[1] Finkel, Steven E. et al. "Effects of U.S. Foreign Assistance on Democracy Building". USAID, 2006, retrieved from http://pdf.usaid.gov/pdf_docs/Pnade694.pdf.

TABLE 4.1 *Annual aid per capita by region (1960–2012), current US$*

Region	1960–1969	1970–1979	1980–1989	1990–1999	2000–2009	2012
Middle East & North Africa	7.0	26.5	32.5	30.3	38.8	35.1
sub-Saharan Africa	3.9	9.0	23.1	29.7	38.1	50.7
East Asia& Pacific	1.0	1.8	3.0	4.9	3.9	3.9
Latin America	3.3	3.8	8.2	12.0	12.2	16.9

Source: World Bank.

the new zeitgeist – and much of it was spent on Afghanistan and Iraq. Nonetheless, by 2010 democracy promotion had become USAID's third largest activity, and the organization had established missions in twenty-three African countries and programs in forty-nine.

Europe did not lag too far behind. The member states of the European Union (EU) collectively spent around €2,500 million on democracy assistance in 2007, and committed a further €150 million per year through the European Initiative for Democracy and Human Rights (EIDHR) of the European Commission (EC). In 2008, democracy promotion represented around 8 per cent of the aid budget of the United Kingdom and one-tenth of aid spending in Germany and the Netherlands. Although some of this money was redirected from other priorities in Africa, aid per capita to the continent increased considerably between the 1980s and the 2000s (Table 4.1).

The growth of international democracy promotion activities was not limited to Africa, but rather reflected the response of Western donors to the end of the Cold War and the opportunity to engage with young multiparty systems in Central and Eastern Europe. From a relatively low base in the 1980s, the amount invested by the international community in promoting democracy around the world exploded in the 1990s: by 2009 the democratization industry was spending around $2 billion a year on funding elections, deepening institutions, and building civil society abroad.

But while donors were often effective at pushing governments to reintroduce multiparty elections, they proved far less capable of shaping subsequent processes of political reconstruction and democratic consolidation. Frustrated by the lack of change on the ground, the most committed democracy promoters – most notably the United

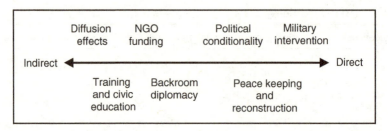

FIGURE 4.1 The spectrum of international democracy promotion activity.

States and the United Kingdom – began to focus their energies on the most obvious barriers to genuine political change. When donors came to realize that elections would not promote accountable and responsive government if they were contested by weak parties that were dominated by their leaders, they sought to promote stronger and more transparent party organizations. In turn, once it became clear that the fragility of electoral and party structures was in part rooted in citizens' lack of awareness of their rights, and limited expectations of their leaders, members of the international community engaged in political education and rolled out programs designed to promote adherence to basic human rights and civil liberties.

Throughout the 1990s, Western donors thus expanded the breadth and depth of their democracy promotion efforts. By the end of the decade, these activities encompassed a broad range of strategies from indirect and low-profile efforts, such as the provision of training to government officials, through to the most direct and high-profile forms of engagement, such as political conditionality and military intervention (Figure 4.1). But the more donors struggled to fix African democracy, the more they became involved in controversial projects of political and social engineering that risked undermining their own legitimacy.

Externally Managed Transitions

The international community became most deeply involved in democracy promotion efforts in countries that had recently experienced civil war. During the 1990s, international mediators increasingly sought to end conflicts in three stages. After first securing a ceasefire, the second stage was to persuade the warring parties to form a power-sharing government. Once this had been achieved, the power-sharing administration was expected to draw up a new constitution and political system, paving the way for fresh elections. Holding elections was understood to be particularly important: the ultimate symbol of a successful transition. Thus, UN Resolution 1885, which extended the UN's mission in Liberia until September 2010, explicitly identified the holding of elections as "a core benchmark for UNMIL's [United Nations Mission in Liberia] future drawdown".

Peace mediators came to fetishize elections because they believed that they would help to prevent a return to war. Elections were understood to be the defining feature of legitimate states, and so it was assumed that if governments in war-torn countries such as Afghanistan, the DRC, and Iraq were elected they would be more legitimate and hence more stable. Moreover, donors hoped that by providing all communities with the opportunity to exercise their political rights, elections would generate more inclusive political systems and more representative parliaments. Such assumptions were underpinned by the belief that multiparty politics would generate more accountable and effective governments, which in turn would give rise to stronger economies, reducing poverty and curtailing some of the long-term drivers of conflict. UN Secretary General Ban Ki-moon neatly summed up this position when, ahead of the Iraqi elections of March 2010, he argued that "a credible election process will greatly contribute to national reconciliation and give Iraqi leaders a new impetus to work together in a spirit of national unity to rebuild their country after years of conflict".

In addition to this at times naive faith in the power of elections, the design of peace-building strategies was also motivated by more practical considerations. The key advantage of elections over other conflict-resolution mechanisms was that they deferred the need to make a decision regarding who would occupy the presidency until polling day. Mediators could thus direct discussions away from issues likely to cause talks to break down, and instead focus on more technical and hence manageable questions such as how the electoral commission should be designed. In turn, this enabled peace builders to secure a cessation of violence, creating sufficient breathing space to begin the process of national reconstruction. But while this strategy brought short-term gains, it had obvious limitations. Most notably, it resulted in elections being held in countries where institutions were weak, the main participants did not trust each other, and there was little commitment amongst the political elite to democratic norms.

In their rush to harness the positive aspects of multipartyism, donors ignored the potential for political competition to exacerbate civil conflict.

Consider the peace-building process in Angola, which suffered a prolonged and brutal civil war between José Eduardo dos Santos's Popular Movement for the Liberation of Angola (MPLA) government and Jonas Savimbi's National Union for the Total Independence of Angola (UNITA) rebels following the collapse of the Portuguese empire in 1974. The conflict proved to be particularly intractable because neither side was capable of inflicting a definitive defeat on its enemy, or willing to lay down its guns unless it was guaranteed control of the state. Support from the United States and South Africa for the "anti-communist" UNITA was offset by the support of Cuba and members of the Soviet bloc for the "communist" MPLA government, resulting in a stalemate that prolonged the war and cost the lives of hundreds of thousands of soldiers and civilians.

Things began to change in the late 1980s, when the thawing of relations between the United States and the Soviet Union created new opportunities to negotiate an end to a number of conflicts in Southern Africa that had been sustained by the Cold War. In 1988, Cuba agreed to remove its troops from Angola if South Africa would end its support of UNITA and grant independence to Namibia. However, hopes that this opening would lead to a ceasefire in Angola were soon dashed after Savimbi rejected claims that he had agreed to go into exile and disband his forces as part of the peace deal. Following the failure of these negotiations it became clear that neither leader would accept a peace process that required them to accept defeat. Because both men were convinced they could win the support of the majority of the population, elections were the obvious solution. A peace deal signed in Lisbon and brokered by the Portuguese government committed UNITA and the MPLA to a process of national reconstruction that would culminate in the election of a civilian government. In support of the process, the UN launched the United Nations Angola Verification Mission (UNAVEM) to monitor the ceasefire and observe the polls. However, the lack of trust between Dos Santos and Savimbi, combined with the absence of democratic institutions capable of operating outside of executive control and the inability of international mediators to enforce the disarmament process, ensured that neither leader had any real confidence in the process. Thus, in the shadow of the election campaign both sides kept their forces battle-ready.

The first round of the presidential elections was held in September 1992 and the results gave Dos Santos – who secured 49.6 per cent of the vote to Savimbi's 40.6 per cent – the upper hand. Because no candidate secured more than 50 per cent, a second round of voting was required. But this election never took place because Savimbi refused to accept the first-round results, claiming that the elections had not been free and fair. As tensions rose, clashes between UNITA and the MPLA broke out in the capital, Luanda, and quickly spread throughout the country. Following a series of UNITA military victories it became clear that Savimbi had retained his forces as an insurance mechanism against the unpredictability of the ballot box. In the absence of the political will necessary to end the conflict, all of the ingredients of a long and bloody civil war remained in place. It was only after MPLA forces killed Savimbi in 2002, leaving UNITA leaderless, that Angola was able to find a pathway to peace.

The Angolan example is instructive, because it demonstrates that while international intervention can pause conflicts, domestic factors ultimately determine the prospects for a lasting peace. But this does not mean that international intervention cannot help war-torn countries to make a fresh start when conditions on the ground are more favourable. No country better illustrates what can and cannot be achieved by international engagement than the West African state of Liberia.

Founded by freed American and Caribbean slaves, Liberia is Africa's oldest republic. However, political stability began to unravel under the government of William R. Tolbert, an Americo-Liberian elected in 1971. As inequalities between the Americo-Liberian elite and the country's indigenous population intensified, the increasingly authoritarian bent of Tolbert's New Whig Party gave rise to mounting public discontent. In 1980, a military coup led by Samuel Doe toppled Tolbert, executing the former president and thirteen of his aides in the process. But Doe's leadership proved to be no more conducive to political harmony than his predecessor, and by the late 1980s a combination of economic decline, his bias towards the Krahn ethnic group, and a fraudulent election in 1985 had undermined the credibility of the new regime. As a result, Doe's government was poorly placed to withstand an invasion by rebel forces in 1989.

The rebels were led by Charles Taylor, who took up arms against Doe after he was removed from his position as director general of the Liberian General Services Agency. But although Doe's authority collapsed under sustained attack, Taylor's National Patriotic Front of Liberia (NPFL) also splintered, and it was a rival group led by Prince Johnson, an ex-NPFL fighter, who found and executed Doe in September 1990. By that point the brutality of the civil war – which ultimately took the lives of one in ten Liberians – and the potential for the conflict to spread throughout the region had prompted the Economic Community of West African States (ECOWAS) to establish a peacekeeping force. But when the resulting Economic Community of West African States Monitoring Group (ECOMOG) was deployed, it struggled to overcome the gulf between its mandate and the reality on the ground because it quickly became apparent that there was no peace to keep and no ceasefire to monitor. Only after further cycles of conflict and negotiation did the warring factions agree to the Abuja Accords and Abuja II, which created a six-member council of state that operated as a proxy government of national unity and, following the dominant peace-building model of the time, scheduled elections for May 1997.

The announcement of the polls triggered a remarkable international effort. The ECOMOG peacekeeping force was expanded to 11,000, while USAID and the United Nations Development Programme (UNDP) created programmes to give ex-combatants jobs, and hence a stake in a peaceful outcome. Largely as a result of the heavy international presence, polling day passed without incident. Rallies organized by the two main candidates, Charles Taylor and Ellen Johnson-Sirleaf – a former supporter of Taylor's who later opposed his handling of the conflict and took up a position with the UN – passed peacefully, despite being held in close proximity. Turnout was impressive with some 85 per cent of registered voters casting their ballots, and the elections produced a clear winner: Taylor secured more than three-quarters of the vote in a poll deemed credible by observers.

Yet although the elections were a technical success it was not clear that they offered Liberians a free and fair choice. Most notably, Taylor enjoyed a significant advantage over his rivals as a result of the territory, equipment, and resources that his army had amassed during the civil war. In particular, Taylor's control over shortwave radio meant that he enjoyed a near monopoly over the media in rural areas. This was not the only problem. Many Liberians feared that if Taylor lost he would reignite the conflict. In the eyes of many voters, this meant that the choice was not really between Taylor and Johnson-Sirleaf, but between Taylor and a return to war. And not just any war. Taylor's troops had committed the most heinous of human rights abuses, raping and amputating their victims. Taylor himself was later indicted by the International Criminal Court for war crimes and crimes against humanity as a result of his support of rebels during the civil war in neighbouring Sierra Leone. The bleak reality of post-conflict elections was demonstrated by the rallying cry of his supporters: "He killed my ma; he killed my pa; I'll vote for him."

As president, Taylor's refusal to establish an inclusive government and to stop meddling in the affairs of other countries set Liberia back on the road to conflict. Within two years of his election, the country was overrun by a number of insurgencies that were backed by the same governments that Taylor had tried to destabilize. When Monrovia fell to rebel forces in mid-2003, Taylor fled to Nigeria. The transfer of power to Taylor's deputy, Moses Blah, enabled a fresh round of negotiations, after which international actors mobilized to support a peace process that, once again, culminated in elections that were scheduled for 2005. It would not have been possible to hold the polls in this timeframe the absence of foreign assistance: the UN deployed a 15,000-strong Mission in Liberia (UNMIL) to relieve the embattled ECOWAS troops, set up 3,070 polling stations, and provided training, transportation, and protection for electoral officials. But what really paved the way for a more successful peace process was that the situation on the ground had changed, creating a much more positive context for democracy promotion.

In contrast to the 1997 elections, members of the transitional government agreed not to stand for election. Along with the absence of Taylor, this meant that warlords did not overshadow the contest. Although a number of parties represented former rebel leaders, and Taylor funded some candidates in a bid to maintain his influence, men in uniform did not dominate the polls. Instead, the main choice facing Liberians was between Johnson-Sirleaf and George Weah – Liberia's most famous sportsman and former FIFA World Footballer of the Year. The more civilian nature of the campaign produced a calmer political atmosphere, while the absence of Taylor freed voters from concerns about an immediate return to war. This is not to suggest that the polls were free of controversy. Although Weah won the first round of voting with 28 per cent of the vote, Johnson-Sirleaf picked up more support from losing candidates and convincingly won the second round run-off. Disappointed by this reversal of fortunes, Weah initially alleged electoral fraud, sparking clashes between some of his supporters and peacekeepers. But ultimately he came to realize that he had more to gain by supporting the consolidation of multipartyism, and hence the opportunity to win the presidency in future elections, than by plunging the country into fresh chaos.

In power, Johnson-Sirleaf's government struggled to overcome the legacy of the civil war and a chronic lack of resources, but managed to avoid both the resumption of conflict and significant democratic back-sliding – a considerable achievement. In doing so, it demonstrated the potential of donors and international organization to strengthen peace processes by acting as external referees, creating a window of opportunity for African leaders to break out of cycles of violence and instability.

The Era of Democratic Dependency

The distinctive feature of externally managed transitions in countries such as Angola, the DRC, Liberia, and Sierra Leone was that, due to low state capacity and the legacies of war, they remained unable to sustain the process of democratization without external support. As a result, these countries entered into a period of democratic dependency, which was no less significant than the period of economic dependency that began in the 1980s (see Chapter 3). African states came to depend on donors in two main ways: first, to fund essential expenditure, from the printing of ballot papers through to the payment of peacekeepers and electoral staff; and second, to provide essential skills and logistical support, from the design of electoral regulations through to the man-agement of polling stations. Such democratic dependency was not a uniquely African phenomenon. The first transitional administration of the modern era was established in Cambodia in 1991. Subsequently, the UN dispatched similar missions to the disputed territories of Kosovo and Timor-Leste in 1999. But the situation in Africa was very different to that in Kosovo, because the sovereign status of most African states was not in question. International actors therefore had to be more careful to be seen to be supporting, rather than leading, transitional administrations. Thus the UN stressed that its role in Angola was solely "to observe and verify the elections, not to organize them". Yet on the ground, the sweeping influence of UN and donor representatives at times empowered international actors to call the shots.

International interventions in African elections were perhaps most intensive and invasive in the DRC. In the 1990s, Mobutu's brutal regime was weakened by economic decline, falling donor support and a series of rebellions. In 1997, his ailing government was finally defeated by a rebellion led by Laurent Kabila. Because Kabila led mainly Tutsi fighters against mainly Hutu forces, some of whom had fled to the DRC following the Rwandan genocide, he attracted support from pro-Tutsi regimes in Burundi, Rwanda, and Uganda. The new president's international sponsors hoped that he would be able to establish a stable government that would be forever in their debt. Instead, Kabila turned his back on his sponsors and set about centralizing power in a manner not dissimilar to Mobutu himself. In response, Uganda and Rwanda threw their support behind a new rebellion, while Kabila fell in with a new set of allies in the form of Angola, Namibia, and Zimbabwe – each seeking to benefit from the country's vast mineral reserves. As different factions fought out a series of complex battles across the country, the situation quickly escalated into the Second Congo War. The number of governments involved, the magnitude of the resources at stake, and the difficulty of establishing order in a country as large and diverse as the DRC meant that conflict became one of the worst ever seen on African soil. Although the figures remain contested, it is thought that the war resulted in more than 5 million deaths, many of which were caused by the spread of disease and starvation.

In early 2001, Kabila was assassinated by one of his bodyguards as the violence unfolded around him. He was succeeded by his son, Joseph, who subsequently entered into a protracted set of negotiations with rebels and neighbouring states, leading to the formation of a transitional government in July 2003. As in Angola and Liberia, elections were identified as a key component of the peace process and were scheduled for 2006. The vast size of the country, history of violence, and depth of mistrust between different leaders meant that the challenge facing international actors was immense. In the lead-up to the polls, more than 16,000 peacekeepers were deployed as part of the United Nations Organization Mission in the Democratic Republic of the Congo (MONUC). By 2007, the Mission had swelled further to a total of 18,400 uniformed personnel including 2,000 civilian staff, at a cost of around $1 billion. During the election campaign itself, this was supplemented by a European Union (EU) military operation that contributed an additional 1,200 troops to ensure orderly elections. All but $15 million of the cost of holding the elections was met by donors.

The activities of foreign actors including the EU and United States were coordinated through the International Committee in Support of the Transition (CIAT). Because CIAT was central to the funding and organization of the electoral process, many Congolese assumed that the decisions of the Independent Electoral Commission reflected the will of donors. This was significant, because the donors were seen to favour the victory of the incumbent, Joseph Kabila, over the two main opposition candidates, Jean-Pierre Bemba and Etienne Tshisekedi. For example, when Tshisekedi decided to abandon his boycott of the polls and to run for the presidency, CIAT administrators refused to reopen voter registration for his supporters, claiming that this would have delayed the elections. Tshisekedi supporters interpreted this ruling as evidence of international sympathy for Kabila, leading to accusations of political bias against the supposedly neutral international intervention. Yet while such critiques were not without foundation, it would simply not have been feasible to hold credible elections in the absence of U.S. and European support.

In the end, polling day passed off remarkably smoothly. Having secured 45 per cent of the ballot in the first round, Kabila defeated Bemba in the run-off, winning 58 per cent of the final ballot. Although Bemba questioned the validity of the results, he ultimately accepted defeat and agreed to lead the opposition in parliament. However, precisely because Western governments had sought to construct a democracy in such an inhospitable environment, they found the country's democratic gains particularly hard to safeguard. Shortly after the elections, the International Crisis Group (ICG) warned that continued progress towards democratization was unlikely unless the level of international engagement was maintained. Yet donors were unable and unwilling to stay so intensively involved after the elections. The dissolution of CIAT shortly after the polls undermined the capacity of the international community to protect the independence of key democratic institutions and the space for opposition parties and civil society groups to operate. In turn, this undermined the faith of opposition leaders in the political system and contributed to the impression that foreign governments were prepared to tolerate democratic backsliding.

Partly in response, Kabila's government progressively removed checks and balances on executive power, undermined the independence of the judiciary, and reduced parliament to little more than a talking shop. The centralization of power, and Kabila's concomitant failure to implement a system of decentralization – originally designed to promote a sense of inclusion among the country's plethora of ethnic groups – exacerbated inter-communal tensions and led to a rapid deterioration in the security situation. The next presidential elections in 2011 passed without a return to outright conflict, but the circumstances surrounding Kabila's re-election further undermined the legitimacy of the political system.

In contrast to 2006, the main opposition leaders rejected the results while election observers from the Carter Centre questioned the integrity of the polls on the basis of variations in the quality of vote counting across the country. Meanwhile, Tshisekedi, who placed second, claimed that he had won the elections and criticized the international community for not doing more to ensure credible elections after incidents of violence broke out around the country. According to his spokesman, "MONUSCO was supposed to [bolster] security for the Congolese people and also to help us through the electoral process", but instead had become part of the problem because "the election figures were all made up with the complicity of the MONUSCO". As with the Congo Crisis fifty years earlier (see Chapter 1), international actors found themselves becoming part of the problem rather than part of the solution, and struggled to exit the country with their reputations intact. The case of the DRC is thus a good illustration of limitation of externally-managed transitions: in the absence of far reaching change on the ground, democratic gains remain dependent on unfeasible levels of international engagement.

Of course, few African governments were as democratically dependent as the DRC. But between 1990 and 2010 elections continued to receive considerable donor support, even in relatively stable and open states. In Zambia, the unexpected death of President Levy Mwanawasa in August 2008 prompted the UNDP to establish an Open Trust Fund, which raised more than $6 million in order to allow the country to hold a constitutionally required presidential by-election within 90 days. Similarly, in Malawi, donors provided almost $30 million to support the electoral process in the three years leading up to polls in 2009. Despite the country's vast oil wealth, donors were even more generous in the run-up to the Nigerian elections of 2015, providing hundreds of millions of dollars worth of support to the electoral process in a country where the government stands accused of stealing and wasting billions of dollars of state resources.

The willingness of the donors to bankroll elections and the reluctance of African leaders to create strong and independent electoral commissions means that, some twenty years on from the reintroduction of multiparty politics, the basic institutions of democracy still lack comprehensive and secure sources of domestic funding in most countries. As a result, they remain vulnerable to executive manipulation and fluctuations in the priorities of the international community.

Mission Creep

Many democracy promotion programmes were requested by African governments, but donors also became drawn into a number of controversial projects that enjoyed far lower levels of political support on the continent and threatened to undermine the legitimacy of Western interventions. This is well illustrated by recent moves to provide foreign aid to political parties. Parties are central to systems of representative democracy because they are the bodies through which the will of the people is supposed to be translated into government policy. Historically, donors left party support to NGOs and Western political parties prepared to support African partners because they feared that engagement in this area would be interpreted as partisan political activity and a violation of sovereignty. However, some donors slowly came to realize that parties' willingness to engage in corrupt and violent activities, coupled with their lack of internal democracy, meant that they were "the weakest link" in African democracies.[2] They therefore began to engage directly with political parties, despite the fact that in most Western countries parties are banned from receiving funds from foreign governments.

An early example of this trend was the donor support offered to the Mozambican National Resistance (RENAMO) rebel movement. Following a long civil war that claimed more than 900,000 lives, a peace accord in 1992 paved the way for the reintroduction of multiparty elections in 1994 under UN stewardship. The rebels faced many pressing challenges, including how to disarm and integrate their forces into the regular Mozambican army, manage disputes between moderates and hardliners over whether to revert to war, and transform the

---

[2] Carothers, Thomas. *Confronting the Weakest Link: Aiding Political Parties in New Democracies.* Washington, DC: Carnegie Endowment for International Peace, 2006.

party's tarnished image: following years of support from the South African government, RENAMO was seen by many to be little more than an apartheid stooge. Meeting these difficulties was all the more problematic because RENAMO had established little by the way of a political or administrative framework prior to 1985.[3]

Donors' concern to ensure that Mozambique developed a viable opposition party that could act as a check to the power of the Liberation Front of Mozambique (FRELIMO) government resulted in an unprecedented level of engagement, including the creation of a trust fund for the party worth $18 million. When RENAMO threatened to pull out of the process in October alleging fraud, donors were persuaded to offer an extra $1 million, effectively paying party leaders off so that they did not sabotage the polls. Donors did not want just any kind of party though, and so they attempted to use their financial leverage to encourage RENAMO to establish internally democratic structures and to focus on substantive issues rather than past grievances and sectional appeals during the campaign. Although such strategies proved largely ineffective, foreign funding was critical to RENAMO's emergence as a credible opposition. Somewhat against the odds, the former rebels took 112 of the 250 available seats in the founding parliamentary election of 1994, enabling them to block constitutional change. Donors thus played a central role not just in rebuilding the political landscape, but in shaping the nature of the party system, the outcome of the elections, and the composition of the legislature. However, this did not last for long: over time the combination of waning donor support and FRELIMO's ability to manipulate the advantages of incumbency resulted in the gradual consolidation of one-party dominance.

Although the intentions of Western governments in the Mozambican case were laudable, there is clearly a danger that if donors start to fund the activities of cash-strapped political parties, Africa's political leaders will have a strong incentive to please foreign governments rather than their own people. This is problematic from the point of view of democratic accountability, and threatens to undermine donors' claims to be politically neutral. It may also result in the emergence of parties that make impressive but unsustainable gains based on foreign support, as in Mozambique. For all of these reasons, the donor

[3] Manning, Carrie. "Constructing Opposition in Mozambique: Renamo as Political Party". *Journal of Southern African Studies* 24, 1 (1998), pp. 161–189.

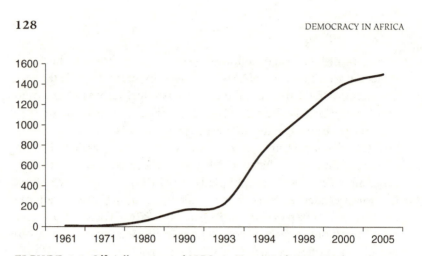

FIGURE 4.2 Officially registered NGOs in Tanzania (1980–2000).
Source: Fitted line to data points in 1961, 1971, 1980, 1990, 1993, 1994, 2005.
Data from the Aga Khan Development Network. "The Third Sector in Tanzania",
available online, 2007; Andrew Kiondo. "When the State Withdraws: Local
Development, Politics, and Liberalisation in Tanzania", in Peter Gibbon (ed.),
*Liberalised Development in Tanzania: Studies on Accumulation Processes and
Local Institutions*. Uppsala, Nordic Africa Institute, 1995; Michael Jennings.
Surrogates of the State, NGOs, Development and Ujamaa in Tanzania. Bloomfield,
CT: Kumarian Press, 2008.

community is deeply divided over the question of whether to provide
support to political parties on a more systematic basis.

Similar concerns have been raised with regards to other more common
practices, such as international support for African NGOs. Frustrated by
the lack of political will to implement reform within many state bureaucracies and ruling parties, and emboldened by the Berg report's damn-
ing assessment of the economic failures of African governments (see
Chapter 3), donors began to look for alternative ways to effect change in
the 1990s. They responded by diverting aid funds to civil society groups.
By the middle of the decade, USAID was channelling almost half of
its assistance through non-state actors in countries where the state was
believed to be particularly corrupt and inefficient, as in Kenya.

African civil society activists responded to this new avenue of
funding by developing the types of NGOs that donors wanted to
support. As a result, the size of the NGO sector expanded rapidly (Figure 4.2). At the same time, parts of the civil society sector
became increasingly dominated by groups that sought to represent
African communities, but received their funding and their priorities

from foreign capitals. While many NGOs had strong domestic roots, and funders later came to take the local ownership of NGO activities seriously, it is clear that these organizations were funded precisely because they enabled donors to push messages and programs that elected African governments were reluctant to endorse. In countries such as Kenya, this created a dangerous divide between the government and Western-funded civil society groups, which were inherently vulnerable to the accusation that they were doing the dirty work of untrustworthy foreign powers. Moreover, because so much of the funding for key public services such as health and education was channelled through NGOs, they were empowered to negotiate with African governments over the direction of public policy. This process of "NGOization", along with the economic demands of the IMF and World Bank (see Chapter 6), meant that unelected NGOs were at times empowered to dictate policy to elected leaders.

Donors also funded NGOs to run civic education programs and to strengthen key democratic institutions. For the most part, such programs were welcomed by people who had campaigned long and hard for democratic reforms. However, at times donors' desire to inculcate democratic norms resulted in mission creep; by the mid-2000s, NGOs were not simply providing information and services, they were engaged in a battle for the hearts and minds of African citizens. In Sierra Leone, efforts to generate a stronger democratic culture focused on shaping the attitudes and beliefs of children because the war had been in part motivated by generational conflicts. A number of international organizations and NGOs, including the United Nations Mission to Sierra Leone (UNAMSIL), offered to fund some of the running and staff costs of radio stations in return for the right to broadcast certain messages and programs. NGOs subsequently developed messages designed to disseminate information regarding the UN Convention on the Rights of the Child. No one would disagree with the intention of improving the lot of African children, but the attempt to push "right" answers to a range of complex questions around issues such as when it is legitimate for children to work and marry was interpreted by many listeners as an unjustified criticism of local norms. As with donor efforts to reform African political parties, such programs appear to have had relatively little effect, but they nonetheless raise difficult questions about when civic education turns into cultural imperialism.

The Inconsistencies of the International Community

It will strike many readers as somewhat paradoxical that during the era of democratic dependency and mission creep the donor community was willing to trade democracy off against other priorities. To understand why this was the case it is first important to appreciate that there was actually no such thing as a coherent "international community". Instead, there were a number of competing players who operated at different levels: non-state groups such as NGOs and democracy promotion organizations, which, although often funded by states, had distinctive aims and methods; multinational companies that operated in a number of African countries; internationally recognized states that variously acted as lenders and debtors, peacemakers, and rivals; and, finally, different assemblages of these states into various international and regional bodies, such as the EU, UN, and World Bank.

It was precisely this complex array of countries and organizations, each with their own priorities and modus operandi, which created the opportunity for African leaders to control the pace of reform. All too often, serious attempts by some actors to promote democracy were undermined by the willingness of others to turn a blind eye to authoritarian excess in order to improve their own security or access to resources. Even if we limit the discussion to the role played by states, the picture in the 1990s was remarkably complicated. While almost all Western donors spoke of the need to promote human rights and democracy, the policies of former colonial powers such as France and the United Kingdom owed as much to historical political loyalties, economic networks, and mutual obligations than a rational evaluation of the situation on the ground. France in particular established deep ties to ruling political elites in its sphere of influence, and frequently prioritized these over the rights of ordinary Africans.

The most shocking illustration of this diplomatic double standard is not the example of Togo discussed in Chapter 3, but the case of Rwanda, where around 800,000 Tutsis and moderate Hutus lost their lives in a government-led genocide (see Chapter 5). It is now clear that the French government was aware that radical factions within the government of Juvenal Habyarimana were planning to massacre hundreds of thousands of innocent Hutus in a desperate bid to keep their Tutsi clique in power. Despite this, France delivered large shipments of weapons to the army, engaged in frontline combat against the Rwandan Patriotic Front (RPF) rebels, and trained many of the militias that would later carry out the killing. Worse was to come. When the atrocities started, the French failed to act decisively and instead intervened to prevent the capture of their allies. This occurred in the same decade that Western governments spoke proudly of their determination to encourage democracy around the world.

Even when donors did set out to prioritize development and democracy, African leaders were often able to use international engagement for their own ends. If manipulating foreign governments was a sport, President Museveni of Uganda would have been World and Olympic champion. As we saw in Chapter 2, after overthrowing Milton Obote's regime in 1986 Museveni constructed a "no-party democracy". Although he subsequently allowed other candidates to contest the presidency in 1996 and 2001, these elections were tightly controlled and political parties remained banned. It was not until 2005 that political parties were legalized, and even then the NRM regime exploited all of the advantages of incumbency to dominate elections in 2006 and 2011. Museveni was so effective at resisting calls to open up the political system because he had an uncanny ability to understand exactly what donors hoped for, and feared. Throughout his early years in power, Museveni emphasized the potentially destabilizing impact of multiparty politics, warning donors that if they forced him to democratize too early they would bring about a return to the chaos of the Idi Amin era. This argument was not without foundation and it was highly effective – the Danish government, among others, argued that a more gradual schedule of reform was necessary given Uganda's history of conflict.

Museveni also proved to be remarkably adept at identifying what foreign governments wanted, and giving it to them. Following decades of failed interventions around the world, European and North American donors were desperate for a success story. By presenting Uganda as a pliant guinea pig on which international aid programs could be tested, Museveni offered donors a chance to show that their policies would have worked if only they had been implemented correctly. Thus, Museveni committed his government to talking about, and tackling, HIV/AIDS at a time when most African governments were refusing to recognize and respond to the danger posed by the pandemic. He also embraced the advice of the IMF and World Bank, accepting economic liberalization as the price of delaying political liberalization.

Initial results were so positive that Uganda became a poster boy for international development agencies. Economic growth increased to 6.5 per cent a year and HIV prevalence rates fell from a high of around 15 per cent in 1991 to around 5 per cent in 2001 (although these figures were later contested). As a result, European development agencies gained a vested interest in maintaining strong ties with the Museveni regime. When the United States began to advocate a more robust democracy promotion approach in the mid-1990s, a number of aid agencies lobbied for criticism to be communicated behind closed doors so that it did not disrupt their positive relationship with the Ugandan government. In doing so, some development agencies clashed with their own foreign ministries, which favoured a tougher approach – demonstrating the potential for disagreements over foreign policy to emerge not only between different governments, but also between different branches of the same government. As a result of these divisions, the same European governments who used their leverage to trigger elections in nearby Kenya (see Chapter 3) publicly argued that it was for the Ugandan people, and not the donor community, to determine the country's political system. Consequently, aid to Uganda came with relatively few political conditions attached. Even before multiparty politics was reintroduced, Uganda received more American aid money per year than Nigeria, despite having only one-fifth the population. Museveni was therefore well placed to resist domestic pressure to democratize.

However, as time went by Uganda increasingly began to look like an embarrassing anomaly, and Museveni came to understand that even he could not keep the winds of change at bay indefinitely. He therefore followed the example of Moi in Kenya, introducing a multiparty system while he still had the authority and resources to control the pace of change. A referendum on the introduction of multipartyism was accompanied by a constitutional amendment that scrapped presidential term limits, enabling him to remain in power. The run-up to the 2006 presidential elections followed in a similar vein, as Museveni secured 60 per cent of the vote, but only after the widespread harassment of opposition candidates and supporters.

Museveni's reluctance to allow for a level playing field finally forced donors to question their alliance with the National Resistance Movement (NRM), prompting the United Kingdom to cancel £5 million worth of aid. Recognizing that the credit he had gained as a good development partner was running out, Museveni looked for other ways to stymie international criticism. He quickly realized that events in Somalia represented the ideal opportunity to once again make his regime indispensable to European and North American governments. Against a backdrop of endemic instability, the United States feared that the absence of an effective central government in Somalia would facilitate the spread of radical Islamic groups within the region. Following a number of deadly bomb attacks in Uganda by the Somali based group al Shabaab, Museveni, and a number of other East African leaders, came to share these concerns. However, although the African Union agreed to provide a peacekeeping force, launching the African Union Mission in Somalia (AMISOM) on 17 January 2007, few countries were prepared to actually contribute troops to the effort. By providing 2,500 peacekeepers, nearly half of the 5,100 total, Museveni cleverly positioned himself as a valuable American ally in the war on terror. Moreover, the failure of AMISOM to secure its original target of 8,000 troops left international efforts in Somalia heavily reliant on Ugandan support, which in turn undermined the willingness of the UK and U.S. governments to censure Museveni for the absence of meaningful reform. Once again, the tail wagged the dog.

Ugandan democracy was not the only casualty of the war on terror. Following the terrorist attacks by al-Qaeda on 11 September 2001 – and with the bombing of the U.S. Embassies in Kenya and Tanzania in 1998 still fresh in the memory – the American government encouraged African states to introduce antiterror legislation. Many leaders did as they were asked, in part because they realised that such policies could be manipulated to empower the security forces, roll back human rights legislation, and facilitate the targeting of minorities. As a result, Amnesty International found major problems with anti-terror legislation in Kenya, Ethiopia, Mauritius, and Uganda between 2001 and 2010. U.S. policy was thus marked by a problematic inconsistency as different departments of the U.S. government worked against each other. While USAID was spending hundreds of millions of dollars supporting good governance programs, the United States was also funding military training in some of the continent's least democratic regimes (Table 4.2). Although much of this expenditure was aimed at increasing the professionalism of the security services, it inevitably strengthened the coercive capacity of a number of profoundly authoritarian governments. Moreover, the willingness of the State Department to channel funds to repressive regimes in Angola and

TABLE 4.2 *American military expenditure in selected countries (2007),* *thousand US$*

	Freedom House rating*	Military & education training	Military financing	Antiterrorism	Total
Angola	Not Free	289	–	4,850	5,139
Chad	Not Free	392	–	795	1,187
DRC	Not Free	–	263	1,375	1,638
Djibouti	Partly Free	3,800	345	356	4,501
Ethiopia	Partly Free	1,900	472	1,150	3,522
Ghana	Free	500	643	38	1,181
Nigeria	Partly Free	1,000	696	1,862	3,558
Sudan	Not Free	96	3,725	84,000	87,821
Tanzania	Partly Free	66	–	2,302	2,368

* The Freedom House overall ratings is based on the average of an average of the country's political rights and civil score. On a 1–7 scale in which lower scores = more free, countries that average 1.0 to 2.5 are considered Free, 3.0 to 5.0 Partly Free, and 5.5 to 7.0 Not Free.
Source: *Freedom House and the US Department of Defence.*

Ethiopia signalled that a lack of democracy was not a barrier to profitable relations with Washington.

It was not just foreign governments that made it easier for authoritarian leaders to retain control – African states also contributed to the inconsistency of the international community. On the one hand, some of the continent's most influential governments have been willing to promote democracy across their borders. Despite its own democratic deficit, Nigeria led peacekeeping and democracy promotion efforts in West Africa through ECOWAS, as demonstrated by its constructive role in Liberia. Similarly, the ANC government in South Africa played an important role in brokering peace negotiations in Burundi and the DRC, and in shaping outcomes throughout southern Africa. Post-2000 there were also increasing signs that African governments were willing to commit themselves to the promotion of human rights and democracy, at least on paper.

In 2001, the Organization for African Unity (OAU), which brought together fifty-three African states, established the New Partnership for Africa's Development (NEPAD) and created the African Peer Review Mechanism (APRM) in 2003. Through NEPAD and the APRM, member states committed themselves to a self-monitoring process in which they would review each other's progress with regards to political, economic, and corporate governance. When the African Union (AU) replaced the OAU in 2005, a pledge to protect human rights was enshrined in the new organization's founding charter. Going far beyond the commitments undertaken by members of the EU and the UN, the AU asserted the right to "intervene in a Member State pursuant to a decision of the Assembly in respect of grave circumstances, namely war crimes, genocide and crimes against humanity".

On the other hand, African leaders have also colluded to insulate each other from external pressure to reform. Part of the reason that African governments were willing to sign groundbreaking agreements to protect human rights at the regional level was that they did not expect the AU to have the institutional capacity and political will to act. To be fair, this has not always been the case. Following flawed elections in 2010 the AU moved to suspend Côte d'Ivoire and recognize the opposition leader, Alassane Ouattara, as the country's "democratically elected president". Two years later, Guinea Bissau and Mali were also suspended following military coups. But all too often African governments have pulled their punches when it came to promoting democracy.

This is well illustrated by the case of Zimbabwe. Following a prolonged liberation war against the white minority regime of Ian Smith, Robert Mugabe came to power through a negotiated transition to majority rule in 1980. For the next fifteen years, his ZANU-PF government dominated the political landscape. But in the late 1990s economic crisis, a failed military intervention in the DRC, and the centralization of power under Mugabe combined to erode the government's popularity. Opposition crystallized around a constitutional referendum in 2000, when critics of Mugabe's "undemocratic" proposals formed the National Constitutional Assembly (NCA) and inflicted a humiliating defeat on the president. The success of the "no" campaign encouraged many groups and leaders that had been part of the NCA to contest the parliamentary elections later that year under the banner of the Movement for Democratic Change (MDC).

Mugabe was quick to recognize the threat posed by the MDC. But despite extensive electoral fraud and voter intimidation, the new party still won 57 out of 120 elected seats. Ahead of the presidential elections in 2002, the Zimbabwe African National Union-Patriotic Front (ZANU-PF) government began a systematic campaign of harassment against opposition candidates to ensure Mugabe's victory. Although the elections were described as "credible, free and fair" by the OAU, commonwealth observers concluded that they had been "marred by a high level of politically motivated violence and intimidation". Zimbabwe was subsequently suspended from the commonwealth and cut off from IMF and World Bank support. The same year, George W. Bush introduced Executive Order 13288, imposing sanctions "against specifically identified individuals and entities in Zimbabwe". Following an intensification of attacks on the MDC, the United States branded Mugabe's regime one of the world's six "outposts of tyranny" and introduced a resolution at the UN to establish an arms embargo.

The strong desire of the United States and Britain to promote genuine reform meant that, in contrast to the strategy that they adopted in similar cases elsewhere in Africa (see Conclusion), they were reluctant to resolve the electoral crisis through a power-sharing deal that would enable Mugabe to retain the presidency. However, regional governments refused to adopt sanctions against the ZANU-PF leadership. Debates at the UN in 2008 revealed a split between the United States, backed by Britain, France, Belgium, Burkina Faso, Costa Rica, Croatia, Italy, and Panama, and a range of governments that spoke against sanctions, including China, Russia, South Africa, Tanzania, and Angola. Because Mugabe was so adept at depicting British intervention as colonial aggression, and because South Africa enjoyed considerable influence in Zimbabwe and the southern African region as a result of its economic power, Western governments were forced to take a back seat in negotiations. This significantly eased the pressure on ZANU-PF to reform.

Although Zambian President Levy Mwanawasa and Botswanan President Ian Khama spoke out against ZANU-PF, the Southern African Development Community (SADC) was more influenced by the South African president, Thabo Mbeki. Significantly, the ANC leader appears to have felt a greater connection to the authoritarian government than to the opposition, despite his country's strong democratic credentials. In part, this was because Mbeki did not respect the MDC's leader Morgan Tsvangirai, who he saw as being uneducated and untrustworthy. The South African leader's stance was also motivated by strategic considerations. His British education, elitist reputation, and neo-liberal economic policies left him vulnerable to the accusation that he was a Western stooge, especially when contrasted to the liberation war credentials of his main rival, Jacob Zuma, who had been a prominent figure in the armed wing of the ANC. Given this, supporting international efforts to force a liberation hero from power would have been a risky strategy. Instead, Mbeki pushed for a strategy of "quiet diplomacy" that would be led by regional governments, in line with personal commitment to find "African solutions for African problems" as part of an "African renaissance". South Africa thus blocked British attempts to extend commonwealth sanctions in September 2002, and consistently followed the same strategy for the next decade.

Unsurprisingly, the general election of 2008 was once again marked by electoral fraud and the widespread repression of opposition supporters. Although the MDC won the most votes in the first round of the presidential contest, the extent of the violence deployed by the government forced Tsvangirai to withdraw from the run-off. Despite this, Mbeki supported proposals for a power-sharing deal that allowed Mugabe to retain the presidency and many key ministries (see Conclusion). Once again, inconsistencies within the international community created just enough wriggle room for an authoritarian incumbent to cling on to power.

Between 1990 and 2010, then, the impact of the international community on the direction of political change on the continent was not unlike a car being driven by multiple drivers. When everyone pointed in the same direction, incumbents faced real incentives to move in the direction of democratic reform. But all too often, rival powers identified contradictory destinations and effectively cancelled each other out, leaving the fate of democracy to be decided by domestic forces.

Enter the Dragon

In the 1990s, China emerged as a global superpower, transforming the complexion of the international community. The rapid escalation of Chinese engagement in Africa was driven by a desire to broadcast power on a global basis and a need for raw materials and new markets. In October 2000, the government of the People's Republic China (PRC) held the first Ministerial Conference of the Forum of China-Africa Cooperation (FOCAC), bringing representatives of forty-four African countries and seventeen regional and international organizations to Beijing to establish "a new long-term and stable partnership based on equality". The speed with which this "partnership" developed was remarkable. As early as 2003, Chinese arms sales to Africa were worth almost $1.5 billion, more than any European country. By 2006, Chinese trade with the continent had surpassed $100 billion, eclipsing all competitors bar the United States. And by 2008, almost 1,000 Chinese state-owned firms were operating in Africa, while more than a million Chinese citizens were said to be living in Africa. Over the same period, rising Chinese demand for natural resources, combined with investment from Chinese firms and small-scale entrepreneurs, transformed the continent's economic outlook (see Chapter 6). In 2013, the value of Chinese trade with the continent topped $200 billion – more than twice the $85 billion traded between Africa and the United States.

African governments found Chinese assistance particularly attractive because it came with less political strings attached and was often delivered in the form of long-term concessionary loans. Although this had the negative consequence of increasing the debt burden of many states, it also meant that African governments enjoyed greater freedom to determine their spending priorities, and were not required to demonstrate democratic credentials in order to receive support. This development was naturally a considerable source of consternation for the democracy promotion community, who feared that it would reduce the dependency of African countries on Western donors, and so undermine their traction on a range of political and economic issues. Most significantly, the absence of democracy back home meant that China had no interest in forcing the pace of political liberalization abroad. China's economic success also worried many European and North American development agencies because it demonstrated that state-directed development within a one-party state could lead to economic growth, and so challenged the IMF and World Bank's favoured policy of simultaneous political and economic liberalization.

Such fears were not without foundation; Chinese support has clearly enabled some African autocrats to resist calls for reform. Most famously, China continued to work closely with the regime of Omar al-Bashir in Sudan despite international criticism of human rights abuses in the Darfur region. In the five years between 2000 and 2005, when condemnation of the Bashir government was at its peak, trade between China and Sudan increased from $890 million to $3.9 billion. During the same period, attempts to build support for action against the Sudanese government within the UN Security Council were undermined by the threat of a Chinese veto. When Bashir was indicted by the International Criminal Court (ICC) for war crimes and crimes against humanity, the Chinese government expressed concern and urged the ICC "not to hear this case for the time being". Sudan was not an isolated case. In 2004, China's Eximbank provided $2 billion in credit to the Angolan government to support projects such as the restoration of the Benguela railway. Combined with a range of other deals and vast investments by Chinese companies in Angola's oil sector, such loans reduced the country's reliance on the IMF and Western donors and strengthened President dos Santos's resolve to resist Western pressure for economic and political reform.

But China's impact on democracy promotion was not as dramatic as has often been claimed. For one thing, the number of countries in which the rise of China has reshaped the political and economic landscape was more limited than is often assumed. According to estimates published by the Department for International Development of the UK government (DfID), between 2006 and 2008 a quarter of two-way trade between China and Africa occurred with just one country – Angola. A further 18 per cent was accounted for by South Africa. In other words, beyond a small number of other countries that included the Republic of Congo, Nigeria, and Sudan, the actual impact of Chinese aid and trade was limited. Overall, direct relations with China substantially changed the economic position of only ten or so resource-rich African states – although many more benefitted from rising export prices as a result of Chinese demand. Indeed, while total African exports to China increased by 110 per cent between 2006 and 2008, the exports of sixteen countries, including Ethiopia, Tanzania, and Uganda, actually fell. Chinese engagement was also tightly concentrated around trade deals and was much less significant in the realm of aid: by 2007 Chinese aid to sub-Saharan Africa was only around half a billion dollars, compared to the $30 billion provided by members of the Organisation for Economic Co-Operation and Development (OECD). As a result, China did not represent a genuine alternative to engagement with Western donors for the majority of African governments.

It is also important to note that in some cases the Chinese government has proved willing to readjust its Africa policy in the light of feedback from the international community. Following widespread criticism of its cosy relationship with Bashir's National Congress Party (NCP), the Chinese government committed itself to playing a more "constructive" role in dealing with his regime. Sudan was subsequently removed from a list of privileged investment destinations for which companies could receive government subsidies. At the same time, the Chinese government took on a far more prominent role in international efforts to bring peace and stability to a range of African countries, providing more than 3,000 peacekeepers for missions in Liberia, the DRC, and Sudan. Whether China will remain true to its policy of "unconditionality", or will gradually start to conform to Western expectations, remains to be seen.

There are other good reasons to question whether the resurgence of China represents a "game changer" for African democracy. Most significantly, China's refusal to apply political conditions to its economic packages did not undermine a pro-democracy consensus among Western donors, because, as we have seen, there was no such consensus to disrupt. China's support for Sudan was no more disastrous to the fate of democracy in that country than French support to the Habyarimana regime was for Rwanda, or South African support to the Mugabe regime was for Zimbabwe. The international community was already deeply divided by the time that China rose to prominence. The addition of another major player on the global scene further complicated an already messy picture, but in terms of the overall impact of foreign governments on African democracy it did not represent a paradigm shift.

Consider Nigeria. The West African oil giant initially turned to China following Western condemnation of Sani Abacha's government for carrying out the death penalty on Ken Saro-Wiwa and other members of the Movement for the Survival of the Ogoni People (MOSOP) in 1995. China's willingness to engage with Abacha's regime in return for access to oil significantly eased the pressure for reform that other international actors had been seeking to build. The relationship between the two countries continued to grow over the next two decades: by 2009, Nigeria was one of China's top ten African trading partners, receiving billions of dollars of investment from the CNPC, and regular visits from President Hu Jintao. Nigeria therefore seems to be a classic example of how Chinese engagement has undermined democracy promotion efforts. But it was not just China that pulled its punches where Nigeria was concerned.

Although the U.S. government was highly critical of Abacha, following the reintroduction of multiparty politics the United States adopted a much more lenient stance towards the government of Olesegun Obasanjo. In part, this was because Obasanjo had been one

FIGURE 4.3 The price of crude oil on world markets (1983–2013), price per barrel in current US$.
Source: Index Mundi.

of the only African military leaders willing to transfer power to an elected government during the 1970s, and because his tenure in office (1999–2007) was significantly more peaceful and democratic than that of his predecessors. But when Obasanjo's People's Democratic Party (PDP) became increasingly corrupt and authoritarian, the United States frequently failed to speak out. It did so for much the same reason as China – the United States was afraid of compromising its relationship with a key regional ally and one of the world's largest oil producers. Instability in the supply of oil from 2003 onward had resulted in a significant increase in prices (Figure 4.3). In response, the United States moved to reduce its dependence on the Middle East by diversifying its sources of oil. One of the countries that it looked to was Nigeria, which by 2006 was servicing around a third of the U.S.'s oil needs.

It should therefore come as no surprise that when Obasanjo presided over a flawed election in 2007 – described by some observers as the worst they had ever witnessed – U.S. criticism was muted, or that relations with the PDP regime subsequently continued much as before. The willingness of the United States to tolerate democratic backsliding reflected a more general trend in which the economic importance of oil, and the financial independence it guaranteed, insulated resource-rich governments from both domestic and international criticism (see Introduction). The argument that petro-states such as Angola, Nigeria, and Sudan would have made real democratic progress had it not been for the rise of China is therefore based on a profound misreading of Africa's recent history. The complex and contradictory nature of the international community today does not represent a new threat to democracy on the continent; it has always been so.

Select Bibliography

Abrahamsen, Rita. *Disciplining Democracy: Development Discourse and Good Governance in Africa*. London: Zed Books, 2000.

Alden, Chris, Daniel Large, and Ricardo Soares de Oliveira (eds). *China Returns to Africa: A Rising Power and a Continent Embrace*. London: Hurst and Co., 2008.

Krishna Kumar (ed.). *Postconflict Elections, Democratization, and International Assistance*. London: Lynne Rienner, 1998.

Ottaway, Marina, and Thomas Carothers (eds). *Funding Virtue: Civil Society, Aid and Democracy Promotion*. Washington, DC: Carnegie Endowment for International Peace, 2000.

For a bibliography for this chapter go to www.democracyinafrica.org

CHAPTER 5

Subverting Democracy: The Advantages of Incumbency and the Politics of Violence

In April 1994, a plane carrying President Juvénal Habyarimana of Rwanda was shot down as it prepared to land in Kigali. Extremist leaders from the Hutu majority claimed that President Habyarimana had been assassinated by Tutsi rebels, and launched a wave of violence against the minority Tutsi community, which ultimately claimed the lives of more than 800,000 people.

As we saw in the last chapter, the international response to the genocide called into question the commitment of western government to promoting democracy and protecting human rights. The scale of the violence also raised questions about the wisdom of introducing elections in deeply divided African societies. At the time, Rwanda was supposed to be pursuing a dual process of peace building and democratization that was intended to pave the way for multiparty elections. But the mass killings and atrocities, more shocking and unforgettable than any horror movie, made a mockery of this plan. Moreover, the sight of neighbour turning on neighbour in the most intimate of conflicts called into question the feasibility of democracy in Africa. If the first crisis of democracy in Africa was the implosion of the Belgian Congo and the Nigerian civil war in the 1960s, then the second was the Rwandan genocide. In the influential formulation of Michael Mann, ethnic cleansing in Rwanda represented the "dark side of democracy". But as we shall see, the reintroduction of multiparty politics was only the latest in a series of events that contributed to the genocide. It was not simply the prospect of elections, but the manipulation and

143

politicization of ethnic identities by successive authoritarian governments, that pushed Rwanda to its darkest hour.

However, while it is far too simplistic to blame democracy for the genocide, it is also clear that the reintroduction of elections exacerbated political instability in a number of African countries. Democratization proved to be such an unsettling process because it significantly increased the level of political uncertainty in fragile and divided societies. Whereas authoritarian rule fixed the identity of the government, multiparty elections made the future less predictable, which in turn transformed the opportunities and challenges facing individuals at all levels of the political system. Leaders were now forced to constantly seek re-election, and many became so focused on retaining power in the short-term that they employed repressive divide-and-rule strategies that aggravated political tensions and encouraged rivals to rebel against the system. Greater uncertainty also impacted on ordinary voters, who were offered the prospects of gaining, or losing, access to resources, often for the first time in a generation. In countries such as Burundi and Rwanda, citizens were used to governments that treated state resources as personal largesse to be distributed only to loyal subjects. They therefore came to expect elections to follow a winner-takes-all logic in which defeat was expected to condemn communities – often living in dire poverty – to a period of exclusion from resources, jobs, and government protection. In countries that were already divided, the combination of political uncertainty, irresponsible leadership, and fearful electorates meant that elections became synonymous with inter-communal tension and disorder.

Of course, there is nothing inevitable about the relationship between multiparty politics and violence. Political competition induces similar strains wherever open elections are held; what matters is the ability of leaders and the political system to manage these pressures. Under certain circumstances, elections can lead to a positive, rather than a negative, cycle. Governments whose options are constrained by independent courts and legislatures, international pressure, and their own commitment to democratic principles are more likely to allow for free and fair elections, and to accept defeat if it comes. In turn, when opposition parties have confidence that the electoral commission will act in a fair and impartial way, they have good reasons to continue to play by the rules of the game. And if ordinary voters believe that whoever takes office will govern

broadly in the interests of all, they are less likely to follow polemical leaders who tout messages of suspicion and hate. The problem
in sub-Saharan Africa was that these conditions were relatively
rare. In countries such as Kenya and Nigeria presidents that had
consistently favoured their own communities in the distribution of
resources and used neo-patrimonial networks to undermine democratic institutions proved able to resist international pressure for
further reform (see the Introduction and Chapter 4). As a result,
electoral competition and violence came to be closely intertwined.

Even in relatively open political systems, heated election campaigns intensified local tensions and political rivalries to dangerous
levels. Although Benin enjoyed one of the continent's smoothest
processes of democratic transition, the presidential election between
Kérékou and Soglo in 1990 was marked by rioting and an ugly incident in which an opposition National Assembly deputy, Valentin
Somasse, alleged that the police had beaten him and severed one of
his fingers. Meanwhile, in largely peaceful Ghana the elections of
2008 exacerbated long-standing tensions over the selection of traditional leaders, leading to clashes in the North and the Volta Region
that resulted in a number of deaths.

Despite the fact that around three-quarters of African elections
witnessed unrest of some form, smaller incidents like these often
went unreported in the Western media because journalists and
commentators became desensitized to election violence in Africa.
As a result, assaults and murders that would have held the front
page in Europe or North America passed without serious discussion. However, while low-level violence was largely ignored, cases
of violent democratic collapse made the headlines, most notably in Rwanda in 1994, Kenya in 2008, Zimbabwe in 2008, Côte
d'Ivoire in 2010, and South Sudan in 2013. Because some of these
countries were perceived to have been peaceful prior to the reintroduction of multiparty politics, their destabilization was seized
on by Afro-pessimists as evidence that it was simply too dangerous
to experiment with democracy in Africa. But as with the Rwandan
genocide, it was never simply democracy that was to blame for these
episodes of violence. It is therefore important to contest claims that
it is too early to hold elections in Africa, because such arguments
typically overlook the important success stories that have emerged
over the last twenty years (see Chapter 6), and the strategies that can
be used to manage ethnic diversity and distrust (see Conclusion).

Elections, Incumbency Bias, and the Presidential Arsenal

In the 1990s, many African leaders responded to the challenge of multiparty elections by refusing to allow free and fair elections. The continent's reluctant democrats drew on their experiences of controlled
elections under colonial and civil-authoritarian rule to cultivate a
powerful arsenal of political weapons that could be used to defeat
the opposition. This arsenal involved four main mutually compatible
techniques: *gerrymandering*, the drawing of constituency boundaries
to favour the ruling party; *corruption*, the misuse of state resources to
support the campaign of the executive, including vote buying and bribing electoral officials; *coercion*, the repression of civil society groups,
the media, and rival parties; and, *electoral fraud*, ballot box stuffing and
the falsification of election results. Each tool had its own strengths and
weaknesses, and incumbents deployed them in various combinations
accordingly. While gerrymandering and corruption were common, the
deployment of high-cost and high-risk strategies such as coercion and
electoral fraud was often an indication of desperation.

The blueprint for how to maintain control through gerrymandering was laid down in the colonial period, when the very governments
that introduced national elections also sought to control their outcomes. In Kenya, Britain was desperate to ensure that elections held
in the wake of the violent Mau Mau rebellion would not result in a
victory for radical nationalism. To prevent this from happening, the
administration deliberately designed constituency boundaries to min-
imize the influence of groups suspected of supporting the uprising and
employed a loyalty test to guarantee that only those who had demonstrated active allegiance to the colonial government could vote. The
British were not alone: there is considerable evidence that the French
government attempted to rig a referendum on the introduction of the
constitution of the Fifth Republic, which was held in its African territories in 1957. The vote was particularly significant, because France
hoped to retain its empire in a rebranded French Community, but by
rejecting the constitution territories could take the option of full independence. French efforts to boost the "yes" vote ultimately failed in
Guinea but were successful in Niger, and set a dangerous precedent
throughout Francophone Africa.

The politicization of electoral administration has remained a central feature of electoral competition ever since. For example, in Kenya
the ruling KANU party prepared for the reintroduction of multiparty

elections in the early 1990s by manipulating constituency boundaries so that its home areas elected a disproportionate number of parliamentary seats. In turn, this enabled the government to retain a parliamentary majority in the 1992 elections even though its presidential candidate, Daniel arap Moi, polled just 36 per cent of the vote.

Electoral corruption also has a long history on the continent. In Nigeria, British colonial officials intervened to tilt the playing field in favour of the Northern People's Congress (NPC) ahead of elections in 1959. The British had established a strong working relationship with the northern elite, having given them considerable leeway to govern their territory as they saw fit under the system of indirect rule, and it was assumed that the NPC would be most amenable to colonial interests. But given Nigeria's fragmented political system (see Chapter 1), the NPC required a supportive coalition partner in order to govern effectively. According to Harold Smith, a colonial officer at the time, the government responded by illegally channelling resources to the National Council of Nigerian Citizens (NCNC), a party the British believed could be pressured into forming an effective alliance with the NPC if it won sufficient seats.

The partisan deployment of state resources continued into the postcolonial period, exacerbated by the combination of the easy availability of oil funds and weak mechanisms for tracking state revenue in Nigeria. Following the reintroduction of multiparty politics in 1999, the great expense involved in running for office placed political leaders under substantial economic pressure. Some Nigerian senators regularly spend upwards of US$500,000 on their campaigns, while presidential elections can cost hundreds of millions of dollars – which is remarkable, given that most voters live on less than $1 a day. Most political leaders were unable to afford to finance such expenditure themselves and so came under great pressure to manipulate their positions to secure funds, or to borrow resources from political brokers who usually demanded political and economic favours in return; it was thus no coincidence that the reintroduction of multiparty elections sparked a fresh wave of political corruption in Nigeria, as it did in countries such as Malawi, Togo, and Zambia.

In the 1990s, the fusion of elections, corruption, and patronage networks led to the rise of vote buying. Indeed, the provision of small "gifts" such as food, money, and T-shirts quickly became an established part of the electoral ritual. In countries such as Kenya, in which political leaders' legitimacy rested in part on their ability to provide financially for their community (see Chapter 2), vote buying played into, and reinforced, established patron-client relationships. However, bribing voters often proved to be a risky way for a candidate to spend their scarce resources, because where voting remained more or less secret it was not easy to work out who had, and more importantly had not, kept their promise. This was not lost on African political leaders. In the founding Namibian election, Hendrik Witbooi of the South West Africa People's Organization (SWAPO) responded to the lavish distribution of food and clothing at rallies by the Democratic Turnhalle Alliance (DTA) by suggesting that voters should "eat DTA, vote SWAPO". Especially in countries where communal identities were politicized and voters were therefore unlikely to be willing to switch sides in return for small handouts, leaders began to place less emphasis on simply buying the support of rival groups in favour of other strategies.

One creative alternative was to purchase the registration cards of people expected to cast their ballot for other parties, thus preventing them from voting and lowering the threshold required for victory. A second was to use existing networks of traditional leaders. In most African countries "chiefs" continued to be paid or subsidized by the state, and governments typically expected them to use their local legitimacy to mobilize support for the ruling party (see Conclusion). Because traditional leaders often enjoyed considerable control over local resources – especially in rural areas – the government's ability to draw on these networks at election time proved to be one of the most effective barriers to the expansion of opposition parties. A related strategy pursued by many incumbents was to establish political machines that could develop more meaningful and permanent relationships with mid-ranking leaders and voters, and so could more reliably deliver support.

In Nigeria, clientelist resources derived from oil revenues were distributed through political "godfathers", wealthy and well-connected individuals who work behind the scenes to place supporters in strategically important positions within political parties and the state, establishing themselves as gatekeepers of political opportunities. The power of godfathers was highlighted in 2003 by Reverend Jolly Nyame, the governor of Taraba State, who claimed that "I am the greatest godfather in Nigeria because this is the first time an individual single-handedly put in position every politician in the state." By working through such figures, the ruling PDP government was able to tap into established political machines that were better placed to detect when voters failed to keep their promises, and hence to ensure their compliance, because they were run by patrons who had intimate knowledge of their clients.

In turn, these patronage networks enabled the PDP to consolidate political control by denying rival candidates the right to compete on a level playing field. But in return for sponsoring the campaigns of certain candidates, godfathers demanded back-door political influence and a return on their investment, facilitating further corruption at the heart of government.

The rise of regimes that looked like democracies from the outside but were run by governments wedded to authoritarian strategies necessitated a new political vocabulary. Borrowing from terms initially used to describe Latin American cases, Africanists began to talk about quasi-democracies, hybrid regimes, illiberal democracies, electoral authoritarian states, and so on. Such labels are in some ways misleading because they suggest that these semi-democratic governments were broadly similar, when in fact they exhibited very different tendencies. As we have seen, how far leaders were prepared to go to retain power – and hence what combination of the presidential arsenal they were prepared to deploy – depended on a range of factors including their access to resources, the strength of the pressure from domestic and international actors for further liberalization, the risks associated with losing office, and their personal commitment to human rights and democracy (see Introduction). Presidents keen to stay in power but willing – or forced – to contemplate real reform typically relied on gerrymandering and corruption, as in Senegal, Tanzania, and Zambia (see Chapter 3). These strategies could be implemented well before the arrival of foreign election observers and so they advantaged incumbents without inviting international criticism.

By contrast, the high-profile nature of coercion and electoral fraud, and their tendency to delegitimate a government both at home and abroad, ensured that these strategies were usually employed either by desperate governments that had run out of other options, or by incumbents empowered to ignore domestic and international protests by their resource wealth, as in Angola, or their geo-strategic importance, as in the case of Uganda (chapter 4). This is well illustrated by the way in which Paul Biya dominated elections in oil- and gas-rich Cameroon. Following his succession to the presidency in 1982, Biya "won" one-party elections in 1984 and 1988 and multiparty elections in 1992, 1997, and 2004, despite his poor economic record. Throughout this period, his capacity to retain office was underpinned by the systematic deployment of coercion. In the 1990s, frequent protests against his Cameroon People's Democratic Movement (CPDM) government were violently put down by the security forces, resulting in hundreds of arrests and deaths, most notably around the deeply flawed 1992 elections when many commentators believe that Biya lost the popular vote. More recently, the United Nations Committee against Torture found evidence of the systematic torture of suspects by the police and gendarmes in 2003, while a report by Amnesty International in 2009 concluded that "the authorities have repeatedly used violence, arbitrary arrests and unlawful detentions to prevent opposition political parties and political activists from holding public or private meetings."

Afraid that intimidation alone might not be enough, Biya backed up coercion with electoral fraud. In the 2011 presidential elections, the way that the voter list was managed created opportunities for multiple voting. Opposition parties reported that some individuals voted three or four times and unsuccessfully appealed to have the elections annulled, alleging "disorder" and "intimidation" at polling stations. According to Robert Jackson, the U.S. ambassador to Cameroon, "On election day, mission observers noted inconsistencies and irregularities in and between almost all polling stations." Yet although these authoritarian strategies empowered Biya to win more than 70 per cent of the vote in three successive multiparty elections, international criticism of his regime has been much less pronounced than in comparable cases such as Kenya and Zimbabwe. In 2003, the year that the UN reported evidence of the use of torture, Biya was invited to the White House by George W. Bush as a reward for his support of the war on terror, while France, the former colonial power and a long-term ally of the Biya regime, rejected accusations that the 2011 ballot had been flawed.

Not all African governments deployed the full range of their arsenal as Biya did, but even so the range and effectiveness of the options available to African presidents meant that the reintroduction of elections led to remarkably few transfers of power. Of all the presidential elections held between 1990 and 2000, opposition candidates won only 15 per cent.

Political Exclusion, Ethnic Cleansing, and the Breakdown of Order

Most electoral authoritarian regimes held on to power in the 1990s, but they were not always stable. Instead, these states tended to follow one of two main trajectories. In countries where the ruling party refrained from or were unable to deploy the full range of its arsenal, opposition parties found it easier to campaign. This created the possibility that the ruling party's hold on power would be gradually eroded over time, intensifying the pressure for genuine political liberalization. Under these circumstances, a virtuous cycle of opposition electoral gains and government reform often emerged, leading to a gradual process of democratic consolidation in countries such as Ghana and Senegal (see Chapter 6).

By contrast, in countries where the sitting president was prepared to use coercion and electoral fraud, a more problematic cycle came to the fore. In these contexts, political exclusion and state sponsored violence disenfranchised large parts of the population. In a small number of countries including Kenya and Rwanda, leaders desperate to retain power at any cost engaged in episodes of ethnic cleansing to displace or eradicate opposition supporters, undermining the very social fabric of their nations. More frequently, the coercive strategies employed by incumbent leaders did not reach such horrific excesses, but nonetheless resulted in a steady deterioration of political stability. One reason for this was that widespread repression encouraged the opposition to form links with militias or factions of the military in order to resist – and in some cases overthrow – the government.

To fully understand this process it is important to move beyond the focus on African governments set out in the Introduction, and to consider the role played by the leaders of opposition parties, the military, and, where they existed, militias/rebel factions. Just as incumbents weighed up whether to repress or reform based on their personal values and the pressure they faced to democratize, so opposition leaders had to decide whether they could best achieve their goals by supporting the status quo or subverting it. When opposition groups felt they were treated fairly, had some access to economic opportunities, and had a chance of winning power in future elections, they faced strong incentives to play by the rules of the democratic game. But when coercion, corruption, and electoral fraud meant that reform could not be achieved by working within the system, the opposition became more likely to embrace violent struggle, and all that this entailed.

We the People? Elections and the Politics of Belonging

One of the main reasons that the reintroduction of multiparty politics intensified ethnic tensions in so many African states was that election campaigns tended to exacerbate existing tensions between ethnic groups who proclaimed themselves to be "indigenous" to a particular area and other groups accused of being "settlers" or "immigrants". Take the Cameroonian capital Yaoundé, where successive waves of immigrants had historically competed over scarce housing, jobs, and land. Disagreements between rival communities had often been fierce, but became particularly violent following the introduction of a new electoral system that threatened to undermine the position of the Beti community, which considered itself to be the rightful custodian of the land but found itself to be in the minority due to the influx of other communities. Fearing political marginalization, Beti "indigenes" questioned the right of Bamileke "immigrants" to rule in the "home of their hosts".[1] In doing so, Beti leaders were effectively rejecting the demand of rival communities to be allowed to engage in the democratic process outside of their own "homeland". In other words, the Beti community effectively argued that there should be geographical restrictions on political rights, implicitly rejecting the notion of a national civic identity.

The growth of ethnic tensions in local political arenas empowered aspiring politicians to manipulate such tensions for their own ends. In the process, they fused local dynamics and national political struggles, increasing the prospects for widespread violence and disorder. In Cameroon, for example, President Paul Biya exploited the competition between indigenes and settlers in Yaoundé to solidify his own support base and foster new divisions within the opposition. In doing so, he further entrenched existing social divisions, exacerbating tensions on the ground.

The Yaoundé example is valuable because it illustrates the way in which multiparty politics brought potentially explosive disagreements over the relationship between territory, indigeneity, and political power out of the shadows and placed them centre stage. During the 1990s, an increasing number of ethnic communities began to assert claims to power and resources that they justified not on the basis of need, but on the principle that being the first community to occupy a piece of land in and of itself gave a group certain political rights – and denied them to others. On this logic, "guests" in a particular area did not have the same right to land and political expression as those who "belonged".

---

[1] Socpa, Antoine. "Indigenous Lessors and Non-Native Tenants: Land at Stake and Political Engagement in Cameroon". *African Studies Review* 49, 2 (2006), pp. 45–67.

This dynamic operated at both the local and the national level, leading to what Geschiere and Jackson have termed a "crisis of citizenship".[2]

It is important to note, however, that this process was not solely driven by the reintroduction of elections. Three other processes unrelated to party politics also focused attention on local politics and communal identities. First, the combined impact of economic decline and the retreat of the state in the 1980s undermined the ability of many African governments to meet their citizens' desire for security and economic opportunities (see Chapter 3). One impact of this trend was to render ordinary people increasingly vulnerable to forces beyond their control. Geschiere and colleagues find that individuals living in a variety of different countries and contexts responded to this development by buying into local sources of identification, which gave them a sense of security and a sense of belonging. The natural by-product of this renewed emphasis on local affiliations was a growing focus on the importance of ethnic and family ties. This tendency was reinforced by the simultaneous rise of an international indigenous peoples' movement, which asserted the right of local communities to be compensated for the use of their land, resources, and collective wisdom, and so encouraged ethno-regional groups to more clearly define and defend their own identities. Local leaders quickly came to recognize that by demonstrating that their communities were the original or rightful occupiers of a particular area or cultural practice they could establish a monopoly over potential revenue streams. In turn, this focused attention on who could and could not claim to be a member of a community, and hence on the dividing line between indigenes and settlers.

The impact of these two processes was exacerbated by a third trend: the NGO-ization of aid in the early 1990s (see Chapter 4), and the subsequent concern of NGOs to demonstrate the projects were locally owned. The rise of NGOs was important, because it created further incentives for communities to demonstrate that they were the true locals, and hence the rightful recipients of funding and assistance. Taken together, these three interrelated developments increased the symbolic and economic value of group identities, created incentives for groups to emphasise their differences rather than their similarities,

---

[2] Geschiere, Peter, and Stephen Jackson. "Autochthony and the Crisis of Citizenship: Democratization, Decentralization, and the Politics of Belonging". *African Studies Review* 49, 2 (2006), pp. 1–7.

and thus further politicized communal identities. When viewed against this background, it becomes clear that the reintroduction of elections in the 1990s was only one of a series of interconnected historical processes that served to complicate ethnic relations.

The interaction between these processes created the conditions for the emergence of exclusionary politics at the domestic, national, and international levels. Multiparty politics opened up governments to popular pressure, which was often hostile to foreign immigrants and refugees. Just how destructive these forces can be is well illustrated by the xenophobic attacks perpetrated by a small but significant number of South Africans on migrants from Mozambique, Malawi, and Zimbabwe, which began in Johannesburg in May 2008. Once the violence had begun it rapidly spread, claiming more than forty lives, despite the support of some of these countries for the anti-apartheid struggle, the multiracialism of the ANC, and the idealism of the supposedly rainbow nation. A Human Sciences Research Council (HSRC) report into the attacks found that in addition to urban deprivation and intense competition for jobs and housing, a popular understanding of "exclusive citizenship" motivated anti-foreigner sentiment.[3]

The South African experience was one of the most shocking examples of a broader trend. Throughout the 1990s, public pressure encouraged African governments, some of which had played host to vast numbers of refugees during the years of pan-African solidarity, to withdraw the hand of friendship. For example, in 2007 Tanzania – which had previously been more willing than most to accept asylum seekers as a symbol of its commitment to pan-Africanism – intensified the forced repatriations of people of Rwandan and Burundian descent. During this process, refugees were "threatened, beaten, and saw their property looted by Tanzanian officials, soldiers, and police officers or militia groups".[4] Of course, there is nothing African about this: during the same period in Europe, the leaders of anti-immigrant parties in countries such as Austria and France exploited economic difficulties to increase their political profile and share of the vote. It should therefore come as no surprise that democratization unleashed

---

[3] Hadland, Adrian (ed.). "Violence and Xenophobia in South Africa: Developing Consensus, Moving to Action". Human Sciences Research Council and the High Commission of the United Kingdom, October 2008.

[4] Human Rights Watch. "Human Rights Watch Letter to President Jakaya Mrisho Kikwete of Tanzania". 9 May 2007, retrieved from http://www.hrw.org/news/2007/05 /08/human-rights-watch-letter-president-jakaya-mrisho-kikwete-tanzania.

similar forces in a number of African countries, in which some of the poorest people in the world host the highest number of refugees.

The politics of exclusion was particularly vicious when local and national xenophobia fused, and political leaders called into question the rights of some ethnic groups not just to be politically active outside their home areas, but to be counted as citizens at all. While some countries continued to enjoy good relations with neighbours and immigrant communities, in others ruling parties questioned the nationality of their rivals in order to prevent them from contesting elections. Perhaps the most striking example of this came in Zambia, where President Frederick Chiluba introduced a constitutional amendment that prevented his main challenger, Kenneth Kaunda, from standing in the 1996 general elections on the basis that his parents were born in Nyasaland, present-day Malawi. What was so remarkable about Chiluba's gambit was that Kaunda had led the country to independence and had been president for some twenty-seven years!

Political exclusion was particularly deleterious to national unity when it was not just individuals but whole communities that were alleged to be "foreign". This was particularly dangerous development because it legitimated ethnic chauvinism on a grand scale and provided marginalized groups with good reasons to rebel against the government. It was this dynamic that underpinned the slide towards civil war in Côte d'Ivoire. Under President Houphouët-Boigny, the Democratic Party of Côte d'Ivoire (PDCI) established a durable and stable single-party system (see Chapter 1). But Houphouët-Boigny's policy that land should belong to those who had developed it encouraged migration to areas with greater economic opportunities and so resulted in fierce competition between "indigenous" groups and "immigrants". Moreover, his government's open and accommodating policies towards migrants, along with the import of forced labour from Burkina Faso during the colonial period, meant that by the 1990s roughly a quarter of the population was of foreign origin. Because the Northern Mandé and Voltaic communities of Côte d'Ivoire were closely associated with migrants from Burkina Faso, Guinea, and Mali, anti-foreign statements implicitly called into question the rights of northern ethnic groups within the Ivorian political community.

The reintroduction of multiparty politics in 1990 exacerbated these long-running debates over the question of *ivoirité* ("Ivorianness") – the criteria for being a genuine citizen. Most notably, Laurent Gbagbo's Front Populaire Ivoirien (FPI) based its election campaign around a promise to "turn back the clock" in order to reverse the process of migration. Others were quick to jump on the bandwagon. President Houphouët-Boigny briefly stood against the tide, appointing Alassane Ouattara – a Malinké of the northern Mandé community – as prime minister. But this moment of inclusion was not to last long. Following the president's death in 1993, his successor Henri Konan Bédié marginalized Ouattara and his supporters. Cast out of the ruling party, leaders from northern communities formed the Rassemblement des Républicains (RDR), which soon became a vehicle for Ouattara's political ambitions, exacerbating ethnic and regional cleavages. The FPI responded by challenging Ouattara's right to contest elections, arguing that he could not be from Côte d'Ivoire as his father was buried in Burkina Faso. The accusation that Ouattara was "anti Ivorian" was particularly divisive because it suggested that the political rights of a range of northern communities with ties to foreign countries could be undermined.

Over the next ten years, successive leaders waded into the debate over citizenship and manipulated the electoral code in order to prevent Ouattara from contesting the presidency. This discrimination, coupled with the policies of Bédié's successor, General Gueï – who interpreted ivoirité in a way that assumed the superiority of the largely Christian south over the largely Muslim north – split the country down the middle. Ahead of elections held in October 2000, Gueï followed the trend of preventing Ouattara from standing, and purged individuals he did not trust from the armed forces, many of whom were of northern origin. This fresh bout of exclusion delegitimized the government and the wider political system in the eyes of northern military and political elites. Thus, instead of working to improve the functioning of the system from within, some northern leaders began to discuss the overthrow of the regime. The aftermath of the elections gave them the perfect opportunity.

When it became clear that Gueï would lose Gbagbo, the general moved to prevent the electoral commission from announcing the results. His intervention triggered widespread clashes with Gbagbo's supporters that resulted in the deaths of 170 people in October alone. Amid the chaos, disgruntled military officers, mostly from the north, took the opportunity to attack, forcing Gueï to flee the country. In turn, this left the electoral commission free to declare Gbagbo the winner. However, the general's defeat did not ensure a more harmonious political landscape. Clashes between Gbagbo and Ouattara's supporters soon followed and although Gbagbo gave the RDR four seats in the new government in a bid to end the instability, he ultimately proved to be no more willing than his predecessors to share political and military power. As during Gueï's tenure, exclusionary politics precipitated rebellion. In September 2002, the demobilization of soldiers sparked a mutiny that rapidly escalated into a civil war as rebels led by former military officers joined the uprising, attacking military installations. In the weeks that followed, the government quickly lost control of the north of the country. Tellingly, the political wing of the main rebel forces, the Mouvement Patriotique pour la Côte d'Ivoire (MPCI), justified its actions with reference to northern marginalization, including concerns over land ownership, election eligibility, and continued political domination by southerners.

Although the attempt to topple Gbagbo ultimately failed, the conflict divided the country in two. The international community moved quickly to deploy a peacekeeping force to patrol the armistice line between north and south and supported the formation of a government of national unity. In line with the dominant peace-building strategy of the time (see Chapter 4), a plan was hatched to establish a power-sharing government that would pave the way for fresh elections. After numerous delays the polls were finally held in 2010. This time, Gbagbo was persuaded to allow Ouattara to stand, but could not be persuaded to let him win. When the electoral commission declared Ouattara the victor with 54.1 per cent of the vote, Gbagbo responded by asking loyalists on the Constitutional Council to reject the results. Recognizing that a transfer of power could only be achieved through force, groups loyal to Ouattara mobilized against the regime and made swift advances, eventually capturing Gbagbo in April 2011. This paved the way for Ouattara to be inaugurated as president in May 2011, briefly gaining a newfound democratic credibility that he quickly squandered by failing to prevent or prosecute human rights violations by his own supporters.

Although election disputes often served to intensify inter-communal tensions, it is important to note that the politics of belonging was not equally pronounced across the continent. Ethnic tensions were less significant in states such as Tanzania, where postcolonial leaders invested time and energy in building a coherent national identity (see Conclusion). By contrast, they were most pronounced in more diverse countries where governments had actively favoured some ethnic groups, and discriminated against others. Let us return to Rwanda. The cleavage between Hutu and Tutsi that received so much attention in the wake of the genocide was not the product of primordial group identities, but reflected more than 100 years of discrimination. What we know of pre-colonial Rwanda suggests relatively fluid "Hutu" and "Tutsi" identities, in which these terms denoted economic status rather than a fixed ethnic identity. The wealthy claimed to be Tutsi, but Hutu could become Tutsi via cattle ownership and moving up the social ladder. The two groups spoke a common language, and the classification was more a way of demarcating class than a reflection of genetic difference. However, Belgian colonial officials bought into the myth, peddled by self-serving Tutsi elites, that the Tutsi were a natural ruling class closer to Europeans than their Hutu counterparts. Consequently, only Tutsis became chiefs, which entrenched the inequality between the two groups and, over time, turned the notion of a ruling ethnic group into a reality. On the eve of independence, a Hutu uprising overthrew Tutsi dominance, resulting in thousands of deaths and the flight of around 150,000 Tutsis. Over time, the actions of successive Hutu-led governments, combined with periods of inter-communal violence, further reinforced social divisions and hostilities, which rendered Rwanda particularly vulnerable to the kind of uncertainty and tension that can be generated by the introduction of multiparty elections. It was only in states that had experienced this kind of divisive politics that ethnic competition escalated into widespread conflict and ethnic cleansing.

The Politics of Fear

Multiparty politics did not just make leaders more vulnerable to a range of external challengers; it also rendered them more susceptible to challenges from within their own parties. It is often assumed that leaders who engaged in electoral violence were solely motivated by the threat posed by new parties entering the political fray. However, in some countries the threat to presidents from within their own governments was just as important. Under the one-party states that proliferated in Africa after independence, the legal prohibition of opposition parties and the use of coercion to punish dissent discouraged divisions within the government and empowered leaders to manage what were often broad and fragmented alliances (see Chapter 1). This changed with the advent of multipartyism, when the legalization of opposition parties created opportunities for disgruntled factions to break away from the ruling party. Many took the opportunity: in countries such as Malawi and Zambia the leadership of the opposition was comprised of individuals who had previously held prominent positions within the government but had subsequently fallen out of favour. In order to retain power, incumbent leaders needed to find a way to prevent their own coalitions from fragmenting. Against this backdrop, violence became a particularly attractive tool for unscrupulous presidents because it promised to simultaneously deal with external opposition and internal dissent.

It was precisely this consideration that made ethnic cleansing such an attractive proposition for Hutu elites in Rwanda once plans had been put in place to reintroduce multiparty elections in the early 1990s. After coming to power in a coup in 1973, Juvénal Habyarimana initially transformed the country into a single-party state under the National Revolutionary Movement for Development (MRND). However, in reality the Habyarimana reign was closer to a military dictatorship, complete with systematic repression and scant respect for civil liberties. The MRND buttressed coercion with ethnic chauvinism, claiming that as Rwanda belonged to the Hutu, and the MRND represented the Hutu majority, the government represented the will of the people. However, in the late 1980s the MRND's control of the political agenda was undermined by economic decline and the invasion of the RPF, a force of mostly Tutsi refugees who sought to overthrow the regime from a base in Uganda, where they enjoyed the support of President Museveni. Habyarimana also faced mounting internal opposition, as the president's willingness to favour his own northern base in the distribution of state jobs and resources led to criticism from disgruntled Hutu in the south and centre of the country.

International actors responded by supporting a dual strategy of simultaneous peace negotiations and political liberalization, in which it was envisaged that a process of conflict resolution between the MRND and RPF would culminate in elections. Over the next two years Habyarimana legalized parties, established a coalition government, and engaged in negotiations to end the war and integrate the RPF into the Rwandan government and army. But the prospect that the ruling party could be outflanked by a coalition of Tutsi and moderate Hutu parties meant that MRND leaders viewed these reforms with a mixture of distaste and trepidation. Indeed, the fear of an anti-MRND Hutu-Tutsi alliance ran deep. In the run-up to the genocide local government prefects wrote to Habyarimana, urging him to "fight openly against what could be called the 'Kanyarengwe effect' which poses a serious threat to the necessary solidarity of the Bahutu." The reference to Kanyarengwe is instructive; he was a Hutu colonel who had fled the country in 1980, joined the rebels, and subsequently risen to become the president of the RPF. The party faithful worried that similar defections from within the Hutu community would spell an end to their hold on power.

In response, Hutu extremists began to articulate a hard line pro-Hutu agenda and to plan an unprecedented program of political violence. The central component of this strategy was the demonization of Tutsis. As the conflict intensified, the government turned RPF successes to its own advantage, manipulating the invasion to create the impression that an all-out war between Hutu and Tutsi was raging inside the country. Through this process, Rwandan Tutsis came to be identified with the RPF, even if they had little to do with the rebellion: the Rwandan army even staged fake attacks on Kigali that they blamed on Rwandan Tutsis in order to bring this particular scapegoat to life. At the same time, newspapers and radio stations such as the notorious Radio Libre des Mille Collines were used to disseminate threats to kill Tutsi and those known to have associated with them. In the background, armed militias, most notably the infamous Interahamwe, were trained to enable the regime to make good on its threats. In contrast to countries in which violence is often deployed as a short-term means to an end, such as Kenya and Nigeria, in Rwanda violence evolved into an end in itself.

It is unclear to what extent this strategy was chosen by Habyarimana or pushed by others, but either way the effect was to polarize the political system into Hutu and Tutsi blocks. The atmosphere of conflict made it easier for hardline Hutu leaders to demand solidarity from their community, and to depict dissenting voices as "sell outs" whose treachery threatened to undermine the group's fortunes. At the same time, many ordinary Hutu citizens who had come to believe the story of a Tutsi plot against the nation demanded that their leaders take action to deal with the political and economic "threat" represented by "outsiders". Taken together, these two developments made it easier for Hutu leaders to escape sanction for violent acts – and harder for more moderate leaders to succeed. In this way the MRND's tactic of increasing the tension and mistrust between the two communities reduced the likelihood that moderate Hutus would join forces with their Tutsi counterparts, shoring up the party's internal unity.

The inevitable consequences of this course of action was that the political system became increasingly divided between a cluster of more extreme parties such as the MRND and the CDR, collectively known as Hutu Power, and a range of increasingly fearful opposition parties. When the president's plane was shot down in April 1994, Hutu Power extremists used his death as a pretext for the onset of the genocide, determined to eliminate "disloyal elements" once and for all. In the days that followed, the Presidential Guard and Interahamwe instigated a wave of killing that was taken up – often under duress – by many ordinary Hutus. The resulting tsunami of violence claimed the lives of hundreds of thousands of Tutsis and those Hutus who bravely refused to participate.

Political bloodshed was most shocking when it involved ethnic cleansing, but it also important to remember that violence was not always expressed in ethnic terms. Take Zimbabwe, where a period of more "ethnic" violence was followed by a period of repression based on partisan, rather than communal, identities. As we saw in Chapter 4, from the late 1990s onward, Robert Mugabe's ZANU-PF came under mounting criticism both at home and abroad. Outside of the party, worsening economic conditions, criticism from veterans of the liberation war that land redistribution was proceeding too slowly, and the evolution of the MDC opposition, proved to be a potent combination. Within the party, established leaders were accused of being out of touch by younger rivals. As in Rwanda, the combination of internal and external threats encouraged the ruling party to deploy violence as a political tool.[5] Fearing that ZANU-PF might eventually lose power to the MDC, Mugabe moved to turn one of his weaknesses into a strength, forming an alliance with war veterans and, in contrast to his previous stance, encouraging the invasion of white-owned farms in order to meet their demands. This change of strategy ushered in a period of intense political repression that had two goals: to make it impossible for the MDC to operate, and to intimidate those within ZANU-PF to stay loyal to the party and its leadership.

This was not a new strategy. From his first days in power, Mugabe had proved to be one of Africa's most adept practitioners of the politics of fear. In the early 1980s, repression took on a more ethnic tone as the new president sought to build a united nation in his own image. The two main nationalist factions during the liberation struggle, Mugabe's Zimbabwe African Liberation Army (ZANLA) and Joshua Nkomo's Zimbabwe People's Revolutionary Army (ZIPRA), had been rooted

---

[5] LeBas, Adrienne. "Polarization as Craft: Party Formation and State Violence in Zimbabwe". *Comparative Politics*, 38, 4 (2006), pp. 419–438.

in different Shona and Ndebele constituencies, respectively. Attempts to integrate these forces into the Zimbabwe National Army (ZNA) resulted in a series of clashes, which, combined with Mugabe's decision to sack Nkomo from the Cabinet in 1982, led some ZIPRA soldiers to desert the ZNA. Determined to hunt down and eliminate these "dissidents", Mugabe deployed his largely Shona forces in a brutal campaign of intimidation against people from the Ndebele community in Matabeleland. When the worst of the violence was over, more than 20,000 people had lost their lives.

The violence that ZANU-PF deployed in the 2000s was very different. The main dividing line between ZANU-PF and the MDC was not ethnic; rather, ZANU-PF elites actively sought to create a sense of "them" and "us" that overlaid group identities. The party's intellectuals had long been engaged in the process of reinterpreting Zimbabwean history, playing on the country's multifaceted liberation struggle to construct a narrative in which ZANU-PF were national saviours, continually defending the country's sovereignty against foreign aggressors. Within official "patriotic history", opponents were demonised as traitors, thus justifying the use of state-led political violence. Following the rise of the MDC and the growing support for the opposition, the focus of patriotic history was tweaked. By aligning ZANU-PF with the war veterans, Mugabe reaffirmed his "revolutionary" credentials, heading off internal criticism. At the same time, ZANU-PF exploited the support of some white farmers for the MDC, cleverly depicting the opposition as tools of Zimbabwe's white minority and, by extension, as representatives of foreign colonial powers. But although Mugabe played heavily on race, the regime also targeted black communities of different ethnicities that were known to have either voted MDC or failed to turn out in sufficient numbers for ZANU-PF. As a result, violence followed lines of party allegiance that cut across communal identities, demonstrating the ability of leaders to shape and reshape the contours of political conflict.

The Diffusion of Violence

Although countries such as Rwanda and Zimbabwe have tended to dominate the headlines, such systematic use of political violence was relatively rare. In the majority of cases, incumbents were either unwilling to destroy their countries in order to retain power, or recognized that they could win elections through a more careful and targeted use of repression. However, even the more cautious deployment of coercion, such as the use of localized gangs or militia, represented a threat to political security in the long run.

The attraction of militias for those in power was that they significantly reduced the cost and risks of repression. On the one hand, such gangs had established local networks that could be co-opted with minimal effort and relatively little expense. On the other, they enjoyed a clear advantage over state security forces when it came to conducting attacks on opposition parties, because they deflected blame away from the government. Culpability for human rights abuses committed by the police or army could be traced back to the executive, or at the very least to the relevant ministries. But when acts of violence were perpetrated by secretive and poorly understood militias, such as the notorious Mungiki gang in Kenya, it was far less clear who was to blame, and far harder to prove it. However, the very advantages of militias were also their key flaw; by enhancing the capacity of these complex social forces for violence, leaders unwittingly undermined their ability to control future conflict.

Again, this process was not simply a product of multiparty politics, but had its roots in a prior set of developments. In the 1980s, the combination of high urbanization, mass poverty, and cuts in government spending undermined the capacity of many African governments to prevent petty crime. In turn, the absence of law and order in many areas inspired the formation of groups such as the Baghdad Boys and the Taliban in Kenya, and the Mapogo a Mathamaga and People Against Gangsterism and Drugs in South Africa, which provided "community policing" in areas where the official police force had ceased to operate. However, once established, gangs often exploited their newfound control over local economies to establish mafia-like practices in which petty traders and bus drivers were forced to pay for their own "protection". Over time, this development began to have a wider political impact. Although vigilante groups were often critical of corruption and the performance of the political elite, and so represented something of a challenge to the status quo, political leaders were frequently able to co-opt them for their own ends, in the process fusing political competition and mob justice.

In Nigeria, the co-option of militias was brokered by wealthy political brokers: the godfathers introduced earlier in this chapter. Chief Lamidi Adedibu, a well-known godfather from Oyo State, was one such "kingmaker". In the run-up to the elections of 2007, the rivalry between Adedibu and his main challenger, Rashidi Ladoja, exploded into violence. Adedibu had helped Ladoja rise to the position of state governor, but the latter's refusal to follow orders had seen the pair fall out. Tensions between the two men first led to violence between rival legislators in the state parliament, and later spilled onto the streets as machete-wielding gangs funded by the two leaders engaged in a proxy war. According to an investigation by Human Rights Watch, both Adedibu and Ladoja had formed their mobs by co-opting factions of the National Union of Road Transport Workers (NURTW),[6] which had originally been created to protect the collective interests of bus drivers but had subsequently been captured by violent touts. By the time of the elections, the NURTW had been transformed into a mob for sale. Through their willingness to sponsor different factions of the union, Adedibu and Ledoja exacerbated this process, leading to the proliferation of gangs and the further spread of violence. Across Nigeria, similar alliances between aspiring political leaders and militias resulted in frequent outbreaks of low-level violence around election time.

One of the most problematic consequences of the use of militias was that it had a ratchet effect: once some candidates deployed election mobs, it became difficult for rival leaders to compete at the polls without employing their own gangs. As a result, the introduction of militias into politics often descended into a dangerous arms race. The more groups were mobilized for political ends, the better organized and armed they became. A case in point is the 2003 general election in Port Harcourt, the capital of Rivers State in Nigeria. The political atmosphere in the Niger Delta, the oil-rich part of the country that has witnessed a series of violent struggles over control of resource revenues, was already tense (see Chapter 1 and Conclusion). Despite this, the PDP government deployed a series of militias to ensure that it retained power. Although this strategy was successful, the party subsequently failed to live up to its promises. Over the next four years, the sense of betrayal and alienation felt by these gangs, combined with the weapons they had secured during the campaign, played into existing tensions and grievances, contributing to a proliferation of gang violence that made Niger Delta one of the most dangerous places in the world.

---

[6] Human Rights Watch. "Criminal Politics: Violence, 'Godfathers' and Corruption in Nigeria". Volume 19, 16 (A), October 2007.

In Kenya, a similar transfer of coercive capacity away from state control also undermined the government's capacity to maintain order. As we saw in Chapter 3, President Daniel arap Moi was one of Africa's most reluctant democrats. His determination to retain power was so great that in the run-up to the elections of 1992 and 1997 he instigated ethnic clashes that were designed to displace communities likely to support opposition parties, most notably the Kikuyu, in his Rift Valley heartlands. As a result, more than 1,500 people lost their lives in clashes that were largely organized through militias such as the Jeshi la Mzee ("The Elder's Army"), which had their roots in Moi's own Kalenjin community.

Seeking an overarching framework through which to market his divisive politics, Moi invoked the notion of majimbo ("regionalism"). Originally understood to refer to a form of decentralized government, Moi and his allies encouraged their supporters to believe that the introduction of majimbo could be translated into a monopoly over local land and resources. This strategy resonated with many communities that had been marginalized at one time or another as a result of successive governments' winner-takes-all practices. During the reign of President Kenyatta, the concentration of resources and key positions within his Kikuyu inner circle frustrated the Luo, Kalenjin, Luhya, Kamba, and Maasai communities. Meanwhile, land in the Rift Valley was made available to Kikuyu settlers, to the great chagrin of the Kalenjin, many of whom saw the Kikuyu as illegitimate settlers. Over time, the significance of such grievances intensified, as political favouritism generated deep inequalities in the living standards of different communities. By the time of Kenya's first multiparty transfer of power in 2002, children in Nyanza Province, predominantly populated by the Luo, were three times more likely to die in the first year of their lives as those in the Kikuyu-dominated Central Province.

The government's adoption of militia groups played into and exacerbated these pre-existing tensions, which radically undermined the formula that had hitherto served to maintain political order. During the 1970s and 1980s, the capacity of elite actors to demobilize or co-opt popular movements protected the one-party state from challenges from below (see Chapter 1).[7] But in the 1990s, this elite consensus was undermined. When political leaders competed against each other for

---

[7] Branch, Daniel, and Nic Cheeseman. "Democratization, Sequencing and State Failure in Africa: Lessons from Kenya". *African Affairs* 108, 430 (2008), pp. 1–26.

the presidency, they became far more willing to give militias funds and direction. It was at this point that the government began to lose control of the use of violence.

The threat that this posed to political stability was initially obscured by the country's first-ever democratic transfer of power. In 2002, presidential term limits forced Moi to stand down having completed two terms in office, and KANU was finally defeated by the National Rainbow Coalition (NaRC), a multi-ethnic alliance led by Mwai Kibaki, a Kikuyu, and Raila Odinga, a Luo. These developments initially appeared to have led the country out of a period of destabilizing ethnic politics. However, Kibaki's failure to honour a pre-election deal to make Odinga prime minister resulted in the fragmentation of the coalition months after it had taken office. The manipulation of the constitutional review process, coupled with concerns about a new period of Kikuyu dominance, reinforced fears among minority communities that they would never receive government support unless one of their own was in power. In the years that followed, Odinga sought to harness this dissatisfaction under the banner of a new political vehicle: the Orange Democratic Movement (ODM).

The ODM brought together prominent Coastal, Kalenjin, Kamba, Luhya, and Luo leaders, who told their communities that it was "our turn to eat". In the run-up to the 2007 polls, the breadth of ODM support, coupled with Kibaki's narrow popular base, created the impression that the main cleavage in the election was the Kikuyu versus "the rest". The rising political temperature was not helped by Odinga's decision to embrace the idea of majimbo. Adopting this rallying cry enabled him to unify his coalition of the dispossessed, but also struck fear into the hearts of the Kikuyu community, who remembered the clashes of the 1990s all too well. For their part, some of Kibaki's supporters likened Odinga to Idi Amin and Hitler, and pledged to prevent him from taking power. This stance, combined with a late move by the government to pack the high court and electoral commission with Kibaki loyalists just days before the election, led ODM leaders to conclude that the government was unwilling to play by the rules of the game. As a result, the 2007 election was a particularly high-stakes event, even by Kenyan standards.

As polling day neared, both sides readied their militias, but the balance of power had shifted radically since the ethnic clashes of 1992 and 1997. Many of the individuals who had helped to organize violence for KANU in the 1990s had left the party to join NaRC ahead of the 2002 elections, and subsequently followed Odinga into the ODM. Consequently, some of Kenya's most feared leaders, such as William Ruto, previously a prominent member of the KANU Youth League, had moved from the government to the opposition. This meant that the country's best organized militias now lay firmly outside of state control, setting the scene for what became known as the Kenya crisis.

Polling day itself was calm. But things began to fall apart during the counting process, when Samuel Kivuitu, the chairman of the Electoral Commission of Kenya (ECK), publicly admitted that he could not locate many of his own returning officers and that he feared that they were "cooking". Although opinion polls and the early results suggested that Odinga might win, the ECK subsequently declared that Kibaki had retained power by a slender margin. The ODM immediately rejected the results citing widespread irregularities, a claim that was backed up by the EU election-observer mission. As shock and anger spread throughout opposition strongholds, a wave of unrest erupted across the country. The worst of the violence came in the Rift Valley, where militias similar to those that KANU had deployed in the 1990s attacked groups that were assumed to have voted for the president. In response, gangs said to be associated with Kibaki's allies, most notably Uhuru Kenyatta, son of the first president, carried out revenge attacks. The slide towards all-out civil conflict was halted by the creation of a government of national unity in March 2008, but by this point more than 1,000 people had already lost their lives and hundreds of thousands of others had been displaced.

Democratization and the Sequencing Debate

As we shall see in Chapter 6, the reintroduction of elections did not always have such devastating consequences. But where leaders were determined to retain power at all costs, the short-term imperative of winning elections led incumbents to pursue strategies that politicized communal identities, compromised democratic institutions, and laid the foundations for civil conflict. The violent breakdown of so many multiparty systems in Africa is strong evidence that in states that lack the effective rule of law, a cohesive national identity, and a monopoly over the legitimate use of force, the rapid reintroduction of elections can have a destabilizing effect. Given this, even the most committed democrat must recognize that there are circumstances in which the long-term promotion of democracy may be best achieved by taking a realistic approach to what is feasible in the short-term. After all, each failed attempt at democratization makes it even harder to build a trusting political community and so renders future transitions less likely to succeed.

However, it is not clear that the way out of this conundrum is to sequence reforms so that elections are only introduced once countries have already developed a successful economy, a strong national identity, and the effective rule of law. Although some contexts are so unfavourable that introducing multiparty politics would seem foolhardy, such as Somalia, there is not a clear alternative to elections. Most obviously, most African nations have already begun to hold elections and Western governments can hardly advocate a return to authoritarian rule. The question of whether or not the introduction of elections should be deferred is therefore only a "live" one for those countries that have yet to make the transition to multipartyism or who suffer further cycles of democratic breakdown and reconstruction. But even in these cases it is not clear that there are any palatable alternatives to democratization in the end. In response to political crises in Côte d'Ivoire, Kenya, and Zimbabwe the international community advocated power-sharing as a means to the end of securing peace. But power-sharing is no alternative to multiparty competition in the long-term. On the one hand, if power-sharing means ceasing to hold elections and curtailing formal opposition to the government, then it is little more than the reinvention of the one-party state and will suffer from the same limitations (see Chapter I). Conversely, if power-sharing means that governments are designed to be more inclusive and representative within a competitive electoral framework, then it is in fact a modified version of multipartyism. In that case, power-sharing is best thought of as one of a number of reforms that can be implemented to help manage the tensions that political competition can generate in new democracies. Either way, power-sharing does not represent a genuine alternative to democratization.

Deferring elections also raises the tricky question of what sort of government should rule over problem states until they are ready to democratize. There is little evidence that investing power in "benign" authoritarian regimes would generate the conditions necessary for successful democratic transitions on the continent. Such a model paid dividends for a number of East Asian countries such as South Korea and Taiwan, which first achieved economic reform and built more effective state institutions under authoritarian governments, and later embarked on a gradual path of political liberalization. But in the universe of authoritarian states, these developmental states are the exception, not the norm. In Africa, authoritarian rule was frequently brutal, exploitative, and arbitrary. Even the civilian one-party states that performed better in terms of inculcating political stability and a viable national identity typically failed to deliver economic growth or establish political institutions that could operate outside of executive control. The only two countries that did tick these boxes were Botswana and Mauritius, both of which have maintained multiparty systems since independence. The conditions needed for the Taiwanese or South Korean model to be successful – a bureaucracy insulated from patrimonial pressures, broad economic equality, and an elite consensus on the importance of generating long-term economic growth – were not present in Africa in the 1970s and in most cases they do not hold now. The idea that some form of benign authoritarian rule could be established to nurse the continent towards democracy is therefore dangerously ahistorical.

The suggestion that Africa should pull back from multiparty politics also flies in the face of the opinions of African citizens according to the data collected by the Afrobarometer survey, which is available at www.afrobarometer.org. In the third round of the opinion poll conducted between 2011 and 2013, over 50,000 Africans across some 34 countries were asked what kind of political regime they would prefer in their country. A clear majority – 71% – preferred a democracy, while only 11% said that a non-democratic alternative might be preferable. Moreover, the survey also found evidence that support for democracy is hardening over time: the proportion of respondents who demonstrated a deep commitment to democracy by both supporting political pluralism and rejecting all forms of authoritarian rule rose from 36% in 2002 to 51% in 2012. African citizens, it seems, may be critical of the performance of their multiparty governments, but have little sympathy for a return to military or one-party rule.

Given this, it seems clear that the twin challenges of electoral violence and state building cannot be resolved by simply curtailing multiparty politics. As Thomas Carothers has argued, this conclusion need not be a defeatist one.[8] The reform of the political and economic

---

[8] Carothers, Thomas. "The 'Sequencing' Fallacy". *Journal of Democracy* 18, 1 (2007), pp. 12–27.

system and the reintroduction of competitive elections can go hand in hand, as the history of democratic consolidation in Botswana, Ghana, and Mauritius demonstrates. These success stories, some of which are discussed in Chapter 6, deserve as much prominence in discussions of African politics as Nigeria, Rwanda, and Zimbabwe. Rather than give up on democracy in Africa, we should therefore turn our attention to the question of how institutional design can be used to make democracy work, a challenge that is the subject of the Conclusion.

Select Bibliography

Des Forges, Alison. *"Leave None to Tell Their Story": Genocide in Rwanda.* New York & London: Human Rights Watch, 1999.

Geschiere, Peter. "Autochthony and the Politics of Belonging" in Nic Cheeseman, David Anderson, and Andrea Scheibler (eds). *The Routledge Handbook of African Politics.* Oxford: Routledge, 2013.

Horowitz, Donald L. *Ethnic Groups in Conflict.* Berkeley: University of California Press, 1985.

Mann, Michael. *The Dark Side of Democracy: Explaining Ethnic Cleansing.* Cambridge: Cambridge University Press, 2005.

For a bibliography for this chapter go to www.democracyinafrica.org

CHAPTER 6

The Democratic Dividend: Political Competition, Populism, and Public Policy

On 2 January 2009, all eyes in Ghana turned to the small and unre-markable constituency of Tain. Because of a problem distributing ballot papers, the people of Tain had not voted in the second round of the presidential election at the same time as the country's 229 other constitu-encies. When they went to the polls four days later, it was in the knowl-edge that their actions would determine the next government of Ghana.

The presidential contest had been close from the start. The can-didate of the ruling New Patriotic Party (NPP), Nana Akufo-Addo, had won the first round with 4,159,439 votes. But the main opposition leader, John Atta Mills of the National Democratic Congress (NDC), had also done well, receiving 4,056,634 votes – just 102,805 behind. As no candidate achieved an absolute majority, Akufo-Addo and Mills contested a run-off. The second ballot turned out to be even closer than the first. Because many of the candidates who dropped out of the race threw their support behind the NDC, Mills was able to fashion a narrow lead of just 23,000 votes. But Tain had not voted, and the number of registered voters in the constituency (53,000) was greater than the margin between the two candidates.

Aware that the NDC had significant support in Tain, and that it was therefore unfeasible to overturn Mills's lead, the NPP govern-ment sought an injunction to delay the poll, claiming that the atmo-sphere was not conducive to a free and fair election. When this strategy failed the NPP, panicked by the prospect of losing power, called on its supporters to boycott the vote, a move that was heavily criticized by opposition parties and civil society groups. As tensions rose, fears of electoral violence increased and the government deployed police and soldiers to keep the peace. During this period a group of filmmakers gained rare access to the "strong room" of the electoral commission where results are transmitted, counted, and verified. The remarkable footage in the resulting documentary, *An African Election*, reveals just how close Ghana came to political meltdown. While party representatives exchanged accusations of electoral malpractice, enraged politicians on both sides made a series of alarming threats about what they were willing to do if their interpretation of the election results did not prevail.

Despite this challenging context, when the Electoral Commission of Ghana announced that Mills had won, the NPP peacefully accepted defeat. As the Mills government began to move into the presidential palace, Ghana became that rare thing: an African country that has experienced two turnovers of power. The only other members of this exclusive club are Benin, Cape Verde, Madagascar, Malawi, Mauritius, Senegal, and Zambia. The peaceful outcome of the election had many roots. An opposition campaign to strengthen the electoral system following disputed polls in the early 1990s increased the confidence of all parties in the electoral process. At the same time, constitutional provisions safeguarding the independence of the Electoral Commission, and the widespread public respect for its longstanding Chair, Afari Gyan, conferred credibility on the management of the process. In *An African Election*, Gyan emerges as the calmest man in the building, his quiet personal authority doing much to persuade party leaders to accept the results. The desire of the outgoing NPP President John Kufour that both candidates should respect the decision of the Commission also discouraged candidates from rejecting the official outcome, as we shall see.

The willingness of the NPP to stand down confirmed the assessment of many commentators that Ghana had become a high-quality and stable democracy. After the first turnover of power in 2005, Freedom House upgraded the country's status to "Free", with a perfect score for political rights. The gradual consolidation of democracy in countries like Ghana has led Staffan I. Lindberg to argue that elections are not simply symptoms of democratic progress, but are actually an important driver of democratization in their own right.[1]

[1] Lindberg, Staffan. *Democracy and Elections in Africa*. Baltimore: John Hopkins University Press, 2006.

According to Lindberg, the repeated holding of elections – even when not fully free and fair – promotes democratic consolidation because it trains voters in democracy, enables opposition parties to learn how to detect and expose electoral manipulation, and creates moments during which pro-democracy organizations, donors, and opposition parties can come together to campaign for further political liberalization. In other words, holding elections facilitates the institutionalization of democratic norms and values, and hence the evolution of freer and fairer elections over time: a virtuous cycle of democratic consolidation.

Lindberg's argument is appealing. But we have already seen that many leaders were able to blunt the transformative power of elections by deploying an arsenal of authoritarian strategies. It is also clear that in countries in which presidents were willing to retain power at any cost the introduction of multiparty politics often exacerbated political instability and civil unrest (see Chapter 5). This suggests that the democratic power of elections is more likely to be unlocked in countries where leaders faced strong incentives to reform rather than to repress (see Introduction). Elections held in uncompetitive and authoritarian regimes are far less likely to have liberalizing effects.[2]

Consolidation Through Competition

The potential for political competition to act as the motor of democratization is well illustrated by the case of Senegal. As we saw in Chapter 2, under Leopold Senghor's UPS Senegal became a de facto one-party state in 1966. Thereafter, the UPS regime remained comparatively open. The tolerant nature of Senghor's administration was shaped by the country's colonial experience and the balance of power between the government, influential social groups, and the international community. The early introduction of elections in the Four Communes of Senegal by the French administration meant that Senegalese elites had greater experience with competitive politics than their counterparts elsewhere on the continent, even if this was confined to urban areas. It was partly this experience that cultivated in

[2] Howard, Marc Morjé, and Philip G. Roessler. "Liberalizing Electoral Outcomes in Competitive Authoritarian Regimes". *American Journal of Political Science* 50, 2 (2006), pp. 365–381.

Senghor a strong personal commitment to plural politics. At the same time, Senegal's lack of significant natural resources limited the government's ability to ignore international and domestic pressure. Most notably, the alliance between Senghor's government and influential Muslim leaders both empowered the regime to mobilize support but also constrained the ability of the UPS to control rural areas in the absence of the support of the marabout.

Taken together, these factors meant that Senghor found the costs of repression to be unacceptable (see Introduction). At the same time, the political dominance of the UPS in the late 1960s and early 1970s meant that he was confident that the party could retain power under a more competitive political system. As a result, Senghor responded to public dissatisfaction by pursuing reform instead of repression, setting in motion a process of controlled political liberalization. In 1974, the political arena was opened up to a new opposition party, the Senegalese Democratic Party (PDS), and in 1976 was further transformed into a three-party system. Multiparty politics Senghor-style was not unconstrained: the UPS enjoyed the advantages of incumbency and each party had to follow an ideological disposition set down by the president. While the UPS was transformed into the PS, the PDS was given a liberal democratic identity and the unbanned African Independence Party (PAI) was to provide a Marxist–Leninist option. Significantly, the National Democratic Rally (RND), the party of Senghor's main rival, Cheikh Anta Diop, was excluded.

Despite the tight constraints under which this system operated, over time elections became increasingly competitive. Senghor stepped down as president in 1981, becoming one of the only African leaders to voluntarily leave power, and was replaced by Abdou Diouf. The new president lacked his predecessor's legitimacy as a founding father and his power base. He also inherited an economy that was in trouble. In 1978, the falling price of peanuts on world markets and an increase in the cost of oil led to an economic crisis. Under Diouf, the PS government sought to manage the twin pressures of economic stagnation and multiparty politics by restricting the inroads that opposition parties could make in presidential contests, but allowing them to win limited victories in parliamentary and local elections so that the political system retained credibility. This compromise enabled the PDS to increase its representation in parliament from 8 seats in 1983 (out of 120), to 17 in 1988 and 27 in 1993. In the process, the PDS gained an important foothold in the political arena, and used victories at the local level to develop its own patronage networks and organizations. Opposition leaders were also able to take advantage of their newfound positions to critique the political system itself, arguing that there could be no democracy without *alternance* – the rotation of power. But while opposition parties made further gains in the 1988 polls and the PDS took 43 per cent of the vote in the capital, the combination of the government's control over the state media and the effectiveness of its political machine in rural areas enabled Diouf to retain power.

However, as the size and hence the authority of the opposition grew, it became increasingly difficult for the government to ignore demands for reform. In 1990, the opposition boycotted local elections in response to the alleged manipulation of the 1988 vote. The fear that a boycott would delegitimize the political process encouraged the ruling party to introduce a raft of changes that included measures to liberalize media coverage. Each reform created greater political space for the opposition to work in, making elections evermore competitive. As a result, it became increasingly unfeasible for the PS to maintain control through coercion and so party leaders faced strong incentives to placate popular pressure by introducing new reforms. Senegal thus entered a virtuous cycle in which reform was followed by opposition gains, creating greater pressure for more far-reaching reforms, which in turn led to more substantial opposition gains, and so on.

Over many iterations, this process moved Senegal towards democracy. In the 1993 elections, the PS once again retained its legislative majority. Fresh demands for reform of the electoral system followed and the government responded by announcing plans for an all-party conference. In 1997, the conference established a new electoral commission, the Observatoire National des Elections (ONEL) that was better insulated from political interference than its predecessor. This reform marked the beginning of genuinely open competition in Senegal; thereafter, the PS lost control of the pace of change. Subsequently, the decision of marabout leaders to withhold their political support, combined with internal divisions within the ruling party, undermined Diouf's hold on power ahead of the presidential elections in 2000. Although the PS emerged as the most popular party in the first round of voting, it was unable to secure the 50 per cent of the vote needed to win outright. This enabled opposition parties to unite against Diouf in the run-off, paving the way for the victory of Abdoulaye Wade and the Sopi ("change") coalition. Twenty-six years on from the reintroduction of multipartyism, Senegal finally enjoyed its first taste of alternance.

The gradual process of change in Senegal illustrates the way in which repeated electoral competition can strengthen democratic rules – even when elections are not initially free and fair, and regimes are not committed to democracy. Where such a virtuous cycle of reform and opposition gains takes place, political change does not require exceptionally virtuous leaders; rather, it occurs as the natural by-product of each of the main parties acting in their own self-interest. This provides clear support for Lindberg's contention that holding elections in and of itself promotes democratic consolidation. But while it is clear that poor-quality elections may contribute to gradual processes of democratic reform, this is not always the case. As we saw in Chapter 5, in countries such as Kenya and Rwanda the divisive impact of multiparty competition encouraged leaders to adopt desperate strategies to retain power that had disastrous consequences for both democracy and national unity. It is therefore important to focus not just on how many elections are held, but the context within which they occur. In Senegal, a lack of natural resources, the comparatively limited development of neo-patrimonial politics, and the presence of influential religious networks outside of state control placed constraints on the actions of the government. Combined with a history of political pluralism, this led Senghor and his successors to favour reform. By contrast, in Rwanda a history of violence and the fear that losing offices would open up members of the ancien régime to economic and political reprisals meant that the government consistently leaned towards repression. It is therefore not possible to get a sense of the likely impact of multiparty politics without first considering the political and economic landscape into which it will be introduced.

The Rules of the Game

The gradual institutionalization of democratic rules was particularly significant because it opened up new pathways of political change. One development of particular importance was the increasing respect for presidential term limits in the 1990s. Although a number of countries including Côte d'Ivoire, Equatorial Guinea, Gambia, Guinea-Bissau, Mauritania, and Zimbabwe did not employ any restrictions on the length of time that an incumbent could stay in office, the majority of the continent's new democracies stipulated that the president could not serve for more than two terms in office. Because of the high-profile nature of term limits, they came to represent an extremely visible issue around which domestic groups and international donors in favour of democratic reform could mobilize, and so evolved into an important new constraint on African leaders.[3] In some countries where ruling parties lacked democratic instincts, or were insulated from pressure to reform by the presence of valuable natural resources, governments rejected term limits, as in Chad, Gabon, Guinea, Togo, and Uganda. But in those countries where governments were less financially self-sufficient, faced stronger opposition movements, or were more committed to plural politics and saw the virtue of a two-term limit, leaders either did not try to seek a third term (Benin, Cape Verde, Ghana, Mali, Mozambique, Sao Tome and Principe, Seychelles, Tanzania) or lacked the power to force through the necessary constitutional changes (Malawi, Nigeria, Zambia).

These different pathways further exaggerated the democratic divide between the continent's more repressive and open political systems, because when term limits were enforced, they created windows of opportunity for opposition parties. Ruling parties won the vast majority of elections in which they were led by a sitting president (Table 6.1). By contrast, in open seat polls (in which the incumbent did not run as a result of term limits, ill health, death, or resignation), ruling parties fared much worse, winning only around half of all contests. Although there have so far been far fewer "open-seat" elections than "incumbent" ones, both account for exactly half of the continent's 24 transfers of power to date (Table 6.1). Moreover, many of the transfers that have taken place during "incumbent" elections occurred in the "founding" polls that marked the reintroduction of multiparty politics, and were made possible by the emergence of a broad but often short lived coalition in favour of political change. Once this moment passed, incumbents became even harder to defeat.

Open-seat polls create fresh opportunities for opposition parties because they generate a series of challenges that ruling parties typically struggle to overcome. The most obvious of these is the selection of a new leader and presidential candidate. In countries where great

[3] Posner, Daniel N., and Daniel J. Young. "The Institutionalization of Political Power in Africa". *Journal of Democracy* 18, 3 (2007), pp. 126–140.

TABLE 6.1 *Presidential transfers of power in multiparty Africa*

	Elections*
Transfers in incumbent polls	Benin (1991, 1996), Cape Verde (1991), Central African Republic (1993), Madagascar (1993, 1996, 2001), Malawi (1994, 2014), Senegal (2000, 2012), Zambia (1991, 2011)
Transfers in open-seat polls	Benin (2006), Cape Verde (2001, 2011), Comoros (2006), Côte d'Ivoire (2000), Ghana (2000, 2008), Kenya (2002), Mali (2002), Niger (1993), Sao Tome and Princippe (2011), Sierra Leone (2007)

* Sample includes all sub-Saharan polities holding direct multiparty presidential elections. Transfers were excluded if they were immediately preceded by a coup and therefore held in the absence of a ruling party.

power is conferred on the presidency and politics remains highly personalized, succession contests can cause irreparable internal divisions. This is particularly likely in cases where party organizations are not strong enough to discipline their members and hold credible leadership contests, as in much of Africa.

Consider the defeat of the formerly dominant KANU in Kenya in 2002, which occurred after President Daniel arap Moi had stood down, having served two terms in office. Following a period of uncertainty in 2000–2001 during which Moi's lieutenants lobbied for the top job, the outgoing president announced that he had decided on Uhuru Kenyatta, son of Kenya's founding father, Jomo Kenyatta, as his replacement. At the time Uhuru was fifty-one, young by the standards of Kenyan politics, and Moi hoped he could both channel the nationalist legitimacy of his father and counteract the "youth factor" that many commentators predicted would benefit the opposition. Moi also believed that Kenyatta's Kikuyu identity would help KANU to mediate its image as a Kalenjin party, pacify those demanding a rotation of the presidency between ethnic groups, and eat into the support base of the party's main challengers.

But Moi had failed to consider the impact that the selection of Kenyatta would have on party unity. Many long-standing party members saw Kenyatta as an outsider and questioned why he had been promoted over their heads. Other prominent leaders who had gravitated towards KANU because they believed that they might be selected to replace Moi were similarly disgruntled. As a result, a number of political heavyweights including the Luo leader Raila Odinga and the Luhya leader Musalia Mudavadi abandoned KANU and established the rival Liberal Democratic Party (LDP). This development marked the beginning of the end for KANU. The LDP subsequently joined NaRC, forming a strong opposition that, as we saw in Chapter 5, went on to inflict a humiliating defeat on Kenyatta in the 2002 polls.

Ruling parties also struggle to win open-seat elections because new presidential candidates face a number of difficult challenges. More specifically, fist-time contenders tend to find it harder to establish a national profile, point to a record of activity, and retain the support of networks developed by their predecessors. Given that many patron-client relationships are rooted in the support of ethnic groups for their leaders (see Chapter 2), this issue is particularly pronounced when the new leader is from a different ethnic group to the outgoing ruler. To see why this matters, let us return to the 2008/9 Ghanaian election introduced above. In the run up to the election campaign term limits prevented the sitting president, John Kufuor, from standing, sparking a divisive contest for the presidential candidacy of the NPP. Despite Kufour's objections, the contest was ultimately won by one of his rivals, Nana Addo Dankwa Akufo-Addo.

The selection of Akufo-Addo, an Akyem, to replace Kufour, an Ashanti, made it more difficult for the ruling party to mobilize support in some of its core constituencies. Although the Ashanti and the Akyem are both subgroups of the larger Akan community, and so are united by similarities in language and customary tradition, tensions between the two groups were not insignificant. Moreover, the bad blood between the Akufo-Addo and Kufour wings of the party meant that the outgoing president refused to campaign for his successor. Taken together, these developments undermined the party's ability to whip Ashanti voters into the political fervour that had accompanied Kufour's successful campaigns in 2000 and 2004. Partly as a result, the turnout of voters in some of the NPP's home areas was lower than the party's campaign team had expected. Given that the NPP only missed out on an absolute first-round majority by 0.87 per cent, and ultimately lost the run-off by just 40,586 votes, it is easy to see why many senior party leaders blamed the party's downfall on internal tensions and the disappointing performance in its homelands.

The third reason that open-seat polls increase the potential for political change is that they give rise to a division of power between the new presidential candidate and the sitting president who, until polling day, retains ultimate control over the machinery of government. This bifurcation of authority is important because outgoing presidents have often proved to be more willing to preside over free and fair polls in elections when their own political future is no longer on the line. This was one of the factors that led to the defeat of the Sierra Leone People's Party (SLPP) in the 2007 general elections. Having been elected in 1998 and served two terms in office President Ahmad Tejan Kabbah was unable to contest the polls. The SLPP moved to appoint his successor well ahead of time, selecting the sitting vice president, Solomon Berewa, in September 2005. President Kabbah initially promoted Berewa's candidacy, but by the time of the election two years later relations between the two had soured. This proved to be critical to the peaceful transfer of power, because Kabbah's refusal to side with Berewa during a controversy concerning the National Electoral Commission (NEC) paved the way for an opposition victory.

The controversy centred on the question of what to do with the votes from polling stations in which more people had voted than were registered. The NEC decided to invalidate all votes from these polling stations, thereby rejecting both fraudulent and legitimate ballots. Because the polling stations in question were largely in SLPP strongholds, the ruling party was disadvantaged and drew up plans to serve the head of the NEC with an injunction to prevent her from declaring the election result. Such a response would have had the effect of undermining the Commission's authority and allowing the regime more time to reassert control over the electoral process. But Kabbah's refusal to support the injunction or otherwise intervene on Berewa's behalf undermined this strategy. Instead, the president's intransigence undermined the SLPP's momentum and emboldened the NEC to declare an opposition victory. At an SLPP conference in 2009, Berewa was clear who he blamed for the party's defeat, telling the party faithful that the "thing that Kabbah did that hurt me a lot was when he broadcast that he was neutral. How can you be neutral against your own party?"

Of course, such rivalries are by no means inevitable. The incoming and outgoing party leaders may pull in the same direction in order to stage manage the elections, as occurred in Nigeria in 2007. In that case, the departing president Olusegun Obasanjo and new presidential candidate Umaru Yar'Adua presided over the most farcical of polls that, as we have seen, were controlled by the government from start to finish (see Chapter 5). But where the relationship between the sitting president and the presidential candidate is not close, the division of authority between the two has the potential to reduce the level of coercion and the degree of electoral fraud.

Taken together, these three factors explain why opposition parties tend to do so much better when sitting presidents do not stand. But while open-seat elections make political change more likely, it is important to keep in mind that they do not render it a foregone conclusion. Significantly, where other conditions remained favourable, ruling parties were often able to overcome the challenge of running a new presidential candidate. In South Africa, for example, the ANC retained power in 2009 and 2014, even though some of President Thabo Mbeki's supporters left the party after he was defeated by Jacob Zuma at the party's fifty-second national conference at Polokwane in 2007. The case of the ANC is an important reminder that open-seat elections are never enough to facilitate opposition victory on their own. In Kenya, the defeat of KANU in 2002 would probably not have occurred if there had not also been a period of economic decline, and if opposition leaders had not learnt from past mistakes and formed a united front. Similarly, in Ghana the defeat of the NPP owed much to economic downturn, a series of corruption scandals, and the sense that it was time for change. In other words, the absence of an incumbent president creates a window of opportunity for opposition parties, nothing more.

These caveats notwithstanding, the effect of open-seat polls on the pace of political change is remarkable. Between 1990 and 2010, the rate of government defeat (turnover) was 35 per cent higher in elections in which the ruling party ran a new candidate (Table 6.2). Even in countries where ruling parties were able to retain power, their average margin of victory over their closest rivals fell from 39 per cent to 29 per cent.

Of course, turnover alone is no guarantee of democratic consolidation. As we have seen in Zambia, it was opposition leader and trade union hero Frederick Chiluba who, after defeating Kenneth Kaunda in the founding elections of 1991, established the most corrupt and venal regime in the country's history (see Chapter 3). But while the impact of turnover has been varied, in some countries alternations of power have played an important role in facilitating reform. Most obviously, transfers of power have removed entrenched, corrupt, and

TABLE 6.2 *Incumbency and election outcomes in Africa (1990–2010)*

	Ruling party runs sitting president (%)	Ruling party runs new candidate (%)	Difference
Ruling party share of the vote	59	44	−15
Winning margin (where ruling party won)	39	29	−10
Voter turnout	67	65	−2
Rate of government defeat	9/61 (15%)	10/20 (50%)	+35%

Note: Sample as in Table 6.1.

authoritarian parties from power. Turnover is also important because it is the most powerful symbol that parties are willing to play by the rules of the game. Every time a ruling party agrees to leave power, political leaders of all stripes are given a new reason to place their trust in democratic institutions. Significantly, this effect is not limited to the elite level. There is now considerable evidence from surveys in a number of different African countries that transfers of power significantly increase popular support for, and faith in, democracy.[4]

Ethnic Voting and "Census" Elections

Even where elections did not contribute to processes of democratization, they transformed the relationship between political leaders and their supporters and so had a profound impact on African societies. This effect varied across the continent. In the continent's democracies, elections resulted in open competition. As a result, electoral success in countries such as Cape Verde, Benin, Botswana, Mauritius, Mali, Namibia, and South Africa, depended on persuading, rather than controlling, voters. This was not the case in the continent's more authoritarian states, where opposition parties struggled to make

[4] Bratton, Michael. "The 'Alternation Effect' in Africa". *Journal of Democracy* 15, 4 (2004), pp. 147–158.

any inroads. Yet despite this, incumbents in places such as Angola, Cameroon, Chad, Sudan, and Togo still demanded that their supporters publicly display their loyalty through high turnout. Opposition leaders – despite operating at a disadvantage – also marshaled what support they could. In between these two extremes lay a group of countries in which the ruling party was prepared to allow genuine competitive elections, but retained an unfair electoral advantage. In states such as Kenya, Malawi, and Zambia, governments were desperate to mobilize support both to boost their legitimacy, and because elections were far harder to rig in the absence of real public support for the regime.

The reintroduction of multiparty competition therefore encouraged political leaders to reconnect with their supporters in a broad range of states with very different levels of political rights and civil liberties. The variety of mobilization strategies this gave rise to has often been overlooked in favour of a focus on the centrality of communal identities. The idea that African elections can be treated as an ethnic (or racial, or religious) census owes much to the work of Donald Horowitz, who suggested that where communal identities are particularly salient political behaviour is largely driven by a psychological attachment to a particular group identity.[5] If correct, this would suggest that elections have little to do with issues, a notion which has far-reaching implications. Classic models of representative democracy assume that poorly performing leaders will eventually be punished at the ballot box, and thus posit a direct relationship between multiparty politics and accountable and responsive government. But if voting is simply a celebration of group identity and leaders and not censored by their ethnic kinsmen for corruption or neglect, then the relationship between multiparty politics and accountability breaks down and there is no reason to think that elections will lead to better government (see Chapter 2).

In the 1990s the apparent willingness of voters to line-up behind ethno-regional leaders in countries as diverse as Côte d'Ivoire, Malawi, Nigeria, and Togo appeared to confirm the census story. Yet even taking into account the rise of the politics of belonging and ethnic chauvinism in the 1990s, this reductive account of electoral competition

[5] Horowitz, Donald L. *Ethnic Groups in Conflict*. Berkeley: University of California Press, 2000.

obscures more than it reveals. As we saw in Chapter 5, ethnic politics is not inevitable; it takes time and effort to generate strong group
identities and hatreds. What this meant in practice was that the degree
to which electoral politics could be said to be "ethnic" varied across
the continent. "Identity politics" was most likely to come to the fore in
those countries where a history of ethnic favouritism and discrimination had created real political and economic inequalities between different groups, as in Burundi and Rwanda. Ethnic voting patterns were
much less pronounced in states that experienced different historical
trajectories. For example, in countries such as Ghana, Mali, Senegal,
and Tanzania, political parties rarely formed on an explicitly ethnic
basis, despite the fact that they were socially diverse.

Even where voting patterns did follow ethnic or racial lines, this
process was often more complex and unpredictable than the "census"
model would suggest. Consider the 1994 elections in South Africa,
where issues of race and ethnicity were never far from the surface of the
campaign. The prominence of communal identities was not surprising.
After taking power in 1948, the National Party (NP) government had
consistently deployed a strategy of divide-and-rule politics to sustain
its rule. In an attempt to fragment black opposition to white minority
rule, the apartheid regime had fostered ethno-nationalism, encouraging different black African groups to form their own semi-independent
homelands, each with their own administrations and flags. As we saw
in chapter 3, alongside this policy of ethnic balkanization, the government sought to isolate black demands for equality by providing
greater political and economic opportunities to Indian and Coloured
South Africans through initiatives such as the Tricameral Parliament.

In the run-up to the 1994 polls many commentators predicted that
the poisonous legacy of apartheid would result in a census election,
splitting the electorate along a "white" and "non-white" cleavage, with
Coloured and Indian voters forming an anti-apartheid alliance with
black South Africans. When the votes were counted it turned out that
they had been wrong: Coloured and Indian communities mainly gave
their support to the NP, and to a lesser extent the Democratic Party,
the forerunner of today's Democratic Alliance. The emergence of a
"black" versus "non-black" cleavage surprised many commentators,
but can be explained by the lingering effect of the divide-and-rule
strategies employed by the national party and the longstanding exposure of whites, Coloureds, and Indians to negative media portrayals
of the ANC. As a result, by the end of the apartheid era these three

communities shared one thing in common: they were all minorities apprehensive about the implications of black majority rule. Understanding African elections thus requires knowledge of history as well as demographics.

The examples Ghana, Senegal, and South Africa demonstrate that in order to explain political outcomes on the continent we need to abandon the census model, and the notion that ethnicity is the only driving force of political behaviour. A more profitable approach is to focus on how pre-existing identities and forms of organization shaped the strategies through which political entrepreneurs responded to the reintroduction of elections. Let us start by looking at how African political parties formed. Many of the broad pro-reform coalitions that emerged in the late 1980s began as multi-ethnic alliances. However, because they typically had little in common bar their hostility to authoritarian rule, these movements struggled to remain united once opposition parties had been legalized. In this sense, they were not dissimilar to the nationalist parties that emerged fifty years earlier.

The extent to which these movements fragmented into a series of ethnic or regional parties depended on the kinds of networks and organizations that were available to political leaders, and whether these rendered the success of a particular leader dependent on their membership of an established party, or empowered them to go it alone. In countries where formal party structures were strong, ethnic identities were weak, and leaders lacked the resources to fund their own campaigns, aspiring presidential candidates faced strong incentives to stay put. By contrast, in those political systems in which political organizations were weak and the distribution of power and patronage under authoritarian rule had created ethno-regional Big Men, leaders had few reasons to stay loyal to their parties, and pro-democracy movements were more likely to break down into their ethnic components.

The Kenyan case illustrates this point well. As we saw in Chapter 2, during the one-party state the Kenyatta and Moi regimes attempted to maintain their popularity by ploughing patronage funds through MPs. In the process, they created a set of ambitious and wealthy regional Big Men who had little need for party branches and members because they were effectively political machines in their own right. As a result, aspiring political leaders did not need to rely on party structures to mobilize support, and demonstrated little interest in cultivating party branches or management structures. The fate of FORD, the organization at the forefront of the campaign for multiparty politics (see Chapter 3), reveals the impact that this had on the political landscape. At the height of its powers, FORD was a powerful multi-ethnic movement led by both Kikuyu (Kenneth Matiba, Charles Rubia) and Luo (Odinga Oginga) leaders. But once Moi agreed to reintroduce multiparty politics, the opposition began to come apart at the seams. The fundamental problem was that neither Matiba nor Odinga was prepared to accept anything less than the presidential nomination. As a result, the party quickly divided into a Luo-led faction, behind Odinga, and a Kikuyu-led faction, behind Matiba. Because the mobilising capacity of FORD rested heavily on the personal networks of these individuals, the party was incapable of disciplining its leaders or preventing them from leaving the party and taking their support base with them. In the end, this is precisely what happened as both leaders insisted on registering their own version of FORD: Matiba called his election vehicle FORD-Asili, while Odinga opted for FORD-Kenya.

The decision to compete as rival candidates handed the election to Moi. The president did not perform well, securing under 2 million votes – just 36.4 per cent of the poll. But this was enough to defeat a divided opposition. The 2.5 million votes that the FORD leaders polled would have given them a clear victory, had they not been split between Matiba (1.4 million) and Odinga (940,000). The collapse of FORD was also significant because it meant that most of the parties that contested the elections were supported by only one or two ethnic groups. This led to a greater focus on ethnic politics, which further entrenched the salience of communal identities and so made it easier for leaders to mobilize support in the absence of effective party structures. Over the next twenty years, major political leaders left parties and coalitions to form new ones with remarkable frequency, safe in the knowledge that they could rely on their supporters to follow them across party lines.

Coalition formation was particularly important in Kenya, because no one ethnic group comprises more than a quarter of the population. This means that leaders have a much better chance of securing power if they could form a multi-ethnic coalition of two or three parties. Once this lesson had been brought home to the political elite by the victory of the NaRC alliance in 2002, Kenyan politics began to follow a regular pattern of coalition formation and collapse, which reshaped the political landscape in complex ways. On the one hand, the need to form partnerships across ethnic lines created a greater imperative towards elite-level compromise than would otherwise have been the case. On the other, the fact that these marriages of convenience rarely lasted long enough to establish an effective internal organization, and relied heavily on their leaders for funding, meant that party supporters and activists were rarely able to exert control over policy or strategy.

The balance of power between individual leaders and party structures was not always so uneven. In countries where the distribution of patronage under authoritarian rule had been less personalized, and so had not created a tier of wealthy ethno-regional leaders, aspiring candidates were poorly placed to fund and organize campaigns. In Ghana, for example, resources were not distributed through MPs under authoritarian rule to the extent that they were in Kenya, and so Ghanaian leaders did not enjoy the same capacity to contest elections outside of the two main parties, the NDC and the NPP. Although the president who reintroduced multiparty politics, Jerry John Rawlings, enjoyed tremendous individual support as a result of his populist policies and personal charisma, this has not been true of his successors. As in Kenya, candidates who fail to secure the nomination of one of the two parties to contest for a legislative seat often contest elections as independents, but in contrast to Kenya relatively few are ever elected to parliament. The same is true of presidential elections, in which the NDC and NPP have consistently won more than 95 per cent of the vote between them. Over the last two decades, the dominance of the two main parties, and the difficulty of contesting for office without their support, has prevented political fragmentation and given rise to one of the continent's only two-party systems (Table 6.3).

It is important to note that this process of political centralization has occurred even though ethnicity and regionalism are not insignificant factors in Ghanaian electoral politics: while the various ethnic groups that make up the Akan people typically vote for the NPP, the Volta region is an NDC heartland. Despite this, the combination of comparatively strong party identities and weak Big Men has ensured that the balance of power does not reside with individual politicians, as it does in countries such as Kenya. At the same time, the ability of the country's two main political parties to trace their roots to ideological traditions that began in the colonial era – the NDC to Kwame Nkrumah's statist and populist politics, and the NPP to the more liberal leanings of J.B. Danquah and Kofi Abrefa Busia – has enabled Ghanaian parties to develop a political language that eschews ethnic appeals.

TABLE 6.3 *African regimes by type of party system*

One-party dominant		Two-party	Multi-party	
Centralized	Fragmented		Centralized	Fragmented
Angola	Botswana	Cape Verde	Lesotho	Benin
Mozambique	Burkina Faso	Ghana	Malawi	CAR
Togo	Burundi	Zimbabwe	Zambia	R. of. Congo
	Cameroon			DRC
	Chad			Kenya
	Djibouti			Liberia
	E. Guinea			
	Ethiopia			
	The Gambia			
	Lesotho			
	Namibia			
	Nigeria			
	Rwanda			
	South Africa			
	Uganda			

Note: A party is classified as dominant if it wins more than two-thirds of the elected seats in the legislature. The opposition is then classified as centralized if one opposition party wins at least half of the remaining parliamentary seats. Where no party secures two-thirds of the seats, a country is classified as a two-party system if the largest two parties in the lower house hold 85 per cent of the seats or more, otherwise it is counted as a multiparty system. A country is classified as a fragmented multiparty system if no two parties secured more than half of the vote between them.

Broader and more durable party structures also emerged in countries where the pro-democracy movement of the 1980s was built on strong pre-existing civil society organizations that could mobilize support across ethnic lines. This was the case in parts of southern Africa, where urbanization and industrialization resulted in the development of vibrant trade union activity in densely populated towns. As we saw in Chapters 2 and 3, the ability of opposition political leaders in Zambia to tap into trade union networks gave them an effective organization that proved to be very efficient at mobilizing support. Combined with the presence of a more cosmopolitan electorate in urban areas, this enabled political leaders to get the vote out without relying on ethnic politics or personal networks. In turn, the greater value of party structures discouraged leaders from going it alone. This effect faded over time as a result of the declining influence of organized labour, but was sufficient to ensure that in the run up to the 1991 election the MMD opposition remained more united, and hence more effective, than reform coalitions in more ethnically polarized countries, such as FORD.

A similar process also played out in countries where white minority rule had only recently been overthrown and so nationalism remained a potent force because. In Namibia, for example, SWAPO was able to translate its struggle credentials into overwhelming electoral dominance because the fight for liberation was so fresh in the minds of voters. Similarly, in South Africa the combination of nationalist sentiment, trade union support, and inclusive government enabled the ANC to both sustain the support of a broad range of black ethnic groups, and to gradually win over many of the minorities that had initially rejected the party in 1994. In turn, the mobilizing capacity of these "struggle" parties increased their value to political leaders, which reduced the likelihood of fragmentation and paved the way for the evolution of one-party dominance. As with the liberation parties of the 1960s (see Chapter 1), SWAPO and the ANC will find it harder to sustain their broad membership base when the unifying force of nationalism begins to wane. In the 1990s, however, they proved to be two of the continent's most effective political organizations.

Populism and Service Delivery

The ethnic census model of African politics is also problematic because it diverts attention away from the issues that candidates actually campaign on. Elections rarely see political parties engage in serious economic debates, but this does not mean that important issues are not at stake. Africa has a long tradition of leaders who have sought to mobilize support by pledging to improve the conditions of the common man. A classic proponent of this strategy was the aforementioned Ghanaian President J.J. Rawlings, whose supporters were so devoted to him that he earned the nickname Junior Jesus. Both under authoritarian and multiparty government, Rawlings portrayed himself as being on the side of those who had lost out under previous regimes. In doing so, he adopted two classic populist tropes: the claim to be one of "the people" and hence the leader best suited to represent their interests, and the promise that by protecting ordinary folk from manipulative elites and foreign exploitation he could make their lives better. This combination is well illustrated by the words that Rawlings used to justify the coup that brought him to power at the expense of a democratically elected government in 1981, when he argued that "the high fees charged as registration for political parties made them a preserve of the rich. At the level of the economy, democracy meant plenty for the rich and a freedom to starve for the broad majority, and a lack of sensitivity to the plight of the poor dominated all our major institutions." Throughout his time at the forefront of Ghanaian politics, Rawlings's rabble-rousing rhetoric drew huge crowds, and large numbers of voters, to his side.

More recently, a number of other leaders have adopted similar strategies. The most successful modern-day populist was the late Zambian leader Michael Sata – popularly known as King Cobra as a result of his reputation as a political "street fighter" – who successfully developed a populist campaign that transformed him from a political no-hoper into the president. Although he had achieved a certain notoriety under the Zambian one-party state, and played a prominent role within the MMD government, by 2002 Sata's career appeared to have stalled. Things started to go wrong when the outgoing president, Frederick Chiluba, refused to anoint Sata as his successor. Frustrated that his service had not been awarded, King Cobra quit the MMD to form his own party, the Patriotic Front (PF), but his first run at the presidency proved to be an embarrassing failure. The 3 per cent of the votes he received all came from the Bemba community, and there was no evidence that his PF party had any kind of national profile.

The defeat sparked Sata into life. Over the decade that followed, he cultivated a highly effective populist appeal, based on his image as a man of action. His manifesto was not dissimilar to that of Rawlings: Sata promised to create jobs, improve working conditions, stand up for Zambian interests, and drive a tougher deal with China and other foreign investors. All of these points hit home. In particular, his argument that MMD elites were colluding with foreign powers to exploit ordinary people chimed with the disaffection of poor Zambians and mineworkers who felt that the country should be receiving more in exchange for its copper exports. Especially in urban areas, where a history of trade union activists and radical politics rendered voters more sympathetic to populist appeals, the PF began to attract a large multi-ethnic support base. In 2006, this propelled Sata to second place in the presidential election, while the PF established itself as Zambia's second largest party, winning 30 per cent of the seats in the legislature and establishing a foothold in local government in the capital city, Lusaka. Five years later Sata was able to build on this foundation in order to inflict a crushing defeat on the MMD's Rupiah Banda, securing 43 per cent of the vote – 12 per cent more than his rival. Given the tendency for incumbents to win elections in Africa (see Chapter 5), this was a remarkable achievement.

Although populist appeals are generally most effective in urban areas, they have also proved to be an effective strategy in some rural locales. Rawlings's populist base in northern Ghana, for example, was predominantly rural. Sata also proved able to mobilize rural votes. In part, this was because he received a strong "ethnic" vote from the rural component of the Bemba-speaking community in northern Zambia. But one of the reasons that Sata could simultaneously mobilize a multi-ethnic base with catch-all appeals and an ethnic base hoping for special treatment was that rural Bemba voters shared many populist sentiments. The preponderance of Bemba speakers in the urbanized and unionized Copperbelt, a legacy of colonial-era migration, resulted in the dynamic exchange of political ideas and remittances between the Copperbelt and northern Zambia. Over time, the depth of linkages with, and dependence on, urban areas made rural Bembas more responsive to populist messages. As a result, they were not turned off by the rhetoric that Sata had to use in order to extend his appeal in urban areas, which enabled King Cobra to run an extremely effective ethno-populist campaign.[6]

Although it can be a very effective way of rallying support, populism does not always make for good policy. The search for a common enemy leads to gross simplifications of complex political realities – such as Sata's scapegoating of Chinese investors – and encourages citizens to believe that governments can deliver more than is feasible. When populists take power, this can lead them to overreach their political and economic capacity, leading to both financial and authoritarian excess. In the Zambian case, many of those who voted for the PF in 2011 had already become disillusioned with Sata before his untimely death in office in 2014. But these caveats notwithstanding, the rise to power of parties such as the PF is an interesting and important development because it demonstrates that you can win power in Africa without resorting to ethnic politics, and that political leaders are constantly looking for new ways to connect to voters.

---

[6] Cheeseman, Nic, and Miles Larmer. "Ethnopopulism in Africa: Opposition Mobilization in Diverse and Unequal Societies". *Democratization*, 22, 1(2015), pp.22–50.

While low levels of urbanization and rural-urban migration limit the potential for populist strategies to be successfully employed in much of East and West Africa, many leaders have nonetheless looked for issues that might enable them to recruit support from across the ethnic divide. For example, parties in countries such as Kenya and Malawi committed themselves to providing free primary education for all. These policies were not conceived of by left wing parties or introduced by leaders with socialist pretensions, and they did not come as part of a broader package of policies aimed to redistribute wealth. Rather, they reflected the efforts of parties to rally support by identifying the issues of greatest interest to the wider population. As the idea spread across the continent, incumbents increasingly promoted free education as evidence that they had responded to the needs and preferences of voters. Although the implementation of this policy was often hampered by low government capacity, it resulted in millions of the continent's poorest children going to school for the first time, demonstrating the potential for competitive politics to generate improvements in the lives of ordinary people.

The Democratic Dividend

The spread of free primary education raises important questions: Has Africa enjoyed a democratic dividend? Is there evidence that democracies are better at providing public services and responding to citizens' needs than authoritarian governments? Sadly for democrats, the answers to these questions are far from straight forward, as the case of South African health care policy aptly demonstrates. By the time that Thabo Mbeki succeeded Nelson Mandela as president in 1999, South Africa had emerged as the continent's largest democracy, whether measured in terms of territory, population, or economic activity. Yet the existence of a free press, a progressive constitution, and active opposition parties was not sufficient to prevent Mbeki's government from failing to provide appropriate HIV/AIDS treatment. Instead, Mbeki dismayed donors by questioning whether HIV was the cause of AIDS, and rejecting the idea that Western medicine could provide the answers to South Africa's health crisis. This was his justification for prohibiting the use of antiretroviral drugs in state hospitals – even to prevent the transmission of the disease from mothers to their children during birth – and for supporting Virodene, a controversial AIDS drug treatment developed in South Africa that was subsequently discredited.

Mbeki's stance on HIV/AIDS has baffled many critics, because it resulted in the deaths of an estimated 350,000 people, the vast majority of whom were ANC voters. It is clear that Mbeki was not ignorant of the depth of the problem. By the end of Mandela's presidency, HIV/AIDS had emerged as one of the most pressing challenges facing the ANC government. Four million people were infected in 1999 alone; by 2000, around 20 per cent of the adult population had contracted HIV. The impact on the nation's health system and economy was tangible. As the death toll rose, many South Africans became used to a depressing ritual of funerals that, in the worst hit areas, began to take over the whole weekend. Given this, Mbeki's stance cannot be explained solely on the basis that he was unaware that a health crisis was occurring on his watch. Rather, his "denialism" must be understood as the product of a complex mixture of his own personal beliefs, public stigma surrounding the disease, and the limited pressure that he could be placed under as the leader of a dominant political party that routinely secured more than two-thirds of the seats in the legislature.

Mbeki's refusal to accept the lessons of Western science was shaped by his experience of the racist medical practices and discourse of the apartheid government, for whom HIV/AIDS was a "black disease" spread as a result of sexual promiscuity. In the 1990s, some doctors and researchers initially pursued a similar line of reasoning, mistakenly arguing that the greater prevalence of HIV in Africa was rooted in higher levels of sexual activity. These theories overlooked the fact that one of the main reasons that the AIDS crisis was particularly bad in Africa was that the disease had already been spreading for decades before it was detected and identified, and that African governments lacked the health care systems and resources to effectively fight it – a weakness that remains a major problem in many countries, as demonstrated by the rapid spread of Ebola in West Africa in 2014. Read against this backdrop, Mbeki's distrust of white medical expertise becomes more comprehensible, if not defensible.

While Mbeki's actions may appear idiosyncratic, they were actually consistent with his broader political project. During his tenure as president, Mbeki also resisted Western criticism of Robert Mugabe and his authoritarian regime in Zimbabwe. As we saw in Chapter 4, Mbeki repeatedly blocked British and U.S. efforts to sanction ZANU-PF and instead argued in favour of "quiet diplomacy" as part of his call for an African renaissance that would be characterized by the search for "African solutions to African problems". Mbeki's ill-fated attempt to promote Virodene rather that follow Western orthodoxy can be read as part of this wider agenda.

The president's ability to sustain his position on HIV/AIDS in the face of international criticism owed much to the fact that he initially faced relatively little domestic pressure to make tackling the disease a priority. On the one hand, ANC supporters were slow to criticize their leader, in large part because of the complex moral economy surrounding HIV/AIDS. The stigma associated with the illness, in which HIV/AIDS is often seen to be a punishment for immoral behaviour or a sign that those infected have been cursed with evil spirits (see Chapter 2), undermined the willingness of those with HIV to speak openly about their needs. Some brave campaigners were prepared to talk publicly about their experiences, including Gugu Dlamini, who was beaten to death by her neighbours after revealing her status on television in 1998, but many more did not. Even Nelson Mandela, with all of his legitimacy and authority, later admitted that he had not talked enough about HIV/AIDS during his presidency because the party was so focused on securing and maintaining power.

On the other hand, the ANC's electoral dominance meant that Mbeki could afford to be stubborn. As we have seen, by drawing on its status as the party of Mandela and national liberation while also providing housing and welfare payments to millions of voters, the ANC established itself as the most powerful political force in post-apartheid South Africa. In dominant-party systems such as Botswana, Namibia, and South Africa, voters remain free to punish the ruling party if they wish, but in practice the limited support for opposition parties means that changes in government policy rarely comes as a result of ruling parties responding to electoral imperatives. Rather, reform depends on the existence of an effective civil society, or change within the ruling party itself.

In the South African case, the reversal of Mbeki's HIV/AIDS policy owed much to the emergence of a vibrant popular movement led by the Treatment Action Campaign (TAC). In 2001, the TAC successfully appealed to the courts to reverse the ANC's policy on mother-to-child-transmissions, challenging Mbeki's approach to the disease. Internal changes within the ANC subsequently opened the door to more far-reaching reform when Jacob Zuma defeated Mbeki at the

Polokwane conference in 2007, replacing him first as party leader and then as president. Thereafter, AIDS denialism began to fade from the mainstream political scene.

It is important to note that Zuma's victory was not the result of Mbeki's reckless policy on HIV/AIDS. Instead, it was the president's economic policies, aloof attitude, and tendency to centralize power that proved his undoing. Nevertheless, the combination of internal party machinations, an effective civil society, and an independent judiciary enabled activists to change government policy over time. In a sense, democracy worked. But that it took so long is an important reminder that poor leadership, social attitudes, and a lack of political competition can lead to policies that are clearly detrimental to the welfare of citizens, even in the most open of political systems. This is important, because we principally value democracy because it allows individuals to participate in the decisions that affect their lives, and because we believe that transparent and accountable governments are more likely to make decisions that are in the public interest. While some Africans have enjoyed these democratic dividends, many have yet to do so.

Indeed, in some cases political competition has further alienated marginalized communities. This has been the case for the San Bushmen of southern Africa, who are often ignored in voter registration efforts, lack effective political representation, and thus remain largely excluded from the political system. The impact of multiparty politics has also been ambiguous with regards to the position of women, despite the support of influential Western donors, who have sought to promote female political participation. It is true that there have been some high profile successes. In a small number of countries that operate proportional representation (PR) systems, such as South Africa, party leaders have used their control over electoral lists to ensure parity between male and female candidates. A significant minority of states including Burundi, Rwanda, Tanzania, and Uganda have also introduced a quota system in which seats are reserved for women. As a result, the proportion of women in these legislatures has increased to world-leading levels (Tables 6.4 and 6.5).

However, in countries without formal quotas progress has been limited. Even in political systems where quotas have been employed, this has rarely translated into women being placed in the most senior ministries such as Finance, Defence, and Foreign Affairs. In 2005, Liberia's Ellen Johnson Sirleaf broke new ground, becoming the continent's first elected female head of state. But to date the only woman

TABLE 6.4 *Female representation in selected African legislatures*

	Quota	% of women in lower house (election year)
Rwanda	Y (30% + 24 appointed)	63.8 (2013)
Sweden	N	44.7 (2010)
Senegal	N	42.7 (2012)
South Africa	N*	40.8 (2014)
Tanzania	Y (20% minimum)	36 (2010)
Uganda	Y (24% + 25 appointed)	35 (2010)
Burundi	Y (30%)	30.5 (2010)
UK	N	22.5 (2010)
Cape Verde	N	20.8 (2011)
S.T & Principe	N	18.2 (2010)
USA	N	17.9 (2012)
Kenya	N	18.6 (2013)
Zambia	N	11.5 (2011)
Liberia	N**	11 (2011)
Ghana	N	10.9 (2012)
Botswana	N	7.9 (2009)
Nigeria	N	6.7 (2011)
Gambia	N	7.5 (2012)

* No formal quota but the Municipal Structures Act 1998 encourages parties to run gender-balanced slates.
** No formal quota but the Political Parties and Independents Registration Guidelines stipulate 30 per cent female composition of electoral lists.
Source: Inter-Parliamentary Union.

TABLE 6.5 *The proportion of women in national legislatures (2014)*

	Single house or lower house %	Upper house or senate %
Europe*	24.6	22.6
Americas	24.2	23.8
sub-Saharan Africa	21.1	18.7
Asia	19.1	13.8
Arab States	17.8	7.7
Pacific	13.1	38.6

* OSCE members, including the Nordic countries.
Source: Inter-Parliamentary Union.

who has emulated her example is Malawi's Joyce Banda, who came to power not by winning an election, but because she was vice president when President Bingu Mutharika died in office in April 2012 – and who subsequently lost power to his brother just two years later (Catherine Samba-Panza became the interim president of the CAR in 2014, but she was elected by the National Transitional Council rather than by the public). Moreover, there is no guarantee that the election of female leaders will actually promote gender equality. African democracies have typically failed to take sexual violence and the right of women to inherit land seriously, whether women are well represented in parliament or not (see Chapter 2).[7] As a result, men have typically retained their position at the apex of traditional leadership and patron-client networks, while the police and the courts have taken little action to defend women's political and economic rights.

Of course, there is nothing African about this story: the United States has never had a female president, the United Kingdom has only had one female prime minister, and women in Switzerland did not even get the vote until 1971. But it nonetheless serves as an important reminder that while political competition may create opportunities for formerly excluded groups to challenge the status quo, in the short-term democracy is as likely to reflect the existing social and political state of affairs as it is to transform it. The capacity for elections to reinforce the established social order is confirmed by the experience of the continent's longest-standing multiparty states, Botswana and Mauritius. Despite their democratic credentials, these states feature some of the lowest levels of female political representation and the largest disparities between female and male pay on the continent.

The Politics of Economic Growth

We have already seen that multiparty politics can exacerbate corruption and inequality (see Chapter 2) and that high-quality democracies may make poor policies. But we have also seen that multiparty elections encouraged leaders to reconnect with their supporters, and were an important driver of the introduction of free primary education

---

[7] Tripp, Aili Mari, and Alice Kang. "The Global Impact of Quotas: On the Fast Track to Increased Female Legislative Representation". *Comparative Political Studies* 41, 3 (2008), pp. 338–361.

across the continent. These contrasting observations raise the question of whether political reform has led governments to make more responsible economic decisions more generally?

Since the early 1990s there has been a steady improvement in the state of African economies. This matters for political as well as economic reasons, because well-managed economic growth can create jobs and enable the government to expand public services, which in turn is likely to boost popular support for democracy. However, is no consensus on why this has happened. The "good luck" school of thought emphasizes the fact that Africa has experienced a fortunate improvement in external conditions. In this interpretation, African resurgence has less to do with changes in domestic policy, and more to do with the rising demand for natural resources from countries such as China and India, which has pushed up the price of African exports. It is difficult to precisely calculate to what extent economic growth has been driven by the rising price of cotton, minerals, timber, and the like, but this has clearly been a significant factor in countries such as Zambia, which remains heavily reliant on copper exports.

A second line of thought is that the continent's improved economic performance reflects the long-term impact of the economic reforms promoted by international financial institutions. The "external expertise" school point out that in many African countries economic policy is strongly shaped by the IMF and the World Bank. Pressure to allow African governments to have a greater say in the running of their countries and to invest more heavily in public services encouraged the World Bank to abandon SAPs in favour of Poverty Reduction Strategy Papers (PRSPs) in 2003. However, the participatory ideal of PRSPs was rarely realized. In Ghana, for example, the proposals "put forward" by the government varied little from the initial document circulated for discussion by the World Bank.[8] Because some governments classify PRSPs as international treaties, which are not debated within parliament, economic policy is often deprived of intense scrutiny, which suggests that external influences on economic policy have been more important than domestic ones.

Although both of these explanations contain elements of truth, they do not tell the whole story. China has played an important role in turning African economies around (see Chapter 4), but private Chinese

---

[8] Whitfield, Lindsay. "Ghana: Aid Dependency and the Limits of Ownership" in Lindsay Whitfield (ed.), *The New Politics of Aid*. Oxford: Oxford University Press, 2008.

merchants have also taken important markets away from their African counterparts. Moreover, even if we only focus on the positive consequences of the rise of China, the high value of primary commodities does not explain why some African exporters are doing much better than others. It is also important to note that while Western financial institutions and governments retain an important role in shaping African economic policy, debt-relief programs have greatly reduced the amount that the poorest African governments need to pay to service their debt obligations. Combined with steady economic growth and the additional revenue generated by more effective tax authorities, this has made African governments less dependent on the IMF, World Bank, and foreign aid. As a result, they have gained greater leeway to determine their own economic priorities, which raises the question of what kinds of governments have managed their economies the most effectively.

Again, there is no consensus. Those who wish to fly the flag for democracy can point to the fact that three of the four fastest-growing African economies in 2012 were democratic: Ghana (8.2 per cent), Liberia (9 per cent), and Sierra Leone (22.3 per cent). The skeptics can retort that many of the countries that maintained the highest growth rates during the 2000s were not, most notably Angola, Ethiopia, and Rwanda. There are good arguments on both sides. David Booth and Tim Kelsall have suggested that democracies do not have a privileged position when it comes to delivering economic growth.[9] What matters, they argue, is whether a government is able to establish centralized control over patronage networks or not. In countries where patron-client networks are highly decentralized, so that everyone is out for themselves, corruption is particularly problematic because it leads to massive waste and inefficiency. Instead of being channelled into productive investments, such as roads and schools, state resources are lost to individual consumption: private jets, yachts, and foreign villas. By contrast, where patronage networks are centralized and well managed, they can be used to kick-start economic activity. This might happen if the ruling party uses state funds to set-up businesses and investment groups that stimulate new industries, for example by providing the funds necessary to get large-scale projects off the ground.

[9] For examples of their research see the website of the African Power and Politics research project, http://www.institutions-africa.org/publications/list.

200 DEMOCRACY IN AFRICA

Booth and Kelsall therefore conclude that patrimonialism itself is not the problem: what matters is the type of patrimonialism that emerges. Where there is tight central control, the pressure that clientelism places on the political system is less likely to spin out of control, and is thus more likely to give rise to productive economic activity – an outcome they refer to as "developmental patrimonialism". This suggests that in some ways authoritarian regimes may have an advantage, because presidents who operate under fewer constraints are more likely to be able to resist the political pressure to expand patronage networks to unsustainable levels. Booth and Kelsall give a range of examples of authoritarian regimes that have achieved something like the kind of developmentally patrimonial system they describe, including Kenya under President Jomo Kenyatta, Indonesia under General Suharto, and Rwanda under the post-genocide government of Paul Kagame.

This is a powerful argument that demands careful consideration, not least because so many efforts to promote sustained economic growth in Africa have met with abject failure. Booth and Kelsall are right to point out that neither authoritarianism nor corruption is incompatible with economic growth. The remarkable rise of China is testament to this. However, when it comes to the overall relationship between regime type and economic performance, the latest research suggests that on average democracies outperform their authoritarian counterparts. According to Musaki Takaaki and Nicolas van de Walle,[10] in the period 1982 to 2012 democracies have enjoyed significantly higher levels of economic growth than their authoritarian counterparts, even when a range of other relevant factors are also taken into account. They also find that the longer a country is a democracy the better its economic performance becomes, which makes sense because reforms take time to translate into outcomes. On the basis of these findings, they suggest that the greater incentives that democratic leaders face to implement policies that benefit their citizens, combined with the higher levels of accountability and transparency under which they operate, lead to more effective and responsible government over time.

The broader democratic dividend identified by Takaaki and van de Walle should make us think twice before we accept authoritarian

---

[10] Takaaki, Musaki, and Nicolas van de Walle. "The Impact of Democracy on Economic Growth in Africa". *UNU–WIDER,* Working Paper 057, 2014.

governments on the basis that they maintain order and have a good development record. As we saw at the end of Chapter 4, it has rarely proved possible to insulate economic gains from political losses in Africa. Authoritarian regimes on the continent have sometimes delivered high-quality economic performance in the short-term, but have rarely been able to sustain this in the long-term. Indeed, it is telling that many of the authoritarian cases of developmental patrimonialism identified by Booth and Kelsall did not actually end particularly well. For example, they highlight President Jomo Kenyatta's government in Kenya (1965–1975), which achieved reasonable levels of economic growth. But in the three years before Kenyatta died (1975–1978), the KANU regime became somewhat erratic. On the one hand, patronage was increasingly used to satisfy private needs. On the other, authoritarian excesses multiplied, as critics of the regime were locked up and in many cases abused. These practices subsequently span out of control under the leadership of Daniel arap Moi, whose excessive deployment of patrimonialism and coercion brought the country to its knees (see Chapter 2).

Similarly, Booth and Kelsall suggest that Uganda was a case of developmental patrimonialism under the first period of President Museveni's rule between 1986 and 2000. This begs the question of what happened after 2000. As we saw in Chapter 4, the answer is that as calls for democratic political reform became louder, Museveni's government became increasingly intransigent. Economic policy and foreign policy were manipulated for partisan political ends, while opposition leaders were regularly harassed. Although this has yet to undermine Uganda's economic performance, there is already evidence that the anticipated returns from recently discovered oil reserves are being misused to bolster the NRM's hold on power, which would represent a real missed opportunity to effect economic transformation.[11] Part of the reason for the deterioration in the quality of governance appears to be Museveni's determination to retain influence and control after term limits force him from the presidency. This does not bode well for the country's political or economic prospects.

The government of Paul Kagame in Rwanda is at an earlier stage of development, but as we shall see in the Conclusion, there are already signs that it may follow in the footsteps of Kenya and Uganda. This

---

[11] Vokes, Richard. "The Politics of Oil in Uganda". *African Affairs* 111, 443 (2013), pp. 303–314.

suggests that these kinds of authoritarian regimes are unlikely to continue to enjoy economic success in the long-term unless they find ways to more effectively accommodate political pressures – which they are rarely inclined to do. By contrast, economic growth in the continent's longest-standing democracies, Botswana and Mauritius, has now been sustained for more than sixty years. We therefore have both instrumental and intrinsic reasons to favour democracy in Africa.

It is important to note, however, that even under democratic conditions economic growth does not necessarily benefit the poor. In many countries, economic expansion has gone hand in hand with rising inequality. According to World Bank data, the five most unequal countries in the world in 2011 were all African: Botswana, the Comoros Islands, Namibia, Seychelles, and South Africa. That three of these countries are regularly listed as some of the most democratic states on the continent should not come as a surprise. As we saw in Chapter 2, leaders have often proved to be able to legitimate vast disparities in wealth, especially if public norms support neo-patrimonial networks in which patrons are always better off than their clients (see Chapter 2). When this is the case, there is no reason to think that allowing the public to have a say over economic policy will result in a more equal distribution of wealth, at least in the short-term. Thus, although the transition to multipartyism facilitated the introduction of important policies such as free primary education, it is likely that – in the short-term at least – the rich will get a lot richer while the poor become a little less impoverished.

Select Bibliography

Kelsall, Tim. *Business, Politics and the State in Africa: Challenging the Orthodoxies on Growth and Transformation*. London: Zed Books, 2013.

Lindberg, Staffan I. *Democracy and Elections in Africa*. Baltimore: John Hopkins University Press, 2006.

Posner, Daniel N., and Daniel J. Young. "The Institutionalization of Political Power in Africa". *Journal of Democracy* 18, 3 (2007), pp. 126–140.

Villalón, Leonardo Alfonso, and Peter VonDoepp. *The Fate of Africa's Democratic Experiments: Elites and Institutions*. Bloomington: Indiana University Press, 2005.

For a bibliography for this chapter go to www.democracyinafrica.org

CONCLUSION

Designing Democracy to Manage Diversity and Distrust

This book has documented the great variety of pathways through which African countries have moved toward, and away from, democracy. It started by highlighting some of the biggest challenges facing the consolidation of democracy in Africa. It ends by considering how new multiparty systems can best be designed to promote democratization while maintaining stability in the African context. This question is as important and pressing today as it has ever been, as the tragic case of South Sudan demonstrates only too well. Back in 2011, South Sudan was a name that inspired celebrations and optimism. Following a prolonged and bloody civil war that pitted the Sudanese government against the Sudan People's Liberation Army (SPLA) and a number of other rebel groups, the South became independent on 9 July amidst great fanfare. In preparation for government, the Sudan People's Liberation Movement (SPLM), the political wing of the SPLA, began the long process of transforming the rebel group into a civilian political party, pledging to put past differences aside in order to focus on the task of national reconstruction.

Just two years later, this early optimism had turned to a deep sense of foreboding. Continuing tension between Sudan and South Sudan remained a serious source of concern, but was quickly overshadowed by mounting tensions between different factions of the SPLM itself. As an internal power struggle between President Salva Kirr and Vice-President Riek Machar spiralled out of control, Kirr dismissed his entire cabinet – including Machar – on 24 July. Just six months later, Kirr accused Machar of trying to seize power in a coup and subsequently charged him with treason. As the alleged coup plotters were rounded up, rebel factions seized several towns, precipitating a descent into civil war.

Many journalists were quick describe the conflict in terms of an ethnic struggle between Kiir's Dinka and Mahar's Nuer, and to interpret the collapse of the government as evidence that South Sudan's fragmented society was not ready for democracy. But much of the academic literature that followed suggested a very different interpretation. Ethnic tensions were clearly important, and hardened as the violence escalated, but this was no re-run of events in Rwanda (chapter 5). Kiir and Machar had friends and allies on both sides of the ethnic divide, and following the outbreak of fighting in the capital Juba, many of those targeted by uniformed units were sheltered by their neighbours, with 'Dinka protecting Nuer, Dinka and Nuer combining to patrol their neighbourhoods'.[1] The collapse of the government of South Sudan was thus not the inevitable consequence of ancient "tribal rivalries", but the product of fearful and irresponsible political leadership. Kiir marginalized Machar not because he was from a different community, but because the president was worried that he would lose control to a rival SPLM faction and wanted to monopolize the political and economic benefits of office for himself. The problem was thus not so much one of ethnicity, but a lack of political inclusion.

The experience of South Sudan and the countries discussed in chapter 5 demonstrates the importance of establishing inclusive political systems in which factions and parties that fail to secure the presidency are still able to participate in government. But what is the right balance between competition and inclusion? History tells us that while elements of competition and inclusion strengthen multiparty systems, too much of either can be fatal to the process of democratization. Let us start with competition. In Côte d'Ivoire and Kenya, where political competition went wholly untamed and losing parties were completely excluded from access to state resources, elections encouraged ethnic conflict and the collapse of political order (see Chapter 5). The experience of these states was so harrowing that it is tempting to conclude that countries should try and be as inclusive as possible, for example by forming a permanent power-sharing government. But maximizing the level of inclusion is also problematic because doing so

---

[1] Douglas Johnson, "The Crisis in South Sudan", *African Affairs*, 114, 435 (2014), pp. 300-309.

inevitably stifles political competition, which is the lifeblood of representative democracy. It is by kicking out bad leaders that voters hold their governments to account. Recall that in Ghana and Senegal democratic reform was driven by opposition parties, who campaigned for freer and fairer elections to improve their own chances of winning power (see Chapter 6). Because power-sharing systems guarantee all parties representation in government, they threaten to undermine the very mechanism through which elections can drive democratization. Excessive inclusion is therefore just as bad for democracy as excessive competition.

The task facing those who draft or adapt state constitutions is thus to decide on the appropriate balance between competition and inclusion – one that allows for sufficient accommodation so that all parties feel they have a stake in the system, while maintaining as much competition as possible in order to promote accountability. Unfortunately, there is no ideal constitutional template that can be deployed across the continent to achieve this goal, because different countries require different degrees of inclusion in order to achieve political stability. Judging whether a given political system can bear the strains associated with higher levels of competition requires an intimate knowledge of a country's demography, geography, and political history. Even then, political scientists, lawyers, and constitutional experts often get it wrong. There are no easy decisions when it comes to designing democracy.

Managing Diversity

Institutional design is not the only way to manage diversity. Following independence, African leaders adopted a number of different strategies of cultural engineering, from pluralist accommodation of sub-national cultures through to the aggressive promotion of a particular national vision. Perhaps the most celebrated was Julius Nyerere's attempt to build a coherent Tanzanian national identity out of the country's mosaic of around 120 small ethnic groups following independence in 1961. Nyerere's strategy involved using the presidency to promulgate a new national identity, underpinned by the promotion of Swahili as a national language, the adoption of a set of national cultural symbols, and a school syllabus that included moral education to teach Tanzanians their "responsibilities". Along with the unifying figure of Nyerere himself, who is still referred to affectionately many years after his death in 1999, these policies supported the emergence of a real sense of "Tanzanianness" which, on the mainland at least, has never been threatened by ethnic or religious cleavages. Nyerere's success demonstrates that top-down nation-building strategies can be effective in even the most diverse of African countries.

However, Nyerere enjoyed advantages denied to many of his counterparts in the 1990s. Most obviously, the colonial period in Tanzania did not politicize communal identities in the way that it did in countries such as Kenya and Nigeria, and so Nyerere did not face the challenge of demobilizing established ethno-regional political networks. By contrast, many of the leaders of African states today have inherited societies that are already deeply divided after decades of conflict. Nyerere's nation-building project also benefitted from being undertaken in the context of a one-party state that suppressed national-level political competition and so empowered the executive to manage dissent (see Chapter 1). Contemporary African leaders face a far greater challenge: to build a nation in the context of divisive multiparty competition.

Another significant factor that assisted Nyerere's project was the widespread use of Swahili as a lingua franca in Tanzania, which meant that language could operate as a force of unity, rather than division. Taken together with the small size of most ethnic groups, this made it easier for Nyerere to persuade Tanzanians to trade in their sub-national identities in favour of a new national identity. Demobilizing ethnic politics has proved to be a far harder proposition in countries where ethnic groups are larger, because aspiring politicians are much more likely to employ ethnic strategies when their community is sizeable enough to confer a national profile on its leaders.

Attempts to impose a particular national culture in more difficult circumstances, such as in the aftermath of civil conflict, have typically relied on greater use of coercion. When the former rebels of the RPF took power in Rwanda following the 1994 genocide (see Chapters 4 and 5), they had to decide how to deal with the legacy of inter-ethnic violence between the Hutu and Tutsi communities. President Kagame's government, which was predominantly Tutsi at senior levels, responded by aggressively promoting a national identity that officially rejected ethnic labels. But while this strategy was presented as ethnically neutral, in reality it served to justify the consolidation of political control. Kagame's official line that there were no

Hutus or Tutsis, just Rwandans, sounded good in principle. However, in practice the RPF's depiction of the genocide only recognized Tutsi victims and Hutu perpetrators. In doing so, it intentionally sidelined discussion of the atrocities committed by RPF troops in the wake of the genocide, and denied the legitimate expression of the hopes and fears of the Hutu community.

Of course, the RPF's nation-building strategy in Rwanda must be understood in the context of the unique horrors of the genocide. As a Tutsi leader in an overwhelmingly Hutu country, it was natural that Kagame would make maintaining political order his number-one priority. The new president was also wary of the danger of being seen to be a foreigner by parts of the Tutsi community, having left Rwanda at the age of three and subsequently enjoyed a relatively privileged life in Uganda. Playing on the narrative of Tutsi victimhood enabled him – and other members of the diaspora who returned to take up prominent political positions after 1994 – to legitimate their positions by identifying themselves with the suffering of those who had stayed behind.

Although the contradictions at the heart of the RPF's nation-building efforts were the product of an exceptional context, they nonetheless reflect the tensions that are likely to arise when governments attempt to impose a single unifying national character onto a set of distinctive and deeply felt ethno-regional identities. In states where citizens feel a closer attachment to their ethnicity than to their country, the adoption of institutions that allow for the interests of each group to be accommodated within a common political framework may be necessary to manage social tensions. One model of how this can be done is provided by Burundi. When multiparty politics was reintroduced in the early 1990s, Burundi stood out as one of the countries in which political competition was likely to exacerbate social division. Although the population was 85 per cent Hutu, the country's first three post-colonial presidents were all Tutsis, and for long periods Hutus were marginalized in both government and the security forces. As in Rwanda, an individual's ethnicity came to determine their political and economic opportunities and this, along with bouts of inter-ethnic violence, served to entrench ethnic divisions. While conflict was often the product of the political calculations of self-interested leaders rather than primordial ethnic animosities, violence was nonetheless expressed in ethnic terms, most notably in 1972 when the predominantly Tutsi military killed between 80,000 and 210,000 Hutus.

Fast forward to the early 1990s, and Burundi was under the control of President Buyoya, who had come to power in a coup in 1987. Despite the salience of identities and the fact that he was a Tutsi leader in a majority Hutu country, Buyoya subsequently agreed to reintroduce competitive presidential elections in 1993. He did so partly as a result of international pressure, and partly because he hoped that his decision to introduce an ethnically balanced cabinet in 1988 would make it easier to mobilize across the ethnic divide. It was a massive miscalculation. At the polls, Hutu voters largely rejected "Tutsi" parties in favour of a predominantly Hutu organization, the Front for Democracy in Burundi (FRODEBU), whose presidential candidate, Melchior Ndadaye, won 65 per cent of the vote. FRODEBU's victory dismayed the Tutsi establishment, who were unwilling to give up their control over key state institutions, most notably control over the army.

Just five months later, President Ndadaye was assassinated by a group of Tutsi soldiers who intended to overthrow his government. The coup was only partly successful, but triggered a wave of violence that left around 50,000 dead and 1 million displaced and led to the creation of a United Nations Office in Burundi (UNOB) to broker peace talks. As usual, power-sharing was high on the agenda of international mediators (see Chapter 4). A series of negotiations led to the signing of the Convention of Government in 1994, which established a form of unity government in which 55 per cent of the ministries were allocated to FRODEBU and 45 per cent to the Union for National Progress (UPRONA), a predominantly Tutsi organization. Provincial governorships and administrative positions were also divided along roughly equal lines.

The use of power-sharing measures was not new. Following Buyoya's example, Ndadaye had appointed an ethnically balanced cabinet that deliberately over-represented the Tutsi community – even though he had secured a significant electoral mandate on the basis of largely Hutu support. The 1994 agreements codified this practice of ethnic accommodation, laying down a blueprint for subsequent peace agreements. However, the deal disappointed many. Most significantly, it did not include key rebel groups, failed to compensate Hutu leaders who demanded that the result of the 1993 elections be upheld, and ducked the critical question of what to do with the Tutsi-dominated army. The situation in Burundi was also complicated by events over the border in Rwanda. When the plane carrying the Rwandan President, Juvénal Habyarimana, was shot down in 1994, the Burundian President

Cyprien Ntaryamira – who had only been appointed by parliament that January – also perished in the crash, leaving the country without a leader. At the same time, the news that Habyarimana's death had triggered the mass killings of Tutsis by Rwanda's Hutu-led government created widespread unease in Burundi, where tensions between Tutsis and Hutus were also on the rise. Given this context, few observers were surprised when conflict resumed with fresh intensity. Against the backdrop of a deteriorating security situation and fresh clashes throughout the country, forces loyal to Buyoya initiated a coup that successfully returned the former president to power.

Over the next ten years, the search for a lasting peace led negotiators to broaden and deepen the provisions of the 1994 agreement in order to encourage rebel groups to engage in the process, shifting the balance between competition and inclusion firmly in favour of the latter. The deal that emerged laid the foundations for the most inclusive political system ever realized in Africa. The 2004 Power-Sharing Agreement and the 2005 constitution ensured systematic ethnic balancing, securing Tutsi support by guaranteeing the over-representation of the minority group. Thus, Hutus were not allowed to comprise more than 60 per cent of the cabinet and the national assembly, despite making up more than 80 per cent of the population. A separate stipulation that legislation could only be passed with a two-thirds majority in the national assembly effectively gave Tutsi parliamentarians a veto over government policy. Ethnic balance in the senate was maintained by a provision that the two representatives to be elected from each province could not come from the same ethnic group. The rest of the political system was governed by similar provisions: under the constitution, the president could not come from the same community as the two vice presidents and political parties had to ensure that no more than two-thirds of their candidates were from the same ethnic group. Significantly, the principle of ethnic balancing was extended to the national police and intelligence services for the first time, offering a partial solution to the issue of how to manage the security forces.

This system effectively reduced the costs of losing an election, because it guaranteed Tutsis political representation and jobs whatever the outcome of the polls. As a result, power-sharing measures helped to generate a more stable political environment ahead of the elections of 2005. This time, the polls were contested by FRODEBU, the National Council for the Defence of Democracy–Forces for the Defence of Democracy (CNDD-FDD) – a Hutu led former rebel group – and a number of smaller political parties. The campaign did not pass without incident: voting in some areas was disrupted by rebel factions that continued to challenge the legitimacy of the process, FRODEBU deliberately attempted to mobilize voters by demonizing the CNDD-FDD, and a number of parties alleged that they had been victims of electoral malpractice. However, voting proceeded smoothly and when Pierre Nkurunziza and the CNDD-FDD emerged victorious the results were quickly accepted by all parties.

The new inclusive political arrangements also had a positive impact on inter-communal relations. Most notably, the strict regulations on ethnic balancing forced parties to recruit candidates and supporters from different communities, leading to the creation of cross-ethnic political networks. Thus, in contrast to the 1993 elections in which most parties were seen to be vehicles for the advancement of a particular ethnic group, in 2005 the largest parties ran multi-ethnic slates, reducing the political salience of the Hutu-Tutsi divide. Of course, ethnic balancing is not a silver bullet. The measures introduced in the Power-Sharing Agreement and the constitution were important, but the 2005 polls would have been far less successful if the population had not been so weary of war, and the international community had not mobilized a 5,500-strong UN peacekeeping force. Moreover, while former rebel factions refrained from open confrontation during the polls, violence continued to be a part of everyday life and the victory of the CNDD-FDD owed much to the party's ability to coerce the countryside. At the same time, one of the rebel groups, the Palipehutu-National Liberation Forces (FNL), did not participate in the elections, and although it officially lay down its arms in 2009, clashes with the CNDD-FDD continued.

The limitations of the new political arrangements became clear in the years following the election, as President Nkurunziza moved to consolidate his hold on power. The checks and balances embedded in the constitution forced Nkurunziza to look for new ways to marginalize opposition, but could not prevent him from finding and pursuing them. As the president sought to stamp his control on an unwieldy political system, his government became increasingly authoritarian, using coercion to intimidate rivals, and purchasing the loyalty of judges and legislators in order to weaken key institutions. This process of democratic backsliding ensured that the general elections of 2010 were much more contentious than their predecessor. Following alleged government manipulation of local polls in May, opposition candidates boycotted the presidential elections, depriving them of legitimacy. Fears of renewed conflict were further exacerbated by violent clashes between rival parties in 2011. All told, the Burundian case thus provides strong evidence, if it were needed, that while a new constitution can help to stabilise multiparty political systems, it is no substitute for political will and the rule of law.

The Politics of Inclusion

The system of political inclusion established in Burundi comes close to the model advocated by Arendt Lijphart, who has spent much of his career arguing that divided societies would be best served by what he calls "consociational" democracy. Although the title is somewhat awkward, the heart of Lijphart's argument is actually fairly straightforward: political systems are more likely to be seen to be legitimate, and hence stable, if different communities feel that they are included in government and that their core interests are protected by the status quo.

Based on the system of government that was introduced in the Netherlands in 1911, and similar systems in Belgium and Lebanon, Lijphart proposed four main mechanisms for promoting inclusion. First, a power-sharing cabinet in which all of the main political parties can experience a taste of executive power. Second, the extension of this principle of accommodation throughout the political system, with all state positions from the bureaucracy to the police force distributed in proportion to the size of ethnic groups within the wider population. Third, a minority veto, which would enable every community to block policies that they find unacceptable. Fourth, a form of federalism in which communities would be given a degree of self-government over issues that only affect them. In terms of government policy, this would involve allowing a community to establish its own schools and to regulate its own cultural and religious practices. In cases where communities are located in different parts of the country, this might take the form of a federal political system in which groups are allowed a degree of local self-government within sub-national provinces or regions.

Ljiphart argued that when implemented together these measures would ensure the representation of minorities at the highest level of government, foster elite cooperation, and render disagreements between different communities less explosive. As a result, he believed that it was the ideal form of political system for Africa's divided societies.[2] However, because ruling parties are rarely prepared to dilute their hold on power, and international donors have little experience of many of these mechanisms, consociational political systems are rare. Indeed, given the potential for winner-takes-all politics to destabilize African states it is remarkable how few inclusive mechanisms have been employed (see Table C.1). Only three countries have implemented a federal system and ethnic quotas are equally rare. A considerable minority of states employ proportional representation in their electoral systems, which make it easier for small minorities to secure representation in the legislature, and this has gone some way to softening the divisive impact of political competition in some cases (although not all, as we shall see later). However, most of the countries that employ PR also feature political systems in which real power resides not with the legislature but with the president. This is problematic, because presidential elections, in which only one person can emerge victorious, are inherently winner takes all (Table C.2).

To some extent the preponderance of presidentialism is mitigated by the fact that the vast majority of African presidents now need to secure more than 50 per cent of the vote to win power: if no candidate wins an absolute majority in the first round, a run-off is held between the top two candidates. This means that leaders cannot be elected on a tiny fraction of the vote. As a result, they often need to build support from across the political spectrum in order to win office. For example, it is not uncommon for the two candidates who qualify for the run-off to compete for the endorsement of those leaders forced to drop out, offering them ministerial positions or other rewards to secure their support. This creates an imperative to form alliances similar to the need to form multi-ethnic coalitions that emerged in Kenya (Chapter 6). However, the limited checks and balances on the executive in many African states mean that once the election is over presidents are often able to avoid keeping their promises, and so there is no guarantee that power will actually be shared.

This is not to say that political inclusion is a panacea. Each of the mechanisms identified by Lijphart has a drawback, and these reveal the costs of inclusion. Constitutional design is such a difficult balancing

---

[2] Lijphart, Arend. "South African Democracy: Majoritarian or Consociational?" *Democratization* 5, 4 (1998), pp. 144–150.

TABLE C.1 *Inclusive political arrangements employed in Africa*

Federalism	Ethiopia, Nigeria, South Africa
Second chamber*	<u>Appointed</u>: Senegal, Somaliland, South Sudan <u>Elected</u>: Kenya, Liberia, Nigeria, Zimbabwe <u>Indirectly elected</u>: Burundi, Cameroon, DRC, Ethiopia, Gabon, Rep. Of Congo, Madagascar, Mauritania, Namibia, Rwanda, South Africa, Sudan <u>Hereditary</u>: Lesotho
Proportional representation in lower house	Angola, Benin, Burkina Faso, Burundi, Cape Verde, DRC**, E. Guinea, Guinea**, G. Bissau, Mozambique, Namibia, Niger**, Rwanda, S.T. and Principe, Senegal**, Seychelles**, Somaliland, South Africa, Togo
Constitutionalized power-sharing	Burundi
Rotation of presidency***	Comoros, Nigeria (informal)
Ethnic quotas/ balancing in legislature	Burundi, Mauritius, Somaliland

Notes: Somaliland is included for illustrative purposes even though its sovereignty is not internationally recognized.

* Elected = majority elected (even if some appointed), Indirectly elected = majority indirectly elected (even if some appointed), Hereditary = majority hereditary peers (even if some appointed), all others are majority appointed (even if some directly or indirectly elected).

** Denotes countries that use parallel voting systems, where a proportion of members are elected using first-past-the-post, and others using proportional representation.

*** Between ethnic groups or regions; constitutionalized unless otherwise stated.

act precisely because it involves a series of difficult trade-offs. To name just a few: power-sharing may generate stability, but can also empower poorly performing and corrupt parties to remain in power; federalism may help to deflect competition away from the political centre, but does so at the risk of relocating conflict to the local level; and, electoral systems can be tweaked to ensure that minorities are never excluded, but this may institutionalize the political salience of ethnicity and so prevent an ethnically blind polity from evolving. Thus, while building accommodation into the political system can be a useful mechanism through which to manage inter-group tensions, it creates new challenges for every problem it resolves.

TABLE C.2 *The executive format of African political systems*

Prime Ministers	Presidents		
	Elected by parliament*	**Directly elected under FPTP****	**Directly elected under two-round runoff**
Ethiopia***	**Angola**	**Cameroon**	Benin
Lesotho	Botswana	**DRC**	**Burkina Faso**
Mauritius	South Africa	**E. Guinea**	Burundi
		The Gambia	**Cape Verde**
		Gabon	**CAR**
		Malawi	**Chad**
		Tanzania	Comoros
		Zambia	**Rep. Of Congo**
			Cote d'Ivoire
			Guinea
			G. Bissau
			Kenya
			Liberia
			Madagascar
			Mali
			Mauritania
			Mozambique
			Namibia
			Niger
			Nigeria
			Rwanda
			S.T Principe
			Senegal
			Seychelles
			Sierra Leone
			South Sudan
			Sudan
			Togo
			Uganda
			Zimbabwe

* Although these countries call their executives "president", in reality they are appointed by the legislature and not directly by the people and so conform to the parliamentary model of government.

** FPTP = first past the post electoral system, in which whoever secures the most votes wins even if they do not have an absolute majority.

*** Like some other countries, Ethiopia has both a prime minister and a president. In the Ethiopian case, it is the prime minister that is the most powerful.

The Perils of Power-Sharing

Despite the increasing use of power-sharing to resolve conflict, its costs are rarely considered. Peace in Burundi, for example, came at the price of rewarding armed rebel groups first by including them in negotiations and then by enabling them to secure political power – even though many factions had little connection to the wider population. Moreover, because the Power-Sharing Agreement over-represented the Tutsi minority in order to secure the compliance of Tutsi elites, many Hutu viewed it as undemocratic. Indeed, one reason that the Palipehutu–FNL rebels continued to fight was that they wanted to realize a political system that would fully reflect the numerical dominance of the Hutu community. Power-sharing helped Burundi to get back on its feet, then, but in many citizens' eyes it left the country with a democratic deficit.

In Burundi, the benefits of political inclusion were worth the costs. The Power-Sharing Agreement was a compromise arrived at through a long process of trial and error because previous less inclusive schemes had failed. But the popularity of power-sharing with international mediators – and some African governments – has meant that it has recently been deployed in countries that have not suffered civil war, and where the costs and benefits are very different. Take Kenya and Zimbabwe. In 2008 both countries suffered an election-related political crisis because sitting presidents refused to accept electoral defeat (for full details see Chapters 4 and 5). In both cases, the crisis was "resolved" by the creation of a government of national unity.

In Kenya, a deal brokered by Kofi Annan and supported by a range of regional and international governments allowed President Mwai Kibaki to retain the presidency. Opposition leader Raila Odinga had to make do with the newly created post of prime minister. Although cabinet posts were split equally, Kibaki's Party of National Unity (PNU) refused to give up control of the more significant positions, including foreign affairs, finance, home affairs, defence, and internal security, and so was well placed to dominate the cabinet and the government. International support for power-sharing thus enabled a discredited leader to remain in office, and in the process set a dangerous precedent that disputed elections would be resolved in favour of the incumbent. A similar power-sharing agreement in Zimbabwe that allowed Robert Mugabe to retain the presidency despite his deployment of brutal violence reinforced this problematic norm. However, it is worth noting that British and U.S. opposition to the Zimbabwe deal, and concerted international efforts to prevent President Laurent Gbagbo from clinging on to power in Côte d'Ivoire following his electoral defeat in December 2010, subsequently demonstrated that there were limits to what the international community was prepared to tolerate.

This is good news, because in Kenya and Zimbabwe the power-sharing arrangements that were put in place strengthened the position of authoritarian incumbents. In both countries, opposition parties struggled to maintain their momentum within the context of governments of national unity. Part of the problem was that ODM and MDC supporters expected that now that their leaders were in power they would be rewarded for their loyalty. However, because the opposition were generally given less important ministries, their influence was limited. Odinga and Tsvangirai also struggled to differentiate their own positions from the governments within which they operated. In Kenya, for example, ODM found it difficult to articulate what they had achieved in office, as opposed to what had been delivered by the PNU. At the same time, power-sharing gave Kibaki and Mugabe the time they required to reorganize and prepare for the next elections. It is thus no coincidence the ODM and the MDC both performed far worse in the post-power-sharing elections than they had done in 2007/2008.

Power-sharing was also problematic because it blunted the capacity for political competition to act as the motor of democratic reform. Towards the end of the presidency of Daniel arap Moi, and during president Kibaki's first term in office, opposition legislators successfully campaigned to free parliament from its financial dependence on the executive, and used their powers of scrutiny to expose corruption within the government. These reforms only scratched the surface of the corruption at the heart of Kenyan politics, but they did suggest that those in power would have to be more careful in the future. As we have seen, in 2005 the ODM even defeated the government in a constitutional referendum (see Chapter 5). But following the creation of the power-sharing administration in which everyone was formally in government, it was unclear who was responsible for fulfilling this role. One reason for this was the remarkable fluidity of Kenyan politics, which led to the rapid breakdown of party identities. This had both positive and negative consequences. On the plus side, Kibaki and Odinga were able to put aside their differences to briefly join forces in support of a new constitution that significantly reduced the powers of the president, rolling the clock back to the heady days of NaRC's 2002 election campaign when the two men had campaigned together.

On the down side, incorporating the opposition into government exacerbated the tendency for Kenyan politicians to protect their own interests at the expense of the public. Because representatives from both of the main parties were implicated in the post-election violence, a broad range of MPs had an interest in maintaining the country's culture of impunity. Most notably, two leaders who feared that they would be prosecuted for their role in the clashes, the PNU's Uhuru Kenyatta and the ODM's William Ruto, formed an anti-reform alliance in the shadow of the power-sharing deal. Consequently, although the two parties traded accusations of corruption and wrong doing, little was actually done to hold ministers to account. Instead, Kenyatta and Ruto marshalled MPs from both sides of the house to protect themselves and their allies. This may have happened even if Kenya had not pursued power-sharing. But the formation of a government of national unity exacerbated this tendency because so many MPs benefitted from being in government – and hence were unwilling to speak out against their colleagues – that there was never a serious attempt to cut down on the misuse of public funds. A similar process undermined the will of the political class to act against the perpetrators of electoral violence. When the failure of the National Assembly to establish a credible domestic mechanism to prosecute those suspected of organizing the post-election violence prompted the International Criminal Court (ICC) to indict seven prominent leaders including Kenyatta and Ruto, Kenyan legislators responded by unanimously voting to withdraw from the ICC.[3]

While power-sharing came at a heavy cost, the benefits it delivered were only temporary. In contrast to the kind of constitutionalized measures advocated by Lijphart, power-sharing in Kenya and Zimbabwe was adopted as an isolated reform in order to persuade elite actors to buy into the formal political process until fresh polls could be held. Because the agreements lapsed before the next round of elections, different communities and parties had no guarantee that they would be represented in any future government. As a result, the stakes of electoral competition remained dangerously high. Thus,

---

[3] This move was largely symbolic as Kenya remained bound by its previous commitments under the Rome Statute.

although the creation of a government of national unity helped to bring political violence under control, it did not lay a strong foundation for long-term political stability. Although the 2013 presidential and parliamentary elections in Kenya passed largely without incident, all of the ingredients for election violence remain. The limited form of political inclusion that was employed following democratic deadlock in Kenya and Zimbabwe was therefore less beneficial than the comprehensive and permanent set of arrangements employed in Burundi.

Federalism and the Decentralization of Conflict in Nigeria

Nigeria is rare in the African context for enshrining a division of power and responsibilities between central government and sub-national states in its constitution. By contrast, most of the rest of the continent remains highly centralized, although countries such as Kenya, Mali, Malawi, and Uganda feature varying degrees of decentralization.

Given Nigeria's astonishing size and diversity it is hard to imagine it being governed by anything other than a federal system: the country covers some 577,355 square miles populated by more than 100 million people that are roughly half Christian and half Muslim, and can be further broken down into more than 200 ethnic groups that speak an estimated 4,000 dialects. Under British rule, Nigeria became a three-unit federal structure in 1954, with the states designed to represent the country's largest ethnic groups, the Igbo (east), Yoruba (west), and Hausa-Fulani (north). As we saw in Chapter 1, this system was ill-advised; it served to entrench the hegemony of these groups within their respective territories and to pit them against each other when it came to electing a national government. It also created a regional power base for each ethnic community that was sufficiently large and powerful to be able to challenge the overall system, and thus contributed to the attempted secession of the Eastern Region and the subsequent civil war.

Just prior to the civil war, General Gowon had moved to reform the design of the federal system, increasing the number of states from three to twelve. The borders of some of the new states were designed to allow smaller ethnic groups to achieve self-government, and hence to reduce the power of the three main ethno-regional blocks. In 1966, this threat to Igbo hegemony had presented the Eastern government with an additional reason to try and break away from Nigeria to form the Republic of Biafra. But following the defeat of Biafra in 1970 and the reassertion of national unity, the new federal dispensation also emerged as a structure through which inter-ethnic mutual accommodation could be more successfully pursued. Over time, the federal government found it far easier to manage smaller states, many of which were financially dependent on the centre. Moreover, a range of regional elites became preoccupied with the opportunities offered by local public office, easing the pressure on central government. Consequently, disputes over the distribution of power and resources became less likely to result in the fragmentation of the state.

In some ways it is a little surprising that federalism captured the public imagination, given the limited powers that were devolved to the states for much of Nigeria's postcolonial existence.[4] During the period 1984–1999 the military government used the cloak of federalism to legitimate the centralization of economic control: although the number of states went up, the proportion of government revenue devolved to state governments declined from 40 per cent in 1983 to 20 per cent in 1995. The share of government resources going to the states later increased substantially following the reintroduction of multiparty politics in 1999, breathing fresh life into the federal structure, but in the 1980s Nigeria remained a centralized state in federal clothing. However, despite the large gap between federalism's promise and its reality, the opportunity to take up lucrative jobs and establish patronage networks through regional and local government enabled aspiring leaders who lost out nationally to win locally. As state revenue increased, so did the capacity of the federal system to divert the energies and attention of a range of political entrepreneurs: by 2010, the budget of Rivers State, where much of Nigeria's oil wealth is to be found, was a staggering $2.82 billion.

As the federal system became embedded in the national political culture, a range of minority groups across the country began to campaign for the creation of new states in which they hoped to become the local majority. Successive governments responded by using state creation as a way to respond to local grievances. But because of Nigeria's deeply fragmented ethnic mosaic, the more states that were formed, the more minorities mobilized for their own opportunity to taste the fruits of self-government, giving rise to a seemingly inexhaustible demand for greater decentralization. Consequently, the number of

---

[4] Suberu, Rotimi. *Federalism and Ethnic Conflict in Nigeria.* Washington, DC: United States Institute of Peace, 2001.

states increased to nineteen in 1976, twenty-one in 1987, thirty in 1991, and thirty-six in 1996. In turn, the proliferation of states undermined the ability of each individual state to check the power of central government and also made it less feasible for any one state to seriously pursue secession.

In terms of conflict management at the national level, the arrangements introduced from the late 1960s onward have clearly been a success. Nigeria is one of the only countries in Africa to have had avoided a second civil war after suffering a first. It is also important to note, though, that federalism was also underpinned by a number of political arrangements that were developed by the Nigerian political class in order to be able to cope with the challenges posed by the country's ethno-regional diversity. Significantly, party competition came to be regulated by a set of home-grown agreements, most notably that the presidency should rotate between the north and south of the country. This informal mechanism gave rise to a political system in which power could be shared between different communities over time, reducing the stakes of electoral competition and the prospects for political conflict at the national level.

There is also a serious question as to whether federalism actually reduced political violence, or just transformed it. The national obsession with state formation, and the principle that local groups could benefit by securing a state of their own, magnified the importance of who could, and could not, claim to be indigenous to a particular area. In turn, this exacerbated existing tensions between different ethnic and religious groups. The focus of questions of belonging, combined with the willingness of political godfathers to bankroll local politicians and their thugs (see Chapter 5), intensified local struggles as self-proclaimed "indigenes" sought to prevent "settlers" from exercising political rights within their area. One consequence of this is that demands for new states, and competition for the control of states, have become increasingly violent.

Consider the protests of the small Ogoni community in Rivers State against the scant benefits the group received from the sale of the oil that is sourced from under their feet. Although much Ogoni frustration was directed at the symbols of their exploitation such as the oil companies, the security forces, and the central government, the episodes of violence have punctuated their campaign were also fuelled by the politics of state creation. The campaign of Ogoni leaders for greater rights for their people initially focused on securing a separate Rivers Province, then later a Rivers State, and more recently a Port Harcourt state, in which the Ogoni would be a majority, free from domination by the more numerous Ijaw group. Although Ogoni rhetoric focused on the environmental destruction of the Niger Delta under their best-known leader, Ken Saro-Wiwa, the attempt to create an Ogoni state brought the group into conflict with other communities who stood to lose out if the country's electoral map was redrawn. In turn, such clashes, some of which Ogoni leaders believe were deliberately aggravated by the government, contributed to the destabilization of the Niger Delta. Thus, while federalism helped to decrease the pressure on the political centre, it exacerbated demands at the local level: political conflict was not resolved, but decentralized.

In the Niger Delta region, the situation remains bleak. When periods of relative peace and stability have been achieved, they have typically been the product of amnesty programmes in which militants are paid considerable sums to cease their activities. The extension of patron-client co-optation to the politics of peacemaking was in some ways a natural development given the neo-patrimonial nature of Nigerian politics. But it nonetheless represents a worryingly expensive and unsustainable conflict management strategy. Federalism can help to maintain national political stability, then, but it is no silver bullet.

Electoral Design and the Mauritius Miracle

Although the people of Mauritius may not consider themselves to be African, the small island located 3,000 kilometres off the Tanzanian coast has much to teach us about how to manage multiparty politics in a diverse society. At the point of independence in 1968, Mauritian society was deeply fragmented. Of the 1.1 million inhabitants, 68 per cent were South Asian, 27 per cent Creole of African ancestry, 3 per cent Chinese, and 2 per cent Franco-Mauritian. Religious divides further complicated the picture: of the South Asian majority, around half were Hindu while about one-sixth were Muslim. It is true that because all of the main ethno-regional communities arrived in Mauritius relatively recently, the country has been saved the kind of divisive debates about which groups are indigenous that drove civil conflict in Côte d'Ivoire, Kenya, and Nigeria. But even so, relations between these groups began poorly and so Mauritius has also had to find innovative ways to manage diversity.

In the last colonial election of 1967, riots between Creoles and Muslims broke out that could easily have been the forerunner of post-colonial conflict. Indeed, the potential for democratic consolidation appeared decidedly shaky in 1971 when rising economic problems and by-election successes for the opposition Mauritian Militant Movement (MMM) encouraged the government to declare a spurious state of emergency and to cancel the first post-independence elections. Yet despite such unstable foundations, a combination of inclusive leadership, clever institutional design, and the emergence of a set of political norms around the way state resources should be shared supported the evolution of one of the continent's most competitive and successful democracies.

Early on, Mauritius adopted a set of electoral laws that were intended to occupy a middle ground between winner-takes-all competition and power-sharing.[5] Legislative elections were organized on the basis of a first-three-past-the-post system, in which twenty-two districts each elected three representatives, with a further two legislators elected by the island of Rodriguez. Because the electorate received three votes (two on Rodriguez) they could split their ballots, which created the opportunity for political aspirants to strengthen their support base by mobilizing across party and/or ethnic lines. Despite this innovation, the numerically dominant Hindu community still tended to dominate elections. However, a second inclusive electoral provision, in which eight seats are allocated to "best losers" by the Electoral Supervisory Commission in such a way as to ensure that the legislature reflects the social diversity of the wider population, has served to ensure minority representation.

Significantly, clever institutional design was reinforced by the willingness of political leaders to compromise for the greater good. Unlike Burundi, successive prime ministers bought into the politics of inclusion. The country's first prime minster, Sir Seewoosagur Ramgoolam, was heavily influenced by Fabian socialist ideals, and pursued a form of social democracy in which the government took on the responsibility of providing public goods such as education and health care. This practice of mutual toleration was critical to the smooth running of government, because the fragmented nature of the social and political landscape meant that parties had to form coalitions in order to

[5] Bräutigam, Deborah. "Institutions, Economic Reform, and Democratic Consolidation in Mauritius". *Comparative Politics* 30, 1 (1997), pp. 45–62.

secure power. Between independence and 2014, a single party won a majority of seats only once and even then the victorious MMM kept a pre-election commitment to form a coalition government.

The glue that held these multiparty governments together was the evolution of an informal norm that the senior party in an alliance would allow its junior partner considerable influence over policy areas of specific concern in return for the support of its broad agenda. Because all parties gained from being included, coalition governments proved to be remarkably stable: Mauritius saw just three prime ministers in the first thirty-two years of independence. Over time, the accommodation of a range of interests within the policy-planning process became entrenched, helping to reduce minority groups' sense of political and economic alienation. The state of emergency between 1971 and 1976 notwithstanding, all of the administrations headed by Sir Ramgoolam were marked by ethnic inclusivity. Ever since, electoral competition has tended to revolve around two main coalitions led by a combination of Hindu and Franco-Mauritian leaders. In turn, the presence of leaders from these communities on both sides of the political divide has helped to mitigate the extent to which political competition exacerbates ethnic and/or religious tensions. At the same time, the willingness of governments to give up power, and to keep their electoral promises, cemented trust in the political system and contributed to the process of democratic consolidation and economic development (see Chapter 5). From shaky foundations in 1968, Mauritius thus emerged as one of Africa's most stable and democratic states. What is more, decades of consistent economic growth have transformed the island from a poor lower-income country to a stable upper-middle-income country.

But while the electoral system facilitated this success by helping to contain ethnic and religious tensions, it did so by institutionalizing, rather than eradicating, identity politics. Under the "best losers" system each candidate is required to state his or her identity so that the Electoral Supervisory Commission knows which candidates it can appoint in order to ensure greater ethnic balance within the legislature. Because only four ethnic groups were recognized by the constitution for the purposes of this exercise (Hindus, Muslims, Sino-Mauritians, and a residual category that rather inelegantly throws together Franco-Mauritians and Creole Christians), the best loser system maintained the political significance of outdated labels, hampering the evolution of a genuinely "identity blind" political process. As in Burundi, this approach assumed a system of ethnically based political representation and so denied citizens the opportunity to reject ethnic politics. Over the last few years an increasing number of parliamentarians have begun to argue that while the system was a necessary evil in the 1970s, the country can now afford to introduce a more classical form of proportional representation that would maintain minority representation without the use of ethnic labels.

Many Mauritian legislators favour the introduction of PR because they believe that it is the type of electoral system that is most likely to promote minority parties, and hence minority communities. Under a first-past-the-post (FPTP) system, whichever candidate wins the most votes in a given constituency is elected to the legislature. This means that if a party's support base is dispersed such that it wins a small amount of the vote in a number of constituencies, it may win no seats at all. This is not the case in a system of proportional representation, where the number of seats a party is allocated within the legislature is adjusted so that it is in line with the total number of votes that the party receives. This means that, other things being equal, proportional systems are more likely to increase the legislative representation of smaller parties, and to reduce the majority of the government.

Such a change would make sense in Mauritius, but it is worth noting that the adoption of different electoral systems in the African context has not always had the impact that political scientists would have predicted. This is largely because many ethnic groups are tightly geographically concentrated, and so their votes do not get "wasted" by being thinly spread amongst a number of losing candidates. Instead, smaller parties that rely on ethnic or regional support are often well placed to win seats in their homelands, even in the absence of proportional representation. Consequently, FPTP electoral systems have typically failed to prevent legislative fragmentation. Indeed, some of the political systems that feature the highest number of legislative parties operate FPTP systems, such as Liberia and Kenya (Table C.3). At the same time, while proportional systems have often helped smaller minorities to secure legislative representation, there are a number of cases in which they have not had the expected effect of reducing the prospects of one-party dominance. As we have seen, in Namibia and South Africa nationalist parties have been able to convert their liberation credentials into electoral dominance, despite the existence of proportional electoral systems with very low thresholds for legislative

TABLE C.3 *Electoral systems and the number of political parties*

	Legislative voting system	Number of legislative parties	Effective number of legislative parties
DRC	PR	105	23.50
Liberia	FPTP	11	5.84
Kenya*	FPTP	20	5.11
Zambia*	FPTP	5	3.03
Benin	PR	8	2.64
South Africa	PR	13	2.26
Ghana	FPTP	4	2.16
Mauritius**	FPTP	3	1.91
Namibia*	PR	9	1.73
Tanzania*	FPTP	6	1.60
Mozambique	PR	3	1.60
Senegal	PR	13	1.57
Botswana*	FPTP	4	1.56
Burundi***	PR	3	1.50

Notes: The effective number of parties is a measure that counts parties and weights their relative strength. When the number is lower it indicates that most of the seats in parliament are controlled by a small number of parties. Calculated on the Laakso-Taagepera Index, using parties not coalitions, with independents combined as if they were one party.

* Additional members indirectly elected/appointed.

** First-three-past-the-post in multi-member constituencies and best loser system where candidates appointed from list of unsuccessful candidates.

*** Remaining seats allocated based on constitutional requirement that 40 per cent filled by Tutsis, 30 per cent by women, and 3 per cent by ethnic Twa.

Source: *African Elections.*

representation. The design of electoral systems can help to promote political inclusion, then, but institutional design must also take into account local realities.

"Africanizing" Democracy

The foregoing discussion of some of the strategies that can be used to promote political inclusion in order to stabilize new democracies demonstrates three important points. First, that more inclusive institutions can enhance political stability by giving a broader range of communities a stake in the system. Second, that the effects of these strategies are rarely straightforward and need to be understood in their domestic context. Third, that some of the most successful innovations on the continent, such as zoning in Nigeria or the best loser system in Mauritius, have been homegrown. Taken together, these findings raise an important question: is African democracy best served by following Western models, or pursuing a more indigenous set of political arrangements?

To begin to answer this question, let us return to Ghana one final time. The constitution that ushered in multiparty politics in 1992 created a House of Chiefs, an unelected body comprised of traditional leaders with the capacity to check parliament on issues relating to chieftaincy and customary law. Some chiefs have caused controversy by transgressing rules that prohibit them from engaging in partisan activity. Despite this, political leaders of the two main political parties agree that the integration of traditional rulers into the formal political system has helped to generate a sense of inclusion, and has made it easier to manage inter-communal tensions around elections. This suggests that adopting more African political arrangements can help to increase the legitimacy, and hence stability, of a political system. Would it not therefore make sense for constitutional draftsmen to draw less on U.S. and British models and to put more time and energy into identifying and incorporating local traditions? The case of Somaliland suggests that the answer might be yes.

Following decades of instability and conflict, elders from northern Somali clans and representatives of the Somali National Movement (SNM) declared their intention to withdraw from war-torn Somalia and to form a new state, the Republic of Somaliland, in May 1991. One of the most significant challenges facing Somaliland's founding fathers was to simultaneously build an effective state while ending inter- and intra-clan conflict. Although pre-colonial Somali life had not featured centralized hierarchical political structures, the brutal reign of Mohamed Siad Barre from 1969 to 1991 served to politicize "clannism", leaving a poisonous legacy for future governments. While group identity has remained relatively fluid, and the community to which an individual identifies may vary according to context, clans have nonetheless become the dominant social structures through which political mobilization occurs.

In their search for a political system that could accommodate the reality of clannism, Somaliland's founding fathers realized that they shared a set of norms about decision-making and conflict resolution that could be used to design a structure of government that would resonate with their people. While pre-colonial Somali life was typically stateless and pastoral, it was not without rules. Governance was based on councils (*shir*) made up of lineage elders (*odayaasha*) who were committed to making decisions by consensus. Inter-clan relationships were defined by contracts (*xeer*), which collectively formed a system of customary rule (*xeer Somali*).[6]

Although the process of state-building was largely funded by remittances from the diaspora, and Britain, the EU, and the United States provided training for Somaliland's politicians and the electoral commission, the fact that international actors did not officially recognize Somaliland meant that the territory never became dependent on foreign donors for the design or the funding of its democratic institutions (see Chapter 4). As a result, the Somaliland state that emerged was a more organic affair, and heavily reflected traditional methods of regulating social relationships. In 1993, a clan conference (*shir beeled*) produced the Somaliland Communities Security and Peace Charter, which established a framework for reconciliation and mutual security that was agreed at a convention of clans and took the form of a national xeer. The Transitional National Charter that emerged from the same meeting established a *beel* (clan family) system of government that effectively fused existing practice with elements of a modern democratic system. Most notably, the charter explicitly identified kinship as a central organizing structure within the politics of Somaliland, creating a bicameral parliament with an upper chamber composed of elders responsible for security, with seats in both houses allocated to clans on a proportional basis. Democratic principles were promoted through the codification of a set of checks and balances not dissimilar to the U.S. system. Political competition was regulated by a constitution that established competitive presidential elections and dispersed power between the parliament, judiciary, and executive.

Although conflict continued until 1996, and the political system went through a series of further modifications, this agreement represented the blueprint on which the polity of Somaliland was subsequently constructed. The constitution of 2001, which was passed in a referendum by an overwhelming majority of the population, explicitly built on the Peace Charter, adding a number of additional

---

[6] Kaplan, Seth. "The Remarkable Story of Somaliland." *Journal of Democracy* 19, 3 (2008), pp. 143–157.

mechanisms designed to boost the representation of minorities and place some limits on the influence of the numerically dominant Isaaq clan. When this process was over, Somaliland had established something akin to a clan-based system of political inclusion.

Tellingly, this organic set of arrangements proved to be more durable and more democratic than any of the internationally sponsored administrations that rose and fell in Somalia over the same period. Most notably, it has proved capable of regulating political competition and of facilitating political change, supported by the evolution of the electoral commission into a competent and professional body and the willingness of leading political figures to play by the rules of the game. When President Mohamed Egal died in office in 2002, power passed peacefully to the vice president, Dahir Riyale Kahin, as stipulated in the constitution – even though he represented a rival clan. Riyale Kahin was subsequently re-elected in 2003 by just eighty votes, and although opposition parties alleged malpractice, they peacefully accepted the result once it had been upheld by the courts. Against all the odds, Somaliland thus emerged as a role model for other countries in the region; an unlikely triumph of political imagination based on shared experiences and values. Not only has political system developed the capacity to collect taxation and issue currency, but foreign observers described the 2005 legislative elections as the most transparent ever to take place in the Horn of Africa.

However, while Somaliland is a valuable case to learn from, it is important not to exaggerate the quality of democracy enjoyed by its citizens. In an effort to prevent the splintering of the party system along inter- and intra-clan lines, Somaliland's 2001 constitution limited the number of parties to three, restricting the choice available to voters. Successive presidents have also relied on neo-patrimonial relationships with clan members to mobilize support, raising questions about whether or not the system is actually as inclusive as it claims. More recently, a government crackdown on political criticism in 2012 and disputes over the timing and conduct elections has served to tarnish Somaliland's reputation as a beacon of plural politics in a repressive region.

We should also be cautious about the extent to which this home-grown model can be generalized to other cases. Although the state-building process in Somaliland had to overcome the same sort of inter-communal tensions experienced by many African states, the fact that the Isaaq clan comprises a majority of the population means that political stability in Somaliland has been underpinned by a national identity that is more cohesive than it appears to be at first glance.

Given that the society of Somaliland is relatively homogenous by African standards, a similar model might not be as successful in more diverse contexts, such as the DRC, Kenya, and Nigeria. Moreover, if African countries are to build more stable democracies by focusing on shared values and established practices, then they need to move away from the idea of importing a model from abroad, whether from Somaliland or elsewhere. The right lesson to take from the experience of Somaliland is therefore not that a new model has emerged that all African states should follow, but that African states should stop being so keen to follow models at all. Democracy is not like an IKEA bookcase that can be mass-produced in flat-pack form and put together in the same way, no matter what country it ends up in. Rather, it requires craftsmen (and women) who can carefully tailor democratic institutions to a country's own distinctive experiences and practices, in order to develop more locally grounded – and hence sustainable – systems of government.

It is important to note that this is not an appeal for moral relativism and should not be taken to imply that African political systems should be held to lower democratic standards. While it is always important to take context into account, it is also important not to fetishize tradition. Appeals to "African" values have too often been used to justify the extension of authoritarian control, rather than to consolidate democracy. As we saw in Chapter 1, nationalist leaders such as Tanzania's Julius Nyerere used the argument that Africans made decisions through the slow building of consensus rather than multiparty competition to justify the introduction of restrictive one-party states. If local traditions are to support democratic consolidation, they must be modified so that they promote open and competitive politics, not the other way around.

Consider the position of traditional leaders. Following the reintroduction of multiparty politics chieftaincy has not gone away. Rather, as the Ghanaian example demonstrates, democratization has given the institution a shot in the arm. Recent research by Carolyn Logan demonstrates that most Africans both perceive traditional leaders to be legitimate and think that they should be given a greater role within the political system.[7] Yet there are a number of limitations with the incorporation of traditional leaders in Africa's new democracies. Even if we ignore the fact that in many countries the emergence of the modern

[7] Logan, Carolyn. "The Roots of Resilience: Exploring Popular Support for African Traditional Authorities." *African Affairs* 112, 448 (2013), pp. 353–376.

"chief" was in part the product of colonial rule (see Introduction) –
which calls into question just how "African" this institution really is –
the functions that traditional leaders perform are sometimes hard to
reconcile with democratic norms and values. Following the reintroduction of elections in the 1990s chiefs, who were typically reliant for
their position and income on the government, have often deployed
their local authority to mobilize support for the ruling party (see
Chapter 5). A few years ago I conducted a short period of fieldwork
looking at the challenges facing opposition parties in Malawi and
Zambia. When I asked rural opposition leaders to set out the most
significant factors that prevented them from being able to compete
fairly in legislative elections, they all put the ruling party's control of
traditional leaders at the top of the list.

The ways in which chiefs resolve local disputes that fall within
their jurisdiction is also a cause for concern. Land and marital disputes are often left to traditional leaders to adjudicate on the basis of
customary laws that do not always allow women to inherit wealth or
property. Moreover, because such cases are heard outside of the formal legal process there are typically far fewer checks on the abuse of
power. Given this, it is particularly problematic that chieftaincy tends
to be a male-dominated institution that in many countries has failed
to recognize the needs and rights of women. There is thus a danger
that the uncritical adoption of "traditional" forms of representation
may further reinforce the exclusion of marginalized communities. In
Somaliland's clan-based system, for example, women enjoy political
rights, but comprise only a tiny proportion of municipal councillors
and MPs. So while there is much to be gained by Africanizing democracy, it is important that "traditional" practices are brought into line
with fundamental democratic principles.

The Limits of Institutional Design

Of course, neither clever institutional design nor the Africanization
of democracy can solve all of the challenges generated by the reintroduction of multiparty politics. For one thing, constitutions typically
reflect the interests of those in power, and electoral systems are rarely
modified to the benefit of the opposition. As we saw in Chapters 4 and
5, ruling parties have typically been able to retain control of the political agenda, which helps to explain why the reintroduction of elections

was accompanied by so little constitutional reform. It is therefore unlikely that the kinds of inclusive measures discussed in this chapter will be introduced. This is a cause for concern, because the failure to develop more independent democratic institutions means that countries such as Côte d'Ivoire, Kenya, Uganda, Togo, and Zimbabwe are consistently holding intensively contested elections within discredited political systems that give opposition leaders little reason to believe in the rules of the game. This is not a recipe for democratic consolidation.

Even when constitutional reform has occurred, it has only led to genuine political change in countries where domestic and international actors were willing to mobilize in order to ensure that the new rules were respected. As we have seen, the national conference in Togo did not serve to put the country on the road to democratic governance because neither the ruling party nor key foreign backers were prepared to change established ways of doing business (see Chapter 3). Without the political will necessary to consolidate reforms, a constitution is not worth the paper it is written on. Unfortunately, such will is typically most lacking precisely where it is most needed: in states with a history of inter-communal conflict and low levels of trust among the elite.

It is also important to be realistic about what institutional reform can achieve even when it is backed up by the necessary political will. The causes of civil conflict and political instability run deep and are rooted in entrenched communal identities, pervasive poverty, inequality, the militarization of politics, and the evolution of cultures of impunity that prevent the prosecution of those guilty of perpetrating violence and corruption. Reversing these trends requires economic, political, and social change over many years; institutional design can help, but on its own it is rarely enough.

These caveats notwithstanding, it is encouraging that the introduction of mechanisms of minority representation and federalism have worked to strengthen democracy in contexts as challenging as Burundi and Nigeria. This shows that African countries do not have to accept their fate: political systems can be designed that combine the right balance of competition and inclusion, reducing the stakes of electoral competition while supporting accountability. Significantly, Africa's constitutional draftsmen do not need to look West for examples of how this can be achieved; as the case of Somaliland demonstrates, alternative forms of democratic design can be located much closer to home. But while it makes sense to draw on a broad range of relevant examples when putting together a new constitution, there is no one-size-fits-all template for how to build a stable multiparty system; rather, each set of political institutions must be carefully designed in the light of a country's own history. Getting this right will take hard work – but it will be worth it. Institutional design is no cure-all, but it can change the incentives facing political leaders, making them more likely to reject authoritarian rule and invest in multiparty politics. It is far too early to give up on democracy in Africa.

Select Bibliography

Ake, Claude. *The Feasibility of Democracy in Africa*. Ibadan: CREDU, 1992.

Berman, Bruce, Dickson Eyoh, and Will Kymlicka (eds). *Ethnicity and Democracy in Africa*. Oxford: James Currey, 2004.

Bradbury, Mark. *Becoming Somaliland*. Oxford: James Currey, 2008.

Reynolds, Andrew. *The Architecture of Democracy: Constitutional Design, Conflict Management, and Democracy*. Oxford: Oxford University Press, 2002 (includes chapters by Lijphart and Horowitz).

Suberu, Rotimi T. *Federalism and Ethnic Conflict in Nigeria*. Washington, DC: United States Institute of Peace, 2001.

For a bibliography for this chapter go to www.democracyinafrica.org

The Fate of Africa's Democratic Experiments 1989–2014

Country	First multi-party pres. election^	First multi-party leg. election^	Interruption of multi-partyism^^	Reason for breakdown	Highest number of consecutive pres. elections^^^	Highest number of consecutive leg. elections	Electoral transfer of power^^^	FH political rights score in 2010	FH civil liberties score in 2010	Holding elections in 2014	FH rating 2014^^^^
Angola	1992	1992	1992	Civil war	2 (2008–)*	2 (2008–2012)	N	6	5	Y	NF
Benin	1991	1991	–	–	5	6	Y (1991, 1996, 2006)	2	2	Y	F
Botswana	–	1965			–	10	N	3	2	Y	F
Burkina Faso	1998**	1992	2014	Coup**	4	4	N	5	3	Y	PF
Burundi	1993	1993	1993	Assassination	1 (1993, 2010–)	2 (2005, 2010)	N	4	5	Y	PF
Cameroon	1992	1992	–	–	4	4	N	6	6	Y	NF
Cape Verde	1991	1991	–	–	5	5	Y (1991, 2001, 2011)	1	1	Y	F
CAR	1993	1993	2003, 2013	Coup	2 (1993–1999 & 2005–2011)	2 (1993–1998 & 2005–2011)	N	5	5	N	NF
Chad	1996	1997	–	–	4	3	N	7	6	Y	NF
Comoros	1990	1992	1995, 1999, 2007	Coup	2 (2006–2010)	1 (2009–)	Y (2006)	7	4	Y	PF
Congo, Rep.	1992	1992	1997	Civil war	2 (2002–)	2 (2002–)	N	6	5	Y	NF
Côte d'Ivoire	1990	1990	1999, 2002, 2011	Coup / Civil war / Civil war	2 (1990–1995)	2 (1990–1995)	2000***	6	5	Y	PF
Djibouti	1993	1992	–	–	4	4	N	5	5	Y	NF
DRC	2006	2006	–	–	2	2	N	6	6	Y	NF
Eq. Guinea	1996	1993	–	–	3	4	–	7	7	Y	NF
Eritrea	–	–	–	–	–	–	–	7	7	N	NF
Ethiopia	–	1995	–	–	–	5	N	5	5	Y	NF
Gabon	1993	1990	–	–	4	5	N	6	5	Y	NF
The Gambia	1982	1966	1994	Coup	4****	4	N	5	5	Y	NF

Country	First multi-party pres. election^	First multi-party leg. election^	Interruption of multi-partyism^^	Reason for breakdown	Highest number of consecutive pres. elections^^^	Highest number of consecutive leg. elections^^^	Electoral transfer of power^^^	FH political rights score in 2010	FH civil liberties score in 2010	Holding elections in 2014	FH rating 2014^^^^^
Ghana	1992	1992	–	–	6	6	Y (2000, 2008)	1	2	Y	F
Guinea	1993	1995	2008	Coup	3 (1993–2003)	2 (1992–2002)	N	7	6	Y	PF
Guinea–Bissau	1994	1994	1999, 2003, 2009, 2012	Coup, Coup, Assassination, Coup	1 (1994, 1999, 2005, 2009, 2012)	1 (2008)	N	4	4	Y	NF
Kenya	1992	1992	–	–	5	5	Y (2002)	4	4	Y	PF
Lesotho	–	1993	*****	Coup	–	5	Y (2012)*****	3	3	Y	F
Liberia	1997	1997	1999	Civil war	2 (2005–)	2 (2005–)	N	3	4	Y	PF
Madagascar	1992	1993	2002, 2009	Civil unrest/ military takeover	2 (1993–2002)	1 (2007)	Y (1993, 1996, 2001)	6	4	Y	PF
Malawi	1994	1994	–	–	5	5	Y (1994, 2014)	3	4	Y	PF
Mali	1992	1992	2012	Coup	4 (1992–2007)	5 (1992–2007)	Y (2002)	2	3	Y	PF
Mauritania	1992	1992	2005, 2008	Coup, Coup	3 (1992–2003)	3 (1992–2001)	N	6	5	Y	NF
Mauritius	–	1976	–	–	–	9	Y (1982, 1995, 2000, 2005)******	1	2	Y	F
Mozambique	1994	1994	–	–	5	5	N	4	3	Y	PF
Namibia	1994	1994	–	–	4	4	N	2	2	Y	F
Niger	1993	1993	1996, 1999, 2009, 2010	Coup, Assassination, Coup, Coup	2 (1999–2004)	2 (1999–2004)	N	5	4	Y	PF
Nigeria	1999	1999	–	–	4	4	N	5	4	Y	PF
Rwanda	2003	2003	–	–	2	3	N	6	5	Y	NF

235

Country	First multi-party pres. election ^	First multi-party leg. election ^	Interruption of multi-partyism ^^	Reason for breakdown	Highest number of consecutive pres. elections ^^^	Highest number of consecutive leg. elections	Electoral transfer of power ^^^	FH political rights score in 2010	FH civil liberties score in 2010	Holding elections in 2014	FH rating 2014 ^^^^^
S.T. & Principe	1991	1991	^^^^^^^	–	3 (1991–2001)	4 (1991–2002)	Y (2011)	2	2	Y	F
Senegal	1978	1978	–	–	7	8	Y (2000, 2012)	3	3	Y	F
Seychelles	1993	1993	–	–	5	5	N^^^^^^^^	3	3	Y	PF
Sierra Leone	1996	1996	1997	Coup/Civil War	3 (2002–)	3 (2002–)	Y (2007)	3	3	Y	PF
Somalia	–	–	–	–	–	–	–	7	7	N	NF
Somaliland^^^^^^^^	2003	2005	–	–	–	2	Y (2010)	5	5	Y	PF
South Africa	–	1994	–	–	–	5	N	2	2	Y	F
South Sudan	2010	2010	2013	Civil war	1 (2010)	1 (2010)	N	–	–	Y	NF
Sudan	2000	2000	2005	–	2 (2000–2010)	2 (2000– 2010)^^^^^^^^^^	N	7	7	Y	NF
Swaziland	^^^^^^^^^^	–	–	–	–	–	–	7	5	N	NF
Tanzania	1995	1995	–	–	4	4	N	4	3	Y	PF
Togo	1993	1994	2005	Coup	3 (1993–2003)	3 (1994–2002)	N	5	4	Y	PF
Uganda	2006	2006	–	–	2	2	N	5	4	Y	PF
Zambia	1991	1991	–	–	5^^^^^^^^^^	5	Y (1991, 2011)	3	4	Y	PF
Zimbabwe	1990	1990	–	–	5	6	N	6	6	Y	NF

Notes: The information presented here was generated by using three separate coders and then comparing their findings. On some close judgment calls, coders did not always agree, such as when a period of violence counts as an interruption of democracy, or the main reason for the collapse of a democratic episode. These results reflect the most common coding. ^First election held following the reintroduction of elections in the 1990s for all countries bar those that did not suffer an authoritarian interruption prior to the 1990s, such as Botswana, Gambia, and Mauritius where we record the first post-colonial election. ^^An authoritarian interruption counts as an event which breaks the flow of multiparty elections, such as a coup that leads to the constitution being suspended – it does not include democratic backsliding in cases where elections continue to be held. ^^^Numbers in brackets indicate the time period over which consecutive elections were held in cases where authoritarian interruptions mean that it would otherwise not be clear in which period the run of consecutive elections occurred. ^^^^A transfer of power refers to a change in the party of the president in presidential systems, and a change in the party of the prime minister in parliamentary systems. Elections in which there is effectively no ruling party, such as transitional elections held after a long period of civil war, are not counted as transfers of power. To count as an electoral transfer the incumbent must voluntarily give up power – transfers that occur only after military intervention are not listed. ^^^^The Freedom House overall rating is based on the average of an average of the country's political rights and civil score. On a 1-7 scale in which lower scores = more free, countries that average 1.0-2.5 are considered Free, 3.0-5.0 Partly Free, and 5.5-7.0 Not Free. *National assembly only, constitution was changed in 2010 to make the president appointed by national assembly, rather than directly elected. **A presidential election was held in 1991 but only the president contested so it is not counted as a multiparty poll here. In 2014, the military took over after mass civil protests against an attempt by the sitting president to change the constitution to allow himself a third term. ***Although Outtara was able to take power after the 2010 election, this was only after the breakdown of the political system and military intervention. ****Multiparty constitution but with severe restrictions on opposition parties until 2001. *****There was a short lived coup in 1994 but this was overturned and the government reinstated in a month. In 2014, the prime minister alleged that the military was attempting to take power in a coup but by the time of going to press he had not yet resigned his position. In 1998 there was a change of party, but the prime minister had earlier launched this new party, and so this did not represent a defeat for the incumbent. ******There was a change of prime minister in 2003 also, but this was the result of a deal among the parties in the ruling coalition and not the product of an election. *******In 2003 a coup occurred, but this was overturned in a week and the previous government was reinstated. ********In 2011 the same president won but on a different party ticket. *********Somaliland is not an internationally recognized state, but is included for illustrative purposes. Although there has not been a clear authoritarian interruption, elections were postponed and the government's tenure extended in both 2007 and 2011. **********The legislative elections of 2000 were boycotted by the opposition. Following elections in 2000, further polls were postponed until 2010. ***********Holds "non-partisan" elections in which multi-party competition is prohibited. ************An additional presidential by-election was held in 2008 following the death of Levy Mwanawasa in office.

Index